THE LIFE
AND DEATH OF
HERMANN

THE LIFE
AND DEATH OF
HERMANN
GOERING

EWAN BUTLER AND GORDON YOUNG

A DAVID & CHARLES MILITARY BOOK

British Library Cataloguing in Publication Data

Butler, Ewan
    The life and death of Hermann Goering.
    I. Germany. Goering, Hermann, 1893–1946
    I. Title II. Young, Gordon

    ISBN 0-7153-9455-X

Previously published by Hodder and Stoughton Ltd,
1951 and by Universal-Tandem Publishing Co. Ltd, 1973
This paperback edition published 1989
by David & Charles Publishers plc
and printed in Great Britain
by Redwood Burn Limited, Trowbridge, Wiltshire
for David & Charles Publishers plc
Brunel House   Newton Abbot   Devon

Distributed in the United States by
Sterling Publishing Co. Inc,
2, Park Avenue, New York, NY 10016

Cover pictures
Front: Reichsmarshal Hermann Goering with Hitler
             (*Military Archive and Research Services*)
Back: Hermann Goering (*Peter Newark's Military
             Pictures*)

DEDICATED
To the fighter pilots of the
Royal Air Force who, in 1940,
first shattered a Marshal's
dream of glory

Beginning and End

"THERE is nothing to be said in mitigation. For Goering was often, indeed almost always the moving force, second only to his leader. He was the leading war aggressor, both as political and as military leader; he was the director of the slave-labour programme and the creator of the oppressive programme against the Jews and other races at home and abroad. All of these crimes he has frankly admitted. On some specific cases there may be conflict of testimony, but in terms of broad outline his own admissions are more than sufficiently wide to be conclusive of his guilt. His guilt is unique in its enormity. The record discloses no excuses for this man."

The pale light of an autumn morning, slanting through high windows, took on an unseasonable brilliance from the scarlet robes of Lord Justice Lawrence, President of the International Military Tribunal at Nuremberg as, standing, he delivered this Judgment. It glinted from the stiff, broad epaulettes of the Soviet Justice and was reflected, dully, from the black robes of the American and French Judges, of Counsel, Allied and German.

No colour relieved the dock, where twenty-two men, pale from long imprisonment, sat ranged waiting to learn their fate. As the President concluded his Judgment, several pairs of lack-lustre eyes were turned, discreetly, towards the bulky man who sat, impassive, at the end of the bench, listening attentively to the chatter of the earphones.

No colour there any more. No brave flash of silk, gilt and enamel from the green-grey tunic which Hermann Wilhelm Goering now wore. Two years ago his chest would have been a-twinkle with stars and crosses, two years ago his name had still meant something in Europe. Six years before—long since, in 1940—the Reichsmarschall's air force had been the hope of Germany and the dread of all other nations; the Reichsmarschall himself had been, or had at least seemed to be, almost inconceivably powerful, a portent. Now he sat a convicted felon in the dock at Nuremberg, while the tinny, impassive voice of the interpreter brought to him, in hasty translation, the verdict of his judges. It was October 1, 1946.

" . . . His guilt is unique in its enormity. . . . " For the man to whom those words were addressed the adjective may have brought some satisfaction. No judge would think of applying it, for instance, to Rudolf Hess, who sat there beside him like a witless dummy; to the fool Ribbentrop, to louts like Streicher and Kaltenbrunner, to poor, flabby Funk, or indeed to any of his companions in the dock. It was, perhaps, something to be unique, even as a criminal.

The verdict came as no surprise to Goering. For the past year he had been a prisoner, under interrogation, and the whole trend of those endless questionings, of the intensely boring conferences with his well-meaning but sadly bourgeois defence counsel, had shown clearly enough that his enemies held all the cards. A few days before the verdict he had commented sarcastically to his lawyer on the solicitous care which the American medical service took of his health:

"They want to have me brisk and lively on the chopping-block!" Goering had said. He did not add that he proposed to cheat his enemies of that satisfaction.

Hermann Wilhelm Goering was not much given to self-analysis. Like that of the wild-boar which he had once loved to hunt, his was a character inclined to rush full tilt at obstacles, to shoot first and if absolutely necessary to discuss the shooting afterwards. These are not marks of an introspective mind. During the trial at Nuremberg Goering had unwittingly given to those who heard his examination several clues to the strange mechanism which lay behind his broad forehead. For an experienced lawyer at least there could be no doubt that the man was animated by a criminal brain.

Criminal brains and criminal temperaments have in all periods of history been distressingly common, although the appetite of the law-abiding majority of mankind to know more about their unfortunate possessors is still insatiable. Hermann Wilhelm Goering was no ordinary felon. On the authority of the most august criminal tribunal ever assembled "his guilt was unique in its enormity." He had once been a hero; he had given to a woman deep, tender love, such as few women are allowed to know; he had shown great ability and had risen to vast power and wealth, if not to eminence, in the face of sorrow, poverty, madness and misfortune; and yet . . . "the record discloses no excuses for this man."

It is not the purpose of biography to excuse or to condemn.

8

Rather does the biographer seek to reassemble, however imperfectly, the fragments which have made up a human existence and from them to allow the reader to deduce, as best he may, the character and temperament of his subject, the influences which turned him into a hero or a criminal, the motives for his actions. That, at least, is the purpose of this book.

"Father of the Man"

It is unlikely that President Paul Kruger, preoccupied as he was in the early days of the century with the war against Great Britain, noticed, among the generous contributions which reached his war-chest from private persons in Germany, the sum of 40 marks, contributed, it seemed, by "Hermann Goering, General of the Boers." The rank claimed by the donor was, indeed, somewhat misleading, since no General officer of that name was fighting in the Transvaal. Yet "General" Goering's devotion to the Boer cause was genuine enough, for the money represented the entire contents of the moneybox of a small boy, and as for fighting – the good people of the Franconian hamlet of Veldenstein could have told President Kruger something about that!

Young though he was, Hermann Goering has assumed unchallenged leadership of the village boys. The stronger and more daring spirits, led by "General" Goering, his rank indicated by an outsized green felt hat with brim suitably upturned, represented the Boer commandos. The remainder of the youthful male population of Veldenstein, unwillingly enlisted as "English" soldiery, suffered a monotonous and painful series of defeats throughout that summer.

Dr. Heinrich Ernst Goering, graduate of the universities of Bonn and Heidelberg, friend of Bismarck and of Cecil Rhodes, himself a distinguished African administrator, strongly disapproved of his son's partisan attitude towards the Boer War. Unlike most Germans of his day he was a convinced believer in the British cause, not from reasons of sentiment but because he wished to see a Great Power solidly installed in South Africa, as a protection to the new German colonies in the South-West.

In the wars of 1866 and 1870 Dr. Goering had served as an officer in the Prussian Army. After the latter conflict he was appointed a district judge in South Germany, and soon his essentially Prussian qualities of orderliness, rigid personal honesty and capacity for hard and intelligent work commended themselves to Bismarck, the founder of the new Reich. Dr. Goering rose steadily in the civil service until, in 1885, he was ordered to South-West Africa, there to conduct, on behalf of Germany, negotiations with the chieftains of the Herero tribes which brought to the Reich a large accession of new colonial territory. The success of these negotiations led to his appointment, in 1888, as first Commissioner-General of German South-West Africa.

True to the traditions of his caste, Dr. Goering was a firm believer in "The Three K's" – *"Kinder, Kirche, Küche"* – "Children, Church, Kitchen" – which governed the women of every respectable German family in the nineteenth century. By his first wife he had been blessed with five children. The effort had killed her. Still in the prime of life, notwithstanding the rigours of service in West Africa, Dr. Goering saw no reason in supposing that a second wife, chosen from healthy stock, might not provide him with five more offspring. In this supposition he was perfectly correct.

Four years in West Africa was, particularly in those days, a long tour of duty for a white official. In 1891 Dr. Goering, due for a change of air, was appointed Consul-General and Minister-Resident at Port-au-Prince, in Haiti. Thither he brought his second wife, Franziska, a gay, temperamental girl from the Austrian Tyrol. Impulsive, deeply emotional, fond of music and acting, Franziska seemed ill-matched with her pedantic, meticulous Prussian husband. Yet they were happy enough, and in Port-au-Prince their son, Hermann, was conceived.

He was not born there, since by Dr. Goering's standards it was improper that a German child should come into the world anywhere but on German soil if that could by some means, however complicated, be arranged. Franziska, accordingly, made the long voyage from the Caribbean to Germany alone, and her son was born at Rosenheim, in Bavaria, on January 12, 1893.

Little Hermann was not long allowed to enjoy his mother's

society. The *Herr Generalkonsul,* alone in Port-au-Prince, needed his wife by his side, and so no sooner was the baby weaned than he was confided to the care of friends in Munich, while Franziska took passage for Haiti. It was the first of many such separations.

The Germany into which young Hermann had been born was an exciting, vigorous place. The nation, newly united, had begun to feel its strength. At Düsseldorf, Duisburg, Essen, Solingen, new mines, new blast-furnaces, new factories, filled the air with their fumes and the ears with their clamour. German goods were successfully invading the world markets, for years past a virtual monopoly of England. German commercial-travellers, their bags filled with alluring samples at extremely attractive prices, ranged the globe, to the growing mortification of their British rivals. The German Army, flushed still by its victory over France, stood at the peak of its power and arrogance. The Imperial Navy, looking out from Kiel and Wilhelmshafen, began to imagine a day when it might engage, on equal terms, the Royal Navy of Great Britain. Queen Victoria would scarcely have recognized now "our dear little Germany" of which she had written so enthusiastically many years before. Her grandson Willie, and that Prince Bismarck upon whose distinguished appearance the Queen had remarked when she had met him, long since, at the Château of Versailles, had changed all that.

Hermann Goering opened his eyes upon a well-ordered Teutonic world. Its pinnacle was the Emperor, Wilhelm II, the "All-Highest." Beneath him came the Army, and, some way behind the Army, the Navy, still a rather neglected service although its power was growing. The hierarchy of German Society was very strict. In the streets, as among the "best people," the cavalry officer, so perfectly and maliciously handed down to us by the drawings of Thöny, in *Simplicissimus,* could do no wrong. Infantry and gunner officers were, to the civilian, hardly less august personages. The supply services, the *Train,* although the butt of cartoonists, who represented them as officered almost entirely by Jewish reservists, still wore the Kaiser's uniform, and were therefore entitled to consideration. The same applied to the Navy.

Thereafter in the social scale came the professors, who enjoyed a prestige altogether out of proportion to their general level of ability, and the senior civil servants. It was from this latter class that Hermann Goering's forebears had sprung.

Below them again stood a general ruck of civilians, ranging from the great bankers, industrialists and ship-owners to the humble artisan.

In the heyday of Nazi power the Party genealogists – those same experts who, during the last war, spent infinite time and labour in seeking to trace Jewish blood in the Royal Family of Great Britain – claimed that Hermann Goering had a "blood relationship" not only with the Royal Family of Hohenzollern, but with Goethe, Bismarck and Count Zeppelin, the pioneer of the dirigible airship. Dr. Heinrich Goering would have been the first to ridicule such claims. He was quite content to trace his descent back no further than 1694, when his great-great-grandfather was born at Rügenwalde, in the Province of Brandenburg.

This Michael Christian Goering was an ancestor of whom any respectable bourgeois family might be proud. A man of great physical strength and of ability as great, he served Frederick the Great as a regimental quartermaster, so well to the satisfaction of the exacting monarch that Frederick appointed Goering his tax collector in the Ruhr, even then an industrial district. Displaying the talent for organization which seems to have been a characteristic of the Goering family, Michael Christian remodelled the local wire industry, at that time the chief business of the area, and proceeded, with the King's full support, to squeeze it dry in the interests of the Prussian war-effort.

During the Seven Years' War, while the Ruhr was occupied by French troops, the peasantry, acting as a local "resistance movement," made a point of pillaging any French stores and equipment which they could safely attack. After one of these raids the French commander seized a number of prominent hostages, including Michael Christian Goering, and released them only after the payment of 7296 *Louis d'Or* – a very considerable sum of money. Although Michael Christian made every effort to recover his share of this ransom when the war had ended, he never succeeded in doing so, and the whole affair became quite a legend in the Goering family.

Michael's son, Christian Heinrich, settled in the Rhineland, lived there in good repute and sired Hermann Goering's grandfather, Wilhelm, who married Caroline de Nerée, member of a distinguished Dutch family of French Huguenot origin.

On his father's side, therefore, young Hermann was descended from a line of officials and officers. His mother's origins were more modest. Peter Paul Tiefenbrunn, Hermann's maternal grandfather, was a Tyrolean peasant, a yeoman well liked and respected in the neighbourhood of Reutte, where the Tiefenbrunn family is still solidly established. The admixture of Prussian official and Austrian peasant in one child is not a common one, and in the case of Dr. Goering and his wife Franziska, *née* Tiefenbrunn, it produced unusual results.

In 1896 Dr. Goering returned for a time from Haiti and the family settled for a time at Veldenstein, in a small house nestling under the ruins of an ancient castle. They found that Hermann, then a child of three, already showed very strong signs of knowing his own mind, and latter-day psychiatrists have sought to ascribe to lack of paternal discipline in his earliest years the turbulent, unbridled character which Hermann Goering displayed throughout his life. In any case the child saw little enough of his father even after the *Herr General-konsul's* return to Germany. Bismarck had constant need of his trusted servant. There were long sojourns abroad and long spells of duty in Berlin. Hermann's two brothers and two sisters were admirably well behaved. Only the youngest boy presented a problem, but with that problem Dr. Goering had little time to deal.

Fortunately a kind friend relieved the Goering family of much of the responsibility for their children. Ritter von Eppenstein, extremely wealthy, a man well known for his generous gifts to charity, had met Dr. Goering in Haiti and had taken an immediate liking to him and to his wife. He was a Jew, but that was a matter of less account in Wilhelmine Germany, where Jewish industrialists and financiers who had done much to develop the Reich stood justifiably high in the Imperial favour, than it later became in Hitler's Reich. Eppenstein's father had been a Dr. Eppeles, Court Physician to the Emperor Wilhelm I, a man already rich from his father's speculations in land and house property around Berlin. The physician had been dignified with the title of *Ritter* (Knight) and his son had now settled down in the Austrian castle of Mauterndorf to live the life of a wealthy country gentleman.

Hermann Goering and his brothers and sisters spent much of their childhood at Mauterndorf, and came to know and love the mountainous Salzburg countryside in which it stood. The young people were spoiled by their host. Guns, horses, guides for mountaineering were theirs to command, and Hermann's

13

brothers and sisters accepted these favours with grace and gratitude. A person who knew the family at that time describes Hermann's behaviour at Mauterndorf as having been "rather arrogant and Prussian" and leaves it to be inferred that of the Goering family Hermann was not Ritter von Eppenstein's favourite.

In its early stages Hermann's education caused his father some anxiety. His first school was at Fuerth, a busy old township not far from Nuremberg and thus close to Veldenstein. Here his violent impulsive character soon became apparent, nor was it, in the eyes of his teachers, counterbalanced by any outstanding aptitude for his books. The German schooling of those days was a grim, earnest business—long hours of work succeeded each other, broken by only the shortest periods of recreation. Organized sport was unknown and the boys were left to fill in what leisure they had as best they might in the playground. Here Hermann Goering soon revealed an inclination for fighting, not to say for bullying, which alarmed the school authorities and caused them to remonstrate with the boy's father. To the disappointment of the more enterprising among his school-fellows and the relief of their weaker comrades the boy was removed from Fuerth.

At Ansbach, the capital of Franconia, whither Hermann was sent to pursue his studies, the same story was repeated. Other schools were tried without much success. "Hermann," as one of his teachers said, "is a good fellow – but a bit difficult. He is a born revolutionary."

"Progressive" methods of education had made no impact whatever in Germany in the first decade of the twentieth century. Discipline was severe and the word of the teacher law. All the more irritating, therefore, was young Goering's habit of arguing persistently about every conceivable topic. One of his masters recalls an occasion on which Goering, in presenting a complaint, launched into a long speech in which he sought to give the whole background to the matter under discussion.

"Cut it short, Goering," said the master, "and come to the point."

"*Aber nein, Herr!*" Hermann cried. "No sir! Unless I tell you the whole story you can't possibly understand what I really mean."

He finished his speech after his own fashion.

As a school report said of him: "This boy always likes to have his own way."

Sharp military discipline, Dr. Goering decided, would be the best medicine for his wilful son, and so he was packed off to a Cadet School at Karlsruhe, and thence, after a reasonably successful sojourn, to the Military Training College at Gross-Lichterfelde, near Berlin. He passed out of this establishment very much more creditably than anyone expected, and in March 1912, just after his nineteenth birthday, was posted as a Second-Lieutenant to Infantry Regiment 112 (Prinz Wilhelm), then stationed at Mühlhausen, or Mulhouse, in Alsace.

On the day before the final passing-out examination Hermann's father had arranged to give a large evening party in Berlin. There would be dancing, pretty girls and plenty of free food and drink. On no account, Dr. Goering decided, should Hermann be invited. The last hours before an examination should be spent, he felt, in final revision rather than in pleasure. As Goering himself told the story, years later:

" 'For heaven's sake, Father,' I said, 'what do you take me for? Let me come along anyhow!' So my father let me come and I danced my feet off, drank a lot and got through the exam next day all the same."

Dr. Goering gave his son 2000 marks (at that time £100) as a reward for this success, and the young man spent the money on a good holiday before joining his regiment.

To be a German infantry subaltern in a good regiment was, in those days, no small privilege. Admittedly one was somewhat despised by the cavalry, but commissions in cavalry regiments were reserved almost entirely for the sons of the nobility and for the offspring of a few very rich *parvenus,* young men whose life was usually made sufficiently miserable for them by their aristocratic brother officers. For a youth of bourgeois birth and upbringing the infantry was the thing, and on the whole a very pleasant thing too.

To young Goering, however, garrison life in Mühlhausen was a trifle boring, nor did he, in the opinion of his senior officers, show from the outset quite the proper degree of respect and awe for the grand traditions of the German Army in general and of Infantry Regiment 112 in particular. To the senior subaltern of the Regiment, an officer steeped in the legend of Frederick the Great, young Goering was quite a problem. His manner was both intolerably cocksure and unpardonably irreverent. The discovery of some trifling fault on the part of the newcomer seemed to afford an excellent opportunity for deflating the young man in front of his comrades. Accordingly the senior subaltern rounded upon Goering in public.

"*Um Gottes Willen!* Leutnant Goering! How dare you! Dash it all, sir, what d'you suppose old Fritz would have said to such goings on? Frederick the Great, God bless him . . ."

The stream of rebuke and exhortation flowed on for some time, the culprit listening quietly, although his manner seemed singularly unchastened. At last he interrupted:

"Might I just comment on that last remark of yours, sir?"

The astounded senior subaltern paused in his discourse; such presumption was quite beyond his experience. Whereat young Goering, not waiting for further permission, proceeded to develop his defence, which consisted in tearing the arguments of his senior officer to pieces.

It was almost inconceivable that such a thing could happen in a German barracks, and the junior officers who listened regarded this termagant with a mixture of respect and alarm. One of them, in particular, was impressed. Young Bruno Loerzer, a year older than Goering and a year his senior in the Regiment, was delighted to find a fellow-spirit. The humdrum garrison life lay heavy on him too, as did the eternal harking back to regimental tradition and the musty stories about Frederick the Great. The two young officers became firm friends, and their friendship was destined to survive many twists of fate.

The Happy War

IF, at some time during the early months of 1914, Second-Lieutenant Goering had served an attachment with a British line battalion at Aldershot or at the Curragh (which he never did), he would probably have enjoyed himself very much. His British brother-officers might, at first, have agreed with Ritter von Eppenstein's circle that he was a little "arrogant and Prussian," but they would have liked him well enough, as British regular officers have always been inclined to like their German opposite numbers.

16

Young Goering was handsome, cheerful and, within his means, generous. Gross-Lichterfelde had taught him to sit a horse adequately, but here British subalterns would have detected shortcomings. On the other hand he was an excellent shot and genuinely fond of an active, outdoor life. He would not, at Aldershot, have found many young men with whom to share his love of mountaineering – he had already at that time climbed most of the great Swiss peaks and was planning a trip to the Caucasus on his next leave – but he might have taken with enthusiasm to Rugby football, a game well suited to his temperament. He liked to drink in pleasant company and knew how to hold his liquor like a gentleman. Goering would no doubt have been popular enough in the Mess.

The life of a British regimental officer would certainly have appealed to the visitor from Germany. In the Imperial Army the club life of a British Mess was unknown. The officers of Infantry Regiment 112 did not sit down, several evenings a week, to formal dinners, at a long table on which silver trophies glowed, gently mellowed by age and much polish, beneath the light of many candles, and the conversation was about anything rather than soldiering, or for that matter, women. Formal dinners there were, of course, at the *Offizierskasino*, the Officers' Club, at Mühlhausen, but they lacked that atmosphere of a well-ordered family which the Mess of a good British regiment provided. The inflexible rule against any discussion of "shop" in the Mess might have been irksome to the guest, but at least he might think it better to talk freely of horses and sport and politics and travel with his contemporaries and even his seniors than to listen, perforce respectfully, to elderly officers recounting hoary legends of Frederick the Great, or tales of the campaigns against France in the last century.

Goering's British comrades would have regretted, perhaps, that this pleasant young German had not been to a public-school, which would have "knocked off his corners" – for he had a number of corners. To a perceptive observer he displayed a strong streak of ruthlessness which, according to the simple philosophy of a British regular subaltern of 1914, could have been cured by a couple of years of fagging. He was rather too firmly attached to material comforts and, in particular, to pleasant, elegant surroundings. However, making all allowances for the fact that the fellow was a foreigner, he was likeable enough. Good-looking, strong, physically fear-

17

less, it would have seemed to his English friends that he might, but for the unlucky accident of birth and education, have made a very reasonable British officer.

Goering, on his side, would have found much to criticize at Aldershot and much that was incomprehensible. The discipline of the British Army seemed to be effective enough in its way, but it was mild compared to that exercised in Infantry Regiment 112. Although he himself was no glutton for work – things had a habit of coming easily to him – the British officer's custom of changing into plain clothes as soon after midday as possible and of devoting the remainder of the day to sport of some kind would have seemed ridiculous to young Goering. One would almost think that they were ashamed of *being* officers. Nor, at Aldershot, was there any trace of that eagerness for war which the German Army displayed during the first decade of the century. True, every British regiment might expect to see action on the North-West Frontier of India, and perhaps, elsewhere in the "Colonies," but that was scarcely war, as the word was understood at Gross-Lichterfelde, and for war of that kind few preparations appeared to be made at Aldershot.

And yet – there were the trophies on the walls of the anteroom to prove that British soldiers had opportunities of sport and travel unknown to the officers of the German Army. There was a regimental plate and the deep armchairs and a kind of intimate comradeship which the Kaiser's officers did not know. It is certain that Goering would have enjoyed all that very much.

Above all there was a sense of permanency, of traditions going back far beyond Frederick of Prussia. Great Britain had been so long united, Germany united for little more than forty years. At home life was rather hectic, in England it was so calm . . . too calm, perhaps, and yet attractive to a young man with a streak of indolence in his character. In a sense it might be pleasant to be a real part of this slow, mysterious society. . . .

It was not until many years after 1914, however, that Hermann Goering set foot in England, and in the meanwhile war came . . . war in the German rather than in the British sense of the word, the war for which Infantry Regiment 112 had trained for so long. Second-Lieutenant Goering, true to his nature, plunged headlong into the new adventure, his opportunities for doing so all the better from the fact that around

Mülhausen the first shots of the conflict were fired.

Infantry Regiment 112 was stationed, in those first days of war, on the right bank of the Rhine. Hardly had the German and French armies begun to move than the company in which Goering commanded a platoon was ordered to board an armoured train and move up to the town of Mühlhausen itself. The train reached the outskirts of the city and halted, while Goering led his platoon forward to reconnoitre. His orders were perfectly clear – he was to obtain what news of the enemy's movements he could but on no account to remain long absent from the main body of the company, since the engine of the armoured train must soon go back down the line for water.

The platoon-commander got his news soon enough. Agitated civilians told him that French cavalry had already entered Mühlhausen, occupied the Town Hall and posted placards declaring the city to be under French martial law. Clearly the German patrol had already fulfilled its limited mission and its commander must now withdraw with all speed and report to company headquarters. Goering, notwithstanding his orders, took precisely the opposite course. Forcing his way through a mob of frightened civilians, he led his little force straight to the Town Hall. The French cavalry had already ridden on. Pausing only to tear down the posters which they had stuck on the walls, the young officer pressed forward in pursuit of the enemy.

He came up with the French near Dornach, on the southern outskirts of the town, unobserved by their piquets, and getting his men down over as wide a front as possible, opened fire. Believing that a strong force of German troops had occupied Mülhausen and that they were now confronted with a sizeable advanced guard, the French patrols withdrew and, as it subsequently became known, the plans of their commander for a general attack on the city were amended in consequence.

Second-Lieutenant Goering secured, in this his first action his first war-booty . . . four French horses . . . and returned, triumphant, to his company. Perhaps the horses atoned, in the eyes of his company commander, for his subordinate's gross disregard of orders. At all events Goering went out on patrol again next day.

On this occasion he commanded a force of six men, mounted on bicycles. Although French patrols were active on the outskirts of Mühlhausen, the German cyclists managed to evade them, entered the city, and were astonished to see before them General Pau, commanding the French forces in that sector, standing in the street with his staff-officers about him. During their ride into the city Goering's party had been joined by a lone German trooper who had somehow become separated from his squadron. This soldier was now ordered to dismount by Goering, who, throwing away his bicycle, proposed, as he afterwards confessed, to gallop up to the unsuspecting Frenchmen, throw the General across his saddle and bring him back captive to his company.

A nervous cyclist ruined this ambitious project by opening fire prematurely. The French replied so briskly that all thoughts of a dramatic kidnapping were abandoned and Goering's party pedalled, as swiftly as possible, back to their own lines.

Hermann Goering's first taste of war had been exciting and entertaining, and his commanding officer had the sense to appreciate in his subordinate qualities of dash and initiative which made him an excellent intelligence officer in the strictly tactical sense of that term. Reconnaissance therefore became Goering's speciality. He made a habit of advancing under whatever cover he could find to a spot as close as possible to the enemy lines, and thence, from some point of vantage, he marked the French positions which he could observe on a map. These excursions often exposed him to greater danger from the fire of German artillery than from that of the enemy, but he was never touched by the missiles of either side.

As the autumn of 1914 approached, Infantry Regiment 112 marched out of Alsace and into France proper, where the regiment fought its way through the Vosges Mountains and was engaged in its first full-scale action at Baccarat, south of Nancy. The rigours of this campaign, the damp, the cold and exposure, did for young Goering what the earnest efforts of the enemy had so far failed to achieve. Now there was no comfortable living, little warmth, often not even a dry change of uniform. To Goering's intense humiliation he was struck down by a sharp attack of rheumatism in the joints of both legs. Evacuated to Freiburg, in the Black Forest, he lay fretting in hospital.

The young officer had but one consolation in his illness. Bruno Loerzer, the comrade who had once been so impressed by Goering's defiance of the senior subaltern of Infantry Regiment 112, had already left that unit some months previously and was training as an airman at the "Aviatik" flying-school, not far from Freiburg. He came to visit Goering in hospital and listened for some time to the invalid's bitter girding at the hard fate which kept him from the front.

"I'll be up in a week, though," Goering said at last. "Only God knows how long I'll have to wait after that before I can get back to the Regiment."

"And when you do," Loerzer answered, putting into words a fear that already haunted his friend; "you'll get an attack of rheumatic fever and then you'll be out of it for good. Why not try the Flying Corps? No foot-slogging there, and a dry bed every night."

The idea appealed to Goering at once. Flying was a tremendous novelty, as yet hardly tried in war. It gave scope for individual initiative, it promised more excitement than Infantry Regiment 112 seemed likely to afford, it offered an opportunity of quick distinction. Goering agreed that he should apply for a transfer from the infantry and that he should then become Loerzer's observer.

"You don't need your legs for that, anyhow," Loerzer pointed out.

Dr. Heinrich Ernst Goering would probably not have approved of this plan, but he was then in no position to oppose it, for he had died in Haiti. Ritter von Eppenstein, a childless bachelor, had now taken the family under his full protection. Frau Goering had become housekeeper at Mauterndorf and it seemed more than probable – indeed almost certain – that a large share of Eppenstein's great wealth would fall to the Goering family in the reasonably near future. The Ritter was already aged 70 in 1914.

It was therefore with the comfortable feeling that his mother was well provided for that Hermann could launch out into the hazardous business of flying. At first his prospects of becoming an airman seemed gloomy enough. The Army authorities blankly refused to agree to his transfer from the infantry. Goering nevertheless persevered, and in October 1914 was formerly commissioned to the Flying Corps.

The recruit's first flight was from Freiburg to Darmstadt, seated in front of Loerzer in a rickety fighter biplane. There both officers awaited their appointment to a squadron at the front, and spent the days of waiting in practice flights. An observer in those early days needed little special training, and Loerzer gave Goering what he required. At last orders came through. Loerzer was to fly to Stenay near Sedan in France, and there report to *Feldfliegerabteilung* 25, a unit under the immediate orders of the Crown Prince, Commander-in-Chief of the Fifth Army, which faced the French forces at Verdun.

At Stenay Goering was subjected to an experience which frequently falls to the lot of young officers of all armies on being posted to a new unit. Nobody was expecting him. Orders had been received concerning Loerzer, but Goering was quite unknown to *Feldfliegerabteilung* 25. It was decreed that he must return to Darmstadt and so be separated from his mentor. Both young men protested vehemently, and the struggle for Goering's continued existence at Stenay lasted for some days. At last the Commander yielded, and Goering stayed.

His comrades of those days recall Goering as a good, reliable observer, with a flair for aerial photography. With Loerzer at the "joystick" he flew over the fortifications of Verdun, leaning out of the cockpit of his aircraft and holding his primitive camera at arm's length while he operated the shutter. On one occasion he succeeded in identifying, at first attempt, a battery of French heavy artillery which was preparing to shell the German positions and in directing German counter-battery fire from the air by visual signals with such success that the enemy guns never came into action. For this feat he received, from the hands of the Crown Prince himself, the first of his decorations – the Iron Cross, First Class, at that stage of the war a very much more coveted award than it later became.

Visual signals were all very well in their way, but the use of wireless telegraphy would save both time, temper and energy. Goering accordingly set himself to master the technique of wireless telegraphy and was one of the first officers of any army to operate a wireless transmitter from an aircraft. By February 1915 he was a competent telegraphist, and he became extremely expert in observing and correcting the fire of German artillery by wireless signals. Here again Goering's impetuous temper and a tendency towards insubordination, which was becoming increasingly marked, got him into trouble more than once. To look down upon the target and see that, in spite of his best efforts, the German guns were still shooting wildly was often more than his rather limited patience could stand.

On one occasion the German artillery was shelling the village of Beaumont, and shelling it with singular lack of effect. Goering tapped back corrections, but the gunners plugged steadily away, ignoring his signals. At last he ordered the guns to cease fire, and as he flew back towards the German lines, delivered himself a blistering signal "in clear" inquiring, impolitely, why the battery persisted in wasting ammunition. This disrespectful message, transmitted in plain language for every enemy operator to hear, brought down a load of trouble upon the head of its sender, and the episode almost ended in a court-martial. But Goering, not for the first or last time, argued his way out of the difficulty and, having done so, reached the conclusion that he had been an observer quite long enough.

In the early summer, therefore, Goering was back at Freiburg, now himself a student on the pilot's course at the "Aviatik" training-school whence Loerzer had graduated some months before. Already accustomed to flying, he took easily to the air. Years later he loved to speak of the sense of power which his first solo flight conferred upon him.

Although the aircraft in which he flew over the rolling hills of the Black Forest were crazy, slow, contraptions by the standards of even ten years later, they were still, in 1915, among the finest fighting aeroplanes in the world, and their pilots members of a minutely small élite among the warring nations, an élite, moreover, which sought, on both sides, to keep alive traditions of chivalry which some of the groundlings, bogged down in Flanders mud, were beginning to forget. Goering displayed in his character three qualities which are more often found allied in men of his race than in those of any other – a muddled idealism, based on a patriotism equally confused, a rather mawkish sentimentality, and a ruthlessness in action which could and did, when necessary, dominate his whole personality. The Flying Corps of the First World War suited him very well.

By the autumn of 1915 Goering was a trained pilot, back at the front with the faithful Loerzer as a member of No. 5 *Abteilung.* His return to active service coincided with the autumn offensive of the French and British armies, and the *Abteilung* was kept busy enough with its own reconnaissance duties and with the interception of enemy aircraft entrusted with similar missions over the German lines.

How many of the stories of Goering's wartime exploits subsequently related by diligent Nazi writers were historically correct is a matter for conjecture. One of the many tales told in Goering's heyday is of a reconnaissance sortie which he is said to have made with two other fighters one misty day in November. They were flying at 2000 feet when Goering observed ahead, well behind the British lines, a Handley-Page bomber of monstrous size. This British aircraft had only just been brought into service, and while the officers of No. 5 *Abteilung* had discussed what little was known about it, none of them had hitherto seen an actual machine. Goering was determined to destroy the great bomber.

So intent was Goering on the prey which lay ahead of him that he failed to observe that he was alone. Less single-minded than he, the pilots of the two machines which had kept him company had perceived, 1500 feet above them, at least twenty British fighters, and had prudently made course for the German lines. Goering had eyes only for the giant bomber. Swooping down on it he killed the rear-gunner, climbed, swooped again and put the forward machine-gun out of action. A third burst from his gun set fire to one of the enemy's two engines, and the bomber began to spiral downwards. Only then did the hunter hear the roar of the British Sopwiths on his tail, and see that a dozen of them were diving to the attack.

A burst of fire holed Goering's petrol-tank, and as he set his hand to the cock which controlled the reserve supply of fuel another burst ripped the fabric of his wings to shreds and grazed his right leg and hip. There was nothing for it but a hazardous nose-dive, in the hope that it might still be possible to pull out of it three or four hundred feet from the ground. The German pilot jerked down the nose of his aircraft as the British fighters almost jostled one another to pursue him, and impeded each other in so doing.

The fighter still answered to the controls. With petrol streaming from his punctured tank Goering hedge-hopped across the German lines and landed somehow in a graveyard, whose church has been converted by the Germans into a field-hospital. Within a minute or two of landing, Goering was on the operating table in the crypt.

His aircraft carried more than sixty bullet holes. The graze to the leg was no more than a flesh wound, but the bullet which had hit Goering in the hip had done more serious damage and left behind it a scar, ten inches long, which he carried for the rest of his days.

Convalescence was long and was followed by light duties

at home. This was a pleasant idle period, enlivened for Goering by the first serious love-affair of which there is any record. Marianne Mauser was the daughter of solid, well-to-do parents. Pretty and attractive herself, she was dazzled by the wounded flyer, and he, if not dazzled, was at least suitably affectionate. Lieutenant Goering was, from the point of view of Marianne's parents, a desirable son-in-law. Not only was his own record and family background to his advantage, but it seemed that he was also one of the heirs presumptive of the wealthy Ritter von Eppenstein. For the present, however, there could be no question of an engagement, let alone of marriage. Flying in wartime was a risky business, as Herr Mauser pointed out to the Lieutenant, who had better reason to know the truth of that saying than had his prospective father-in-law. And so, in the late summer of 1916, Goering went back to the front, leaving his "Mausi" enamoured but not engaged.

Once again Bruno Loerzer awaited his friend, this time near Colmar, near Alsace. Loerzer had now achieved command of a crack *Staffel,* manned by flyers carefully chosen from almost every unit of the German Flying Corps. Hardly had the two old comrades come together than the unit, ordered to Mühlhausen, took up its quarters on the very field where Goering and Loerzer had drilled together in the old, peaceful but unregretted days of Infantry Regiment 112.

All that winter Goering and Loerzer flew together, and on one occasion at least Loerzer saved his friend's life by forcing down a French fighter which would otherwise inevitably have destroyed him. But by now the pupil had overtaken the master. Goering's reputation as a pilot grew steadily, and in May 1917 he was posted, in command, to No. 27 Fighter *Staffel.* For the first time in his life since "Hermann Goering, General of the Boers," had led the urchins of Veldenstein, he had an independent command, and the new commanding officer lost no time in asserting his authority. The *Staffel,* thoroughly overhauled and reorganized, began to win an impressive series of victories. Those who flew with the Allies in that war, now so remote, may recall the unit from the black and white checks which its aircraft displayed on the underside of the lower wing, markings which caused British troops to nickname them after a celebrated brand of whisky.

One British officer had good reason to remember Lieutenant Goering at this time. Captain Frank Beaumont, a pilot of No.

56 Squadron, Royal Flying Corps, which had fought many bitter battles with Goering's flyers, was extremely irritated when one day, after he had shot down two German aircraft, the wing of his own machine, for some reason which he could not understand, disintegrated. He was, nevertheless, able to bring his machine down behind the German lines with no more injury to himself than a slightly damaged foot, and was delighted to find the first days of his imprisonment alleviated by several visits from a Lieutenant Goering, who brought him cigarettes, chocolate and other comforts, spoke with warm admiration of 56 Squadron and, without ever trying to draw military information from him, contrived to have several pleasant conversations on matters of interest to airmen on both sides of the front – conversations which he kept on extremely general lines.

"For God's sake," Goering said to the young officer, "don't get into the Army's hands. Stay with us if you possibly can. We'll look after you, and you'll have a much better time."

Captain Beaumont, however, was not the master of his own fate and soon he was taken away to a prisoner-of-war camp and for the present saw the kindly young German officer no more.

Now a full lieutenant, Goering meanwhile succeeded in overcoming the scruples of the Mauser family and in the autumn of 1917 he and Marianne were officially betrothed.

At the same time the German High Command undertook to reorganize the Flying Corps. It was decided to form a number of large fighter formations, each of forty-eight machines divided into sub-units of four aircraft. The privilege of commanding the first of these relatively large formations – No. 1 *Geschwader* – fell upon Captain Freiherr Manfred von Richthofen.

The experiment was an immediate success, and more formations of the same types were promptly raised. In March 1918 Goering's No. 27 *Staffel* was incorporated in No. 3 *Geschwader* and moved to Ypres.

Richthofen's successes became legendary, the admiration of friend and enemy alike. By April 1918 he had shot down personally eighty enemy aircraft. On the 21st of that month he took off as usual in his Fokker, but this time the hero did not return. For two days anxiety and consternation ran like an undercurrent through the minds of all German airmen. Then Reuter's Agency gave the news that they feared to learn:

"Reuter's Special Correspondent with the British Army reports that the German airman, Captain von Richthofen, has met his death in an air battle over the Front. The body will be buried with military honours. The funeral will be in keeping with the remarkable and impressive record of this airman."

Two days later a British aircraft flew over the German lines and dropped a confirmation of this message, together with a photograph of von Richthofen's grave which his British enemies had smothered in flowers.

A great airman had died, and among officers of Goering's seniority and experience the question of his successor was one of the utmost personal interest. "A military testament," scrawled in pencil on a scrap of paper, answered the question which was uppermost in their thoughts:

"10.3.18.

If I should not return Lieutenant Reinhard will assume command of the *Geschwader.*

FRHR. V. RICHTHOFEN, Capt."

Reinhard was promoted Captain and took over the *Geschwader,* but Goering, too, had his reward. He was now one of Germany's most celebrated pilots. His score of enemy aircraft destroyed stood at twenty-one. In May 1918 the Kaiser recognized the fact by conferring upon him the highest military award within his gift – the coveted *Orden "Pour le Mérite".*

This decoration, instituted by Frederick the Great, was not usually given, as is its nearest British equivalent, the Victoria Cross, for a single deed of supreme courage. Rather was it the reward of consistently gallant service. At all events the officers of the Imperial Army coveted the little white enamel cross worn below the opening of the high tunic-collar no less than do British officers the V.C., and between 1914 and 1918 only some 900 of them earned the right to wear it.

With the award of this distinction young Goering officially entered the Valhalla of Germany's war heroes. His cold, blue eyes looked out upon the civilian world from picture postcards which were sold by the thousand up and down the Fatherland. *Backfische* – the German counterparts of the British "flappers" of 1918 – set the portrait of "Our successful Fighter Pilot" on their dressing-tables besides those of other young Siegfrieds, and wrote impassioned letters to its original. For the first time Goering was tasting glory, and he liked the taste very much indeed.

There is no evidence, however, that "Mausi," for whom the sudden eminence of her fiancé must have been a matter for mingled pride and anxiety, had anything to fear from the thousands of girls who now shared, vicariously, her admiration of Hermann. Goering had little time, and for that matter small inclination, to take advantage of his opportunities. He was seeing a good deal now of Reinhard, Richthofen's successor in command of the *Geschwader*. On July 3, 1918, the two men took off in succession from the Aldershorst aerodrome, near Berlin, to test a new Fokker fighter. Goering took the aircraft up first, banked, looped and landed safely. He clambered out and Reinhard replaced him in the cockpit. The Fokker climbed sweetly to 3000 feet and then the watchers on the ground saw the wings disintegrate. Its wing-struts snapped, the aircraft plummeted crazily to earth. Five days later *Oberleutnant* Goering was posted to the Richthofen *Geschwader* in command. He had achieved a great ambition.

The new commanding officer came to Beugneux, where the *Geschwader* was stationed, with his reputation already established. The officers knew that their new leader had certain peculiarities. In particular, reports of his insistence in choosing always the most comfortable and elegant headquarters available had preceded him. Goering was especially fastidious in his selection of wallpapers. No room whose wallpaper was not clean, bright and attractive would serve as *Geschwader* headquarters. The whole business was quite a joke and Goering had to put up with a good deal of chaff from his brother-officers on the subject.

Yet Goering's pleasure at succeeding to the Richthofen *Geschwader* was somewhat marred by an occurrence which had infuriated his whole family. At the age of 74 Ritter von Eppenstein had taken it into his head to fall in love with a Fräulein Lilli von Schandrowitz, forty years his junior, and to marry her. Frau Goering was forced to leave the comforts of Mauterndorf and all hopes of inheriting the old man's wealth must be abandoned. Hermann was furiously angry and, typically, launched into a vicious quarrel with his former benefactor. All was of no avail. The new Frau von Eppenstein was definitely installed and the Goerings very definitely out, the more definitely thanks to Hermann's outburst of spleen. It is interesting to speculate what effect the Indian summer of a Jewish philanthropist may have had upon Goering's subsequent career. At all events the new commander of the Richthofen *Geschwader* had no very great love for the Jewish race when he took up his duties at Beugneux.

Goering assumed command of the *Geschwader* on July 14, a day of low cloud and drizzle, while across the lines such French soldiers as had the time for celebration were drinking to the anniversary of the fall of the Bastille. The whole unit was on parade to welcome their commander, who was introduced to them by Lieutenant von Wedel. Goering replied in what was his first important speech, his tone and manner crisply military.

"It is a splendid honour," he concluded, "to command a unit of such traditions. We have grave days ahead of us."

Then Lieutenant Bodenschatz formally presented the new commanding-officer with the "Richthofen walking-stick," a cherished relic which Manfred von Richthofen had himself given to poor Reinhard and which now descended to the *Geschwader's* third, and last, commander.

The unit lost no time in resuming its business. On the following day, July 15, 1918, the War Diary read as follows:

"*July* 15. Attack by VII Army. *Geschwader* engaged large numbers of enemy aircraft in the Marne valley. Morn. Moderate flying activity. Aftn. Considerable enemy activity at all heights. Strong formations of English single-seater fighters particularly active. Individual Groups of these squadrons concentrated into half-groups. Closest cooperation maintained with No. 3 Fighter *Geschwader*. *Casualties: Enemy:* – 1045 hrs. one balloon by Lieut. Wenzel Paul (his 6th). 1307 hrs. one Sopwith Camel by Lieut. Loewenhardt (his 36th). 1640 hrs. one 'Spad' by Lieut. Meyer (his 3rd). *Own:* – Lieut. Frieerichs shot down in flames (dead). Good visibility, 99 sorties. Enemy activity increasing."

The German retreat from the Marne had begun and the enemy activity which had been recorded in the War Diary continued to increase. On July 18 Goering shot down his twenty-second enemy aircraft, and the *Geschwader's* total bag was nine French and two British machines. But the greatly improved quality and equipment of the Allied machines was a constant worry. As Goering himself wrote at the time:

"The enemy biplanes are very well armed and fly in

exceedingly good formation, even when attacked by a number of German fighters. They are equipped with armoured or fireproof petrol tanks."

At the end of July Goering managed to snatch some leave, and the command of the *Geschwader* was assumed by Lothar von Richthofen, the brother of its first leader. A few days later he was wounded, and until Goering's return the *Geschwader* was commanded by a certain Lieutenant Ernst Udet, of whom more will be heard later in this narrative.

By August the Germans were in full retreat, hotly pursued by the armies of the Allies. It became increasingly difficult to replace the German aircraft lost, harder still to find the successors of the skilled men who had died in them. Anti-aircraft guns for the defence of aerodromes were at a premium. Day after day the Richthofen *Geschwader* lost one or two of its best airmen, and sometimes Goering, looking down his nominal-rolls, observed with consternation that his command was at no more than half strength. Nevertheless the *Geschwader's* total score of enemy aircraft destroyed since its formation, some nine months before, was 500.

The end was very near now, but there was one more brief spell of good hunting reserved to the heirs of Manfred von Richthofen. Around Metz the American Army was advancing, and most of their airmen had, as yet, little experience of aerial combat. The Richthofen *Geschwader,* quickly transferred to the American front, shot down in a few days almost 100 aircraft. Lieutenant Udet, having gained his sixty-first and sixty-second victories in one of these dog-fights, reported cynically, on landing, that he had allowed a single American to escape "so that there would be one mourner left to tell the tale".

The autumn set in and to the gloom of the weather was added the gloom of a mounting sense of defeat. The *Geschwader* moved back to Marville, where its officers listened drearily to reports of unbroken American successes and, what was worse, of German mutinies. The depleted unit fought and withdrew, only to fight and withdraw again. The War Diary tells the story:

"*November* 7th. Heavy fighting on the eastern bank of the Meuse. Further enemy advance eastwards. Marville aerodrome must be evacuated. Withdrew in own lorries to Tellancourt. Aerodrome on to west of town. Conditions poor, ground bumpy, few grass patches. Billets moderate. Rain and clouds.

November 8th. Arranging aerodrome and billets. Misty. Heavy cloud.

November 9th. Weather bad. All quiet. Preparing to withdraw. Visibility bad."

From Tellancourt the withdrawal proved to be unexpectedly long. On November 8 news so ominous as to be almost incredible had began to filter through to the *Geschwader*. The Kaiser was abdicating, mutiny had broken out in the Navy at Kiel. In Berlin rioters were at large in the streets and German troops had opened fire on their own officers.

At noon on November 9 Goering called his officers together. At all costs, he said, they must stand fast, as a body, one for all and all for one. If attacked by their own troops they would defend themselves. In the meanwhile they would stand together. Piquets were posted and the officers of Richthofen *Geschwader* spent a wakeful night gathered in their headquarters. They were not attacked.

Next morning brought a series of contradictory signals from a series of German authorities. The *Geschwader* was to withdraw to Darmstadt. It was to stay where it was. It was to hand over its aircraft to the American Army. It was to withdraw to Darmstadt.

Both because it had been twice repeated and because it involved at least the postponement of surrender, Goering decided to obey this latter order. Bodenschatz would bring the ground-crews and stores to Darmstadt by the *Geschwader* transport, while Goering led his beaten flyers home. For a day fog lying thick on Tellancourt aerodrome made take-off impossible, and the officers mooned dismally about the sodden field, their only hope now that the Americans would not arrive before the sky cleared. It was very quiet.

The next day brought the end of fighting. As the bells in Paris and London pealed out to welcome the Armistice, the remnants of the Richthofen *Geschwader* took off from Tellancourt. While 250 rattled away in the 35 lorries which comprised Bodenschatz's transport, the Fokkers, one by one, bumped over the hummocky meadow and turned eastwards.

Arrived at Darmstadt, Goering found that one *Staffel* of his *Geschwader* was missing, but presently the laggards appeared and told their story. The *Staffel* had lost its way and, having made an emergency landing at Mannheim, had found its aircraft surrounded by members of the local "Soldiers' Council," typical of hundreds of revolutionary cells which had sprung up from the rotting body of the German Army in the last, agonizing days of defeat. The self-constituted commanders of Mannheim aerodrome forced Goering's men to surrender their arms and then allowed them to proceed to Darmstadt. The members of the lost *Staffel* told their ignominious little tale sheepishly, and were not surprised to observe the fury of their commander as he listened to it.

The whole *Geschwader* was at once ordered into the air, and made course for Mannheim. There the members of the disarmed *Staffel* landed, bearing to the "Soldiers' Council" a message from Lieutenant Goering who, with the remainder of the *Geschwader*, circled overhead. Unless the confiscated arms were immediately restored, the aerodrome would be systematically bombed and strafed from the air. The threat was effective, although the aircraft which threatened the mutineers were not bombers, and could, in fact, have done little damage to resolute troops on the ground. Fully armed once more, the entire *Geschwader* returned to Darmstadt.

A staff-officer awaited them there with orders. The *Geschwader* was to fly to Strasbourg and surrender to the French Army. Goering refused to obey the order. Let some other officer surrender the *Geschwader*. By a curious coincidence his pilots had shown far less than their usual skill when landing at Darmstadt. An array of wrecked undercarriages made it quite impossible for a large proportion of the *Geschwader's* aircraft to take off for Strasbourg. A few were, in fact, delivered there, but the bulk of the unit and its commander remained at Darmstadt. That night Goering sat down and wearily wrote the last entry in the War Diary:

"*November 11th.* Armistice. *Geschwader* flew in bad weather to Darmstadt. Misty.

Since its establishment the *Geschwader* has won 644 victories in the air. Losses by enemy action totalled 56 officer-pilots, 6 other ranks. Wounded, 52 officer-pilots, 7 other ranks.

(Signed) Hermann Goering,
Lieutenant O.C. *Geschwader.*"

The *Geschwader* flew back to Aschaffenburg, where, on November 19, Goering took leave of his comrades in the

Stiftskeller public-house. He spoke to them at some length of their unit's history, of its victories and losses and of the strange time which lay ahead, an epoch in which they could already see all the values which they had cherished crashing to the ground, all the old loyalties shattered. He spoke with feeling understandable in the circumstances, and many of those who listened wept a little. Then the speaker raised his glass.

"To the Richthoven *Geschwader*," he cried, and they all drank.

Goering drained his own glass and, with a savage gesture, dashed it against the wall.

Two Meetings

THEY demobilized Hermann Goering with the honorary rank of Captain. That, his decorations and his skill as an airman were the sole legacies of four years' service in the German cause, and neither rank nor the medals could be regarded as assets in the Germany of 1919. To have been an officer was to have earned the hatred of the mob and the mistrust of those who sought to exercise a precarious Government. A heavily decorated officer was doubly suspect.

Germany seemed to have fallen to pieces. Until the Armistice the morale of the civilian population had, on the whole, been very much better than that of the troops at the front. Now, shabby, beaten, filled with a bitter sense of grievance, the soldiers returned home, and there quickly infected with their own hopelessness those who had awaited the victors for four years. Goering himself went through an experience familiar to those who still wore the uniform of an officer of the Imperial Army in the last days of 1918. He was set upon by a crowd of ex-soldiers, girls and women, hungry and haggard, whipped up by a Bolshevik agitator. They shouted "No more war" and tried to tear the decorations from his tunic, as he thrust his way through the press. Only a few weeks before the incident Goering had been one of Germany's heroes. Now the very decorations which testified to his service were a provocation to many of his countrymen. The collapse of Captain Goering's world was almost too painful to be borne, nor was Captain Goering, the war hero, the lover of the good things of life, a man to resign himself to such a catastrophe.

There was indeed little connection between the Germany of late 1918 and the arrogant nation which had plunged Europe into war four years earlier. In Berlin the Spartakists flaunted their red flags and their machine-guns in the streets of the capital. The sinister Karl Radek was hurrying from Moscow to advise the German Communist Party, while Communists fought with their opponents in the streets and political murder became a commonplace. For a few pfennigs anyone could buy a rifle from a war-weary soldier, and in Bremen and Hamburg troops were forcibly disarmed by the workers. The potato ration for Berliners stood that winter at 5lb. a week.

Wilhelm II, Emperor of Germany, after contemplating a last desperate resistance, had realized that none would fight for his dynasty, and had withdrawn to Holland, muttering futilely to all who would listen that at least he was King of Prussia. He had still failed to grasp that even Prussia would have none of him.

In Munich King Ludwig III was already driven from the throne of Bavaria and the Republic proclaimed.

The despised mob of civilians was taking its revenge, albeit a half-hearted one, upon the society which had plunged Germany into war, a society of which young Captain Goering was a sufficiently typical representative. Time would show that the German leopard had not, in fact, changed his spots, and Goering was destined to play a leading part in that demonstration, but for the present, at least, the collapse seemed to be complete and beyond remedy.

At the age of 25 Goering stood quite alone in a Germany which had rejected him and his class. He was trained for nothing save only soldiering and flying, and for men of that craft there now seemed to be no place whatever in the defeated Reich. Ten years of his life had been given to the worship and service of a system which, once as seemingly immutable as the Alps which he loved, had now vanished utterly in a chaos of defeat and ignominy. For the demobilized officer – even for the regular officer – there was no gratuity, let alone pension. Captain Goering had not even any civilian clothes worth mentioning. Mauterndorf, where but for the belated infatuation of Ritter von Eppenstein for Fräulein von Schandrowitz he might have taken refuge, was now closed to him, thanks to his own bad temper. Frau Goering, living meagrely in Munich on a pension whose value dwindled daily, could do nothing to help her son, nor were the other members of the family in any better case.

Among the first Allied officers to reach Munich was Captain Beaumont, who spoke perfect German. He had been sent ahead to prepare the way for the British authority which was to control the dismantling of the German Air Force, and his first action was to requisition suitable accommodation in the luxurious *Hotel Vierjahreszeiten*. Hardly had he settled in with his rations, his cigarettes, his British gin and whisky, when two German officers presented themselves at his door; he was delighted to recognize one of them as Lieutenant Goering who had been so kind to him during the early days of his imprisonment. Goering's companion was Ernst Udet.

Here at least was an opportunity to repay past kindness which the British officer would not miss. For several weeks he virtually supported the two Germans. They ate his food, they smoked his cigarettes, and when the weekly ration of liquor arrived they shared it out between them until it was finished and then lived soberly until the next consignment reached them. Neither Goering nor Udet ever asked for money, nor did Beaumont feel that he should offer them any. They were content to live in an atmosphere of comradeship till, at last, since Munich seemed to be no place for demobilized German officers, they both departed, with hearty thanks to their host, to seek their fortunes elsewhere.

Goering never forgot this episode and never did Captain (later Air-Commodore) Beaumont fail to receive a card from him on his birthday and at Christmas. Even in the first year of the Second World War these little remembrances continued.

Goering decided that he must leave Germany for some place abroad where he might yet make use of his only skill – the ability to fly an aircraft extremely well.

Here again there were obstacles. The Allied nations and their overseas dependencies were closed to German immigration. The United States, once the hope of the younger sons of Germany, gave them no welcome now. South America offered certain possibilities to the soldier of fortune, but that remote half-continent had little appeal for Goering.

In January 1919 Herr Mauser inquired in a telegram to his prospective son-in-law just what young Goering had to offer his daughter. The answer was "Nothing," and the engagement with Fräulein Mauser was thereby ended. Goering had no choice but to accept his dismissal, although he did so with ill-grace. He was not, as even he may have admitted to himself, a particularly hopeful prospect as a husband. Less than a year had passed since the Kaiser had hung the *Pour le Mérite* about his neck, since his face had become familiar to the German people as one of their great war-heroes, since Mausi had been beside herself with pride at being engaged to such a man. Now he was a person without any certain means of livelihood.

German industry came to Goering's aid now, as it was often to do in the future. Denmark was organizing an aeronautical exhibition at Copenhagen and German aircraft manufacturers, not yet put out of business by the Allies, were eager to display their products. Goering accepted an offer to demonstrate the Fokker F7 in Copenhagen on condition that the aircraft might remain his personal property after the display had ended. He flew the machine from Berlin to Denmark in the spring of 1919.

The first demonstration flights were relatively dangerous. On one occasion, as Goering was stunting over the Copenhagen airfield at Kastrup while a gaping crowd watched him from the ground, a seagull hit his propeller and shattered it. The little aircraft came spiralling down from 7500 feet, while the watchers held their breath and waited for the inevitable crash. At the last moment the German pilot somehow regained control of the machine – to his dying day Goering never knew how that was done – and glided down safely to barracks below.

Money came in fairly comfortably, and was quickly spent. On Sundays Goering visited one provincial town after another offering short flights at 50 kronor (£3) a head, and the evening of each Sunday spent in this fashion saw him with enough money in his pocket for a week of comparatively lavish living. He was able to reside in a fashionable Copenhagen hotel, often for weeks at a time sleeping by day and spending each night in the bars and nightclubs of that gay city. The Danes called Goering the "Mad Flyer," and they rather liked him.

Goering found that the glamour of his war-service, a liability in war-shattered Germany, did much in neutral Denmark to make up for an empty pocket-book. The young women of Copenhagen are celebrated for their charm and gaiety, and in 1919 not a few of them were prepared to console a German

36

hero fallen upon evil times. Captain Goering was not the man to reject these satisfactions, and his loneliness as the rejected suitor of Marianne Mauser was greatly mitigated by the affection of several Danish ladies.

One of them still has good reason to recall the signature of the Treaty of Versailles. The terms of that covenant, conscientiously reported by the Danish newspapers, spoiled for her a romantic afternoon. Captain Goering, upon hearing the terms of his country's submission, "raged like a madman," ran upstairs and locked himself into an attic. There he sulked and brooded until he felt himself fit for human society again. But the magic of the afternoon had been lost and, incidentally, the future of a petulant, ill-instructed virile young German had been sealed. And with it, in some degree, the future of the world.

This careless hand-to-mouth existence in Copenhagen lasted for a year. Yet Germany still exercised her attraction upon an exiled son, and Franziska Goering, to whom Hermann was sincerely devoted, longed for a visit from her hero. Accompanied by a woman friend, Goering flew, without passport, to Berlin and thence journeyed to Munich, where his mother's welcome was warm but that of the outside world as chilly as ever. There was no work in Bavaria, and after a few days Goering returned to Denmark.

In Sweden, richest and most powerful of the Scandinavian nations, young Goering's flying had, however, not passed unnoticed. A number of progressive Swedes were engaged in establishing a civil air service, and in 1919, as again in 1945, they needed pilots with war experience to man their aircraft.

The world of aviation in Scandinavia then was even smaller than it now is, and there was talk of those Swedish projects among the people with whom Goering consorted in Copenhagen. If anybody was going to take advantage of Swedish enterprise, the Captain decided, it should be he, and so in December 1919 he put his F7 down on the airfield of Ljungbyhed in Southern Sweden, where he smashed his undercarriage and was forced to travel on to Stockholm by train.

Here he presented himself to Aktiebolaget Svensk-Lufttrafik, the newly formed airline with which Sweden proposed to enter the lists as a pioneer of civil aviation. Would the company accept him as a pilot? The company would not. Goering persisted through the remainder of a harassing winter, during which he managed to sell a few parachutes, and in the spring of 1920 he had his way.

In the meanwhile lack of money was, to some small degree, compensated by certain satisfactions of *amour-propre*.

Deprived by her neutrality of the practical experience in matters of aviation which the belligerent Powers had obtained at such great cost, Sweden had few experts in aeronautics, and Goering found that his opinions, which he was never behindhand in giving, were listened to and quoted with some respect in Stockholm. In 1920 the pioneers of civil aviation were all too frequently paying with their lives for the privilege of being first in a new field of human progress. The Swedish Press made much of these incidents, and in doing so drew down upon itself the somewhat contemptuous criticism of young Captain Goering. In an interview with a Swedish newspaper he declared that these air fatalities were accorded an altogether ridiculous amount of notice in Sweden. In his own experience of stunt-flying, all aerobatics carried out at a height of less than 1500 feet entailed a strong element of risk, but that must be accepted as a matter of course. "The art of flying must always have its victims."

During the winter Goering's faithful F7 was overhauled and refurbished, and in April it was ready to take the air again. On April 11, 1920, he took it up from Gärdet. The newspaper *Svenska Dagbladet* commented approvingly on this display of stunt-flying, one of the first ever seen in Sweden.

"The German fighter-pilot, Captain Goering, has now obtained his long-awaited fighter – a veteran of the Western Front. It is a Fokker with a 185 h.p. B.M.W. engine, with which he made a trial flight over Gärdet today, executing a series of loops and other aerobatics at heights of between 3000 and 1800 feet. Next Sunday Stockholm's popular 'air chauffeur' will continue his passenger-carrying flights."

To be a pilot of Svensk-Lufttrafik, on a strictly unsalaried footing, was not the path to riches, but the months in Sweden were, nevertheless, pleasant ones for Goering. He was doing a job which he knew and enjoyed, he was a person of some consequence in the narrow world of Swedish aeronautics, he earned enough money to keep himself and to buy, occasionally, some "nice things" for his sittingroom. Although his heart was in Germany, where things seemed to be going from bad to worse, Goering was not unhappy in Stockholm. He made many friends in good society, and was, in a small way, quite a figure in Stockholm, a popular man at dinner-parties and dances.

He was, moreover, agent for Sweden of a brand of German parachute, the Heinicken, a spring-loaded affair designed to open automatically as soon as the pilot of an aircraft baled out. In a rare pamphlet, now preserved in the Royal Library in Stockholm, Goering sought to induce Swedish clients to adopt the Heinicken parachute, and in so doing gave, all unwittingly, several clues to his own, character.

Remembering, no doubt, the bitter days of 1918 when his *Geschwader* was drained by casualties of good pilots for whom replacements could not be found, Goering, who described himself grandiloquently on the fly-leaf of the pamphlet as "Formerly Commodore of Baron von Richthofen's Flying Geschwader No. 1," says:

"The purpose of the parachute is to save the airman from disaster. . . . One can always obtain new aircraft, but it is a matter of far greater difficulty to replace the airman since, *pro prima* to get a man fit for military service transferred to the air-force is a matter of considerable difficulty in any case, *pro secundo* his training, once transferred, takes a long time. Thus the parachute, quite apart from its essential purpose of saving a valuable human life, has become a very important factor in air-defence."

The writer goes on to defend the merits of "automatic" parachutes, such as the Heinicken, as against the "non-automatic" system, as represented by the "Irvin," his chief American competitor which was actuated by the pilot's pulling the "rip-cord."

"In order that the 'non-automatic' parachute may function," says Goering, "the aviator must be able himself to release the parachute. He must therefore have perfect control of mind, nerves and body . . . but of one thing one can never be quite certain – the workings of the human mind and soul . . . I make bold to state that I have shown, in the many aerial acrobatics in which I have taken part, that fear and slackness are not numbered among my qualities, yet I should never be so pretentious as to guarantee that, in making a jump in the circumstances which I have mentioned, my own nerves would be under control."

Early one afternoon in the winter of 1921 a certain Count

Eric von Rosen presented himself at the Stockholm aerodrome. This young man had already won some celebrity in Sweden as an explorer and as a dashing fellow, always ready for a bit of adventure, a person of sudden whims and enthusiasms. He was in a whimsical mood now. Rather than travel in a sluggish train which would take two hours or more to carry him from Stockholm to Sparreholm, when he must drive to his estate of Rockelsta, he proposed if possible to fly to Rockelsta direct. The weather was, admittedly, vile; snow was falling heavily from a leaden sky, but this, in von Rosen's eyes, only made the whole plan the more amusing. He had, as he explained cheerfully to the people whom he found at the aerodrome, never flown in a snowstorm and was anxious to sample the experience. Would any pilot undertake to bring him to Rockelsta? Captain Goering declared he was perfectly prepared to do so.

The flight was sufficiently unpleasant to satisfy even Count von Rosen. A headwind drove the snow into the faces of pilot and passenger as the aircraft battled over pine-clad hills. At last the frozen surface of a lake lay beneath them, and in the last light of a short winter afternoon Goering landed on the ice. He had landed on the wrong lake, as Count von Rosen pointed out as soon as he was able to collect his wits. Goering took off again and this time landed on Lake Baven, close to the red-stone walls of Rockelsta Castle.

Pilot and passenger were half-frozen as they entered the hall of the house, but the welcome they received soon atoned for the discomforts of the flight. Both men were hurried into hot baths, and then Countess von Rosen set them in front of a blazing fire and brought hot toddy. To Goering, staring about him, the place seemed a perfect expression of comfort – not unlike Mauterndorf – the sort of house, in fact, which he had always liked. Ancient weapons hung on the walls of the great hall beside the heads and antlers of elk and deer. At the foot of the staircase which led from the hall into the darkness above stood a great stuffed bear, which as Count von Rosen explained, he had himself killed with a spear. Goering was admiring this beast when a woman came down the staircase. Slim and dark, she advanced into the hall and was introduced to the young German as Carin von Kantzow, the sister of Countess von Rosen. Goering looked her up and down and thought her very beautiful.

The four of them had supper after that and Goering, in

halting, imperfect Swedish, told his hosts stories of the war and spoke bitterly of the present humiliation of his country. They sympathized deeply – particularly Carin von Kantzow. Then all four gathered round the piano and sang – Swedish folk-songs of which Goering did not know the words, but could pick up the melody, and a few German airs, it was all very nostalgic and sad and, to the German taste, beautiful. As their eyes met across the piano, Carin and Hermann were both deeply moved.

Goering managed to prolong his stay at Rockelsta by one day. When at last the noise of the Fokker's engines died away behind the snow-clad hills which lie about the castle the air-man took with him a new interest in life.

Carin von Kantzow was five years older than Hermann Goering. Her father, Baron Carl von Fock, had served in the Swedish Army and she had military connections on her mother's side also.

At the age of 21, Carin married, in 1910, Captain Nils von Kantzow, a lieutenant in the Army. The first years of their life together were spent in a northern garrison and in Paris, where von Kantzow was attached to the Swedish Lega-tion. Just before war broke out in 1914 the young couple returned to Stockholm.

Although Sweden was not at war, the four years of conflict were busy ones for Captain von Kantzow, and he had little time to spare for his wife and their son Thomas. Carin grew lonely and restless. She made friends quickly and as quickly dropped them. She posed for painters; musicians and poets dedicated their works to her; but Stockholm was a small town and Sweden a small country. Out in the world great things were happening, and Carin, a fervent partisan of Germany, longed to have some part in them.

The end of the war did not bring with it for Carin an end of restlessness. When, on that winter's night of 1921, she met the young German who had so bravely served the cause in which she had believed, and who was now exiled from his own country, her heart went out to him. She determined to see Hermann Goering again.

They did not meet often in the three months which followed, but soon Hermann and Carin knew that they were in love. Goering wrote long, passionate letters to the Countess and even tried his hand, clumsily, at poetry. For him, typically, the whole affair was perfectly simple. He loved Carin and

Carin loved him. Obviously, then, she must divorce von Kantzow and they would be married. For Carin the matter was more complicated. She had strong feelings of loyalty, if no longer affection, towards her husband. Hermann, for all his charm and romantic past, had a future little less assured than it had been when Herr Mauser had broken off the engagement with Marianne. To marry him would be to exchange comfort and security for poverty and uncertainty.

Moreover, Goering too was restless. He had come to feel that he could no longer stay away from Germany. Somehow he must work for her regeneration. Yet, utterly untrained as he was, he realized that he could be of little service until he had done something to fill the many gaps in his education. He had already resigned from Svensk-Lufttrafik, and was merely sole agent in Sweden for Heinicken parachutes. Now he abandoned this job and, leaving Carin to battle with her conscience in Sweden, went down to Munich early in 1922, and enrolled himself, a somewhat mature student, at the University there.

At last Carin made her decision. Better poverty with Hermann than the cramped life of a Swedish aristocrat. She announced her intention of visiting Goering's mother in Munich, but still left her ties with the old life unsevered. If she did not like Germany, which she had so long admired from afar, she could still return to Sweden.

She did like Germany, and she liked Franziska Goering. A short stay confirmed her determination to break with the past. She returned to Stockholm and asked Captain von Kantzow for a divorce.

Carin's husband, although deeply upset, behaved like an officer and a gentleman. He put no obstacles in the way of his wife, save only to dispute with her the custody of their son Thomas, and soon Carin was free to go to Germany, this time for good.

So handsomely indeed did Captain von Kantzow behave that he provided his wife and the man who had supplanted him in her affections with a basic sum sufficient to support them both in a modest way. For the first time since the end of the war Goering had secured, thanks to his future wife, a little capital.

The marriage in Munich was a simple business – there was a wedding-breakfast at the Park Hotel with beer and singing, led by Bodenschatz, the last adjutant of the Richthofen *Gesch-*

wader. Carin's eldest sister was present, and a few of Goering's wartime comrades. Afterwards the bride and bridegroom travelled up into the Bavarian Alps, to a little hunting-box near Bayrischzell, where their first months of married life were spent. The honeymoon passed in long rambles through the mountains. Goering would lie on the grass of some upland pasture, reading poetry to his beloved, the very picture of the German romantic, and in the evenings there were cheerful gatherings at the local inn, and much singing, to zither and accordion.

Always, at that time, Goering's talk returned to politics. He had already picked up a good deal of dangerous learning at the University, since in him professors and students found a ready convert to the heady, desperate nationalism which was then fashionable in German academic circles. For the Weimar Republic Goering had conceived a profound hatred. The humiliation of Germany's defeat still rankled bitterly in him – perhaps the rather smug atmosphere of Sweden had not been the best balm for his wounded pride. The Government under which Germany now lived was, he declared to Carin, no Government at all – a mere administration. Somehow determined men must chase these pantaloons from power and give Germany a really firm Government which would stand up to the sneering, triumphant enemies who, according to the best thought in the University of Munich, now took a fiendish pleasure in keeping her in degradation.

The fact that at Versailles for the first time in history, save for the Peace of Vereeniging which ended the Boer War, the victors had tried to make a peace founded upon right rather than upon force, had made singularly little impression in Munich or anywhere else in Germany. Had the Reich won the war, her peace terms would not have been dictated on that basis – the treaty imposed on Russia by Germany at Brest-Litovsk in 1917 showed that clearly enough. Yet Goering, in common with the vast majority of his politically idiotic countrymen, allowed himself to be persuaded that the Treaty of Versailles was a monstrous instrument of oppression, a *Diktat,* imposed upon an innocent Germany by malevolent conquerors who had somehow won their victory by fraud. At the time of his marriage Goering was ready for any wild adventure which might wipe out the shame of defeat. By one of those sinister coincidences of which there are so many in history, the fellow-freebooter whom he, half-unconsciously, sought was there in Munich awaiting him.

One Sunday afternoon in November, Goering went down alone to Munich from Bayrischzell to attend a political meeting in the Königsplatz. The purpose of this demonstration, ironically enough, was to protest against the delivery of certain German military leaders to the Allies as "war criminals." Goering felt strongly about this question – for a time France had demanded his own extradition as a war criminal. To him, as a military man, it seemed intolerable that a German Government should surrender to the enemy soldiers who had done no more than their duty towards Germany. The meeting was being held under the auspices of the Centre Party, the "Democrats," and of a strange little organization called the "National Socialist German Workers' Party," of which Goering knew nothing whatever, save that it was led by a fellow named Hitler, a man generally described, when people troubled to speak of him at all, as a fanatical mystic. Nevertheless, so heartily did Goering approve of the purposes of the meeting that he dug out his old uniform, strung the *Pour le Mérite* round his neck and, defying the stares of his fellow-passengers, took train and tram to the Königsplatz.

When he reached the meeting Goering found that his uniform was not the only one on the Königsplatz, although it was certainly the most distinguished. About the platform stood a shabby squad of young Nazis, whose dark breeches and brown wind-breakers constituted a uniform, of a sort. They did not strike Goering as a very impressive lot.

Nor was he impressed by the worthy bourgeois, felt-hatted, warmly overcoated, who presently mounted the platform and began to protest, plaintively, against the wickedness of the Allied plan to try German officers as "criminals." His wandering attention was soon attracted, however, by a man who stood by him in the crowd, a man in a crumpled trench-coat, bare headed, a lank brown lock plastered across his forehead, a rather ridiculous little moustache giving originality, if not distinction, to a face at first sight insignificant. This personage was surrounded by a crowd of followers and Goering inquired of a neighbour who he might be. When he learned that this was the "fanatical mystic," Adolf Hitler, Goering looked at him with a new interest.

Hitler was no less interested in the conspicuous figure of the young ex-officer. While the orators droned and bellowed on, the two men sized one another up, although they did not

44

speak to each other. Hitler's supporters were urging him to mount the platform himself, but the National Socialist leader refused to accept the suggestion.

"I don't want to break up the unity of this pretty, bourgeois demonstration," Goering heard him say. "If I were to speak now, my speech would be such a contrast to what those fellows are saying that all unity would be hopelessly wrecked."

Until men learn a great deal more than they at present know about the human mind, it is unlikely that any very satisfactory explanation of the sudden affinity which Goering felt that afternoon for Adolf Hitler will ever be given. Goering himself could never explain it save in vaguest terms.

"All at once," he said to a friend afterwards. "I felt *instinctively* that there was a Leader whom Germany needed."

Evil genius Hitler was, but genius none the less. Within a few days of that first wordless encounter, Goering discovered several reasons, both of patriotism and of self-interest, which led him to reaffirm his belief in Hitler. But of those first minutes of silent communion there seems to be no "normal" explanation. When Lucifer appeared to Faustus, the Doctor needed no introduction to his visitor. Is it too fanciful to suppose that Lucifer made himself known, by his own means, to another disciple that afternoon on the Königsplatz in Munich?

At all events Goering went back up the mountain to Bayrischzell, his head full of the strange man in the crumpled trench-coat. He noted in his diary that night that he had seen Hitler, and he and Carin talked about him for some time before they went to bed.

Next day Goering went again to Munich, taking Carin with him. A National Socialist meeting had been advertised at which Hitler himself spoke. They sat together while the flood of oratory swept over them, oblivious to the bad German, the Austrian accent, the essential commonness of the orator. For the first time since the war, Goering felt, the voice of defiance was heard again in Germany. This man was trying to *do* something to raise his country from the shame into which she had been cast by defeat.

"I'm for that man, body and soul," he declared to Carin.

Next day he went to Hitler and offered himself to the Nazi cause.

The Importance of Being a Hero

For Adolf Hitler the accession of Captain Goering to the Party was providential. It might be said, by the well-disposed, that the Nazis of 1922 made up in enthusiasm what they lacked in numbers, yet not even the kindest critic could have maintained that Hitler's followers possessed distinction – and distinction, as their Leader realized, was now needed.

Hitler had a strange attraction, peculiar to himself, which affected most of those with whom he came into contact, an attraction which could rouse large audiences of simple strangers to almost hysterical excitement. He possessed, to an extraordinary degree, the tricks of the born demagogue, the *Bauernfänger,* or "peasant-catcher," in the German phrase. Yet Hitler was after bigger game than peasants, and for that style of hunting his own equipment was, as he fully realized, still inadequate. The industrialists of Ruhr and Rhineland, whose money might, if properly coaxed, replenish the empty Treasury of the Party, senior officers of the Reichswehr, whose moral support would be so welcome, politicians, who must be flattered and cajoled – men of this type were inclined to base their judgment upon the past record of the man with whom they negotiated, and Hitler's record was not impressive.

In the first place Hitler was not a gentleman. In the Germany of 1922 that might seem to be a matter of little moment, so completely had the face of society changed during the past eight years. Yet it was precisely the last remaining citadels of birth and privilege (and, incidentally, of traditional nationalism) that the Nazi Leader had set himself to invest; to be the son of a very insignificant Austrian customs officer was not, even in 1922, an adequate introduction to those fastnesses. Moreover, Hitler was a foreigner – he did not become a German citizen until ten years later.

An impressive war-record might have done something to atone for humble origins, but this, too, Hitler lacked. Although, after the Nazi seizure of power in 1933, Party "historians" spent much time and ingenuity in glorifying the

"Front-Service" of the Führer, the results of their best efforts were meagre enough. Hitler, scorning the Royal and Imperial Army of Austria-Hungary, had volunteered for the German Army. There he failed to rise above the rank of *Gefreiter* (Private, 1st Class), although he had won the Iron Cross of the Second Class, a decoration, it may be observed, which, particularly towards the end of the First World War, was distributed to the German Forces with prodigal liberality. Indeed, it was generally said, in 1918, that a soldier who failed to sport its black-and-white ribbon should, on principle be placed under instant arrest, since there must be something wrong with him.

These modest achievements, the fruit of four years' service, did not, to the colonels and generals of the Reichswehr whose favours Hitler now discreetly sought, indicate any outstanding qualities of courage or military acumen, nor did the fact that Hitler had, for a time after the Armistice, agreed to spy on his comrades in the Army for evidence of "Bolshevik" tendencies in any way endear him to the officers upon whose behalf that espionage had been carried out. The "stool-pigeon" may, in certain circumstances, be a useful member of society but his task is generally an ungrateful one.

Yet now all this might, Hitler hoped, be retrieved, for in Captain Goering he had perhaps found the key which might open for him doors hitherto stubbornly bolted against the National Socialists. To a private soldier—even to such a private soldier as Hitler – the *Orden "Pour le Mérite"* was a dazzling decoration. When to that little cross were added the Iron Cross, First Class, the Zaehring Lion with Swords, the Karl-Friedrich Order and the Hohenzollern Order with Swords, Third Class ... why the display was enough to make the stuffiest general, the stiffest colonel take notice of their holder. Moreover, the fame of the Richthofen *Geschwader* was, in 1922, still very much alive.

Better still, this young ex-officer had been born a real gentleman. He was no jumped-up reserve officer, but a man who had been educated at the Cadet School, who had served as a regular in peacetime, whose father had been a distinguished colonial Governor and a friend of Bismarck at a time when Hitler's father was rummaging among the hand-baggage of country folk on the Austro-Hungarian frontier. Captain Goering would be more at home in the world which Hitler intended to penetrate than any other follower whom the Nazis had at that time recruited. Captain Goering, therefore, should

47

lead the *Sturmabteilungen*, the S.A. or Party Shock Troops. His birth, glamour and decorations would serve to impress both the potential friends, whom Hitler sought to influence, and the raw recruits who, under Goering's leadership, were to be moulded into a body of fanatical political soldiery.

Goering was flattered and pleased. He had met this extraordinary man only two days previously and here he was already at the head of the Party, or almost so. Yet caution – for here there can be no question of modesty – led the new recruit to put in a demurrer. Showing already some of that suppleness which was to make him one of the best of Nazi diplomats, Goering suggested that the announcement of his appointment as "Commander of the S.A." should be delayed for two months. in order that there might be no excuse for spiteful and envious gossip within the ranks of the Party; he would, however, in fact, take up his duties forthwith. Hitler fully approved of this tactful proposal, and so the alliance was sealed.

Goering had fallen under the spell of the *Bauernfänger* in a sense, albeit he was no peasant. Here at least was a man who really knew what he wanted! He did not look impressive, he was not the kind of man who would have been received at Veldenstein, or in the Officers' Mess of Infantry Regiment 112, or, for that matter, at Rockelsta. But then in none of those places were revolutionaries welcome – even Goering's restrained tiltings at the established order had got him into trouble in two of them – and this man Hitler was essentially a revolutionary. Captain Goering decided that he had at last found the right outlet for his energies.

In later years some of the Führer's more prominent followers loved to describe the mystical experience which had been theirs when they first met Hitler in those early days. If their accounts are to be believed, these encounters partook more of a religious revelation than of a meeting between an obscure politician and a recruit to his obscure Party. Captain Goering was, perhaps, a tougher character than the Fricks, the Leys, the Rosenbergs. At all events he made no bones about admitting, twenty-four years later, after Hitler had elevated him and cast him down, that ambition and his hatred of Weimar Germany had, after that first strange encounter with Hitler, decided his entry into the National Socialist Party:

"I joined the Party because it was revolutionary," he said

in 1946. "Other parties had made revolutions, so I thought I could get in on one too, and the thing that attracted me to the Nazi Party was that it was the only one that had the guts to say, 'To Hell with Versailles!'"

Young Captain Goering wanted to wipe out the disabilities which defeat had laid upon Germany and, incidentally, to build in the process a career for himself. With a degree of perception unusual in a man of 29 he saw in this strange fellow Hitler the man who might enable him to achieve both ambitions.

Yet, Goering's ambition notwithstanding, the respective positions of the two men were perfectly clear from the first days of their relationship, and so they remained until it fell to Goering to appear in the dock at Nuremberg as the sole sur- viving Nazi of first-rate importance, the last defender of the Party's doctrine and achievement. Always and in all things, Hitler was the Leader, Goering his loyal subordinate. Although Goering came to display a pretty talent for intrigue – and without that talent he would probably not have survived the attacks of his powerful enemies within the Party – against Hitler he never dared to plot.

In 1922 the slogan *"Führer befiehl! Wir folgen!"* (Führer command! We follow!) had not yet been launched by Josef Goebbels, yet it was Goering's motto from the first. The lessons of the Cadet School and of the Army had left their mark on the ex-officer. Like every German cast in that mould, Goering had learned to obey, without question, the orders of superior officers. The courtroom at Nuremberg and the cham- bers of many less august tribunals, charged with the trial of minor war-criminals, were later vibrant with that plea. How, the defendants asked with unfeigned indignation, could a man be put on trial for having done his duty as a soldier by obeying the order of his superior officers? Goering himself advanced this argument in his own defence at Nuremberg, but in his case it took an unusual and characteristic form. He pleaded, in effect, that he had always acted under Hitler's orders, as his subordinate, but denied that any orders which he had received from Hitler were wrong in themselves.

On that autumn day of 1922 Hermann Goering deliberately allowed Hitler's boot to be set upon his neck, and from the consequences of that action he never sought to turn back.

And so, at the beginning of November 1922, Goering

slipped, unobtrusively, into the National Socialist Party, and began to take stock of the *Sturmabteilungen* – the Stormtroops – from which he must forge a decisive political weapon. Carin greeted her husband's new occupation with enthusiasm. Even more emotional than he, she quickly fell under the charm which Hitler had always known how to exercise upon women. At last Hermann had found work worthy of him, at last his wife could truly help him in what must be a great career!

The first thing was to move house. Hermann would be busy, and for a busy man the little hunting-box near Bayrischzell would be far too remote and inconvenient. Now it was no longer a question of theoretical discussions about the future of Germany during long rambles with Hermann in the mountains. The men with whom her husband had cast his lot were men of action, and close to the scene of action she and Hermann must now live.

Somehow the money for a mortgage and a down-payment was found, and the Goerings left Hochkreuth for a small house, still smelling of new plaster and fresh paint, in the Munich suburb of Obermenzing. From here Hermann had only to catch a tram to be in Hitler's office and right in the heart of things. Nor did Carin intend that her suburban villa should be ignored by Hermann's new colleagues. At the cost of much prowling and haggling in the cheaper second-hand shops of Munich she assembled enough decent furniture, most of it in the good, solid Biedermeier style, to furnish the upper rooms of the new house. Her own flower-paintings took the place on the walls of the more formal pictures which the couple did not possess and could not afford.

Downstairs the little house had one long, cellar-like room, with an open fireplace. Here Carin installed no more than a bare, unpolished wooden table and a set of rough peasant chairs. It was quiet in that room, and cosy, it felt almost as though one was underground, yet the fire crackled cheerfully and the country pottery on the mantelpiece brightened the place up splendidly. The conspirators found it an admirable meeting-place.

To the cellar-room they often came in the winter months of 1923 and in the spring. . . . Hitler, Hess, the Führer's faithful shadow, the muddled philosopher Alfred Rosenberg, Frank, the young lawyer who was one day to rule Poland. These types were new to Goering, but in Ernst Julius Günther Röhm he found for a while a kindred spirit.

At the time of this first meeting Röhm was aged 36. In the war he had served with distinction, had been three times wounded and risen to the rank of Captain. In that he differed in no respect from many other ex-officers. But for Hitler, sitting by the fire at Obermenzing and looking across at the ugly, scarred, pugnacious face of Röhm, the man had a special attraction—he was a friend of General Ludendorff.

The friendship between the Captain and Imperial Germany's last Commander-in-Chief dated from the final, desperate German offensive in the West of 1918. Röhm, transferred from the Eastern front just in time to take part in this enterprise, had been ordered to report on conditions in his corps area to the Commander-in-Chief in person, and he faithfully fulfilled his mission. Undeterred by the grim old soldier who faced him and by the inevitable fury of his corps and divisional commanders, the Captain told a tale of crippling and unnecessary casualties, of shortages of arms and ammunition, of hunger and partial breakdown of the supply services. Ludendorff liked the young man's candour and did·what he could to put matters right. The offensive failed, Germany was beaten to her knees, but the General and the Captain remained friends.

Röhm had many friends, too, among Reichswehr officers of his own age and seniority. To a man they were ardent nationalists, eager to start at once, in defiance of the Treaty of Versailles, upon the task of avenging Germany's defeat. Yet neither they nor their hero, Ludendorff, knew much about politics – they loved to pose as the simplest kind of simple soldiers, and indeed with most of them it was no pose. A political party whose aspirations corresponded with their own must, therefore, be found, and in National Socialism Röhm believed that he had found it.

He persuaded friends to believe it too, and himself took charge of the Party "Defence Sections." Early in 1921 these political soldiers were formed into companies of 100 men each, and in August of that year the *Sturmabteilungen* – the S.A. – were formally created:

"The Nationalist Socialist German Workers' Party," so ran the announcement, "has set up within its organization a special section for gymnastics and sport. It is intended to serve as a means for bringing our young members together in a powerful organization, so that their strength may be used as an offensive force at the disposal of the

51

Movement. . . . Moreover they will be taught loyalty to one another and joyful obedience to their leaders. . . . The leaders of the Party expect all to join. Your services will be needed in the future."

By the autumn of 1921, when Hermann Goering joined the Party, Captain Röhm was already in charge of a promising body of gymnasts and sportsmen, most of whom had learned the rules of the game the rough way. Young, hard-faced men came to the S.A. fresh from fighting against the Bolsheviks in the various German "Free Corps," those strange bodies of patriot freebooters who in East Prussia, Upper Silesia and around the eastern shores of the Baltic had, since the Armistice, battled against the Poles and the Russians, while in Munich, Berlin, Leipzig and elsewhere other "Free Corps" were engaged in counter-revolutionary activity. Less enterprising officers, who for three years past had kicked their heels in enervating, hopeless idleness, saw in Hitler's private army the very hope of that action and discipline which they so sorely missed, and they flocked to the swastika banner.

Röhm had more sinister recruits too, some of whom were by their talents destined for rapid promotion in the Party. To a very small number of Germans such commonplace names as Heines, Schmidt and Schulz had, even in 1921, a very particular significance, for the men who bore them were members of the *Fehmgericht,* an evil seed sown during the Napoleonic Wars, and now, after the convulsions of 1918, taking root and thrusting out rank shoots in Germany. The *Fehme* itself was, by 1922, a word of ill-omen to many hundreds of thousands in Germany.

The *Fehme* was, originally, a German resistance movement against the French invader Bonaparte. Its members, sworn to utter secrecy, exacted terrifying retribution from any German whom they found, after a summary "trial," to be guilty of "collaboration" with the enemy, to use the modern phrase. For young men with minds of gangsters and a fancy for cruelty, the revival of the *Fehmgerichte,* in the years which immediately followed the First World War, provided a convenient outlet for sadistic tastes under a pleasantly patriotic camouflage. Heines, Schmidt, Schulz and their like stole out, night after night, with whips, bludgeons, rope and pistols. Black hoods and masks added to the amusement of the adventure, and in the morning the body of a man or woman, flogged to death or hanging mutilated from a tree, testified that the evening's sport had ended satisfactorily.

In the S.A. many *Fehme* members believed that they saw the possibility of still more ambitious undertakings of the kind which they enjoyed, and Captain Röhm welcomed them into his ranks, since these represented the very type of gymnast whom he sought to enlist. Of Heines, Schmidt and Schulz, who have been mentioned by name as typical of many another recruit of those early days, there will be more to say later.

By the autumn of 1921 there was already friction between Captain Röhm and Hitler, his Leader. Röhm, who on his own admission "looked at the world from a soldier's standpoint, one-sidedly," had, nevertheless, wide views in certain respects. For him, the ex-army officer, there could be only one future for the S.A. – they must become the nucleus of a great, secret army which would replace, under the very noses of the Allies, that military machine which, smashed three years before, was now cruelly denied to Germany by her conquerors. Almost immediately after the defeat, patriotic societies had sprung up like fungi throughout the Reich. Their members paraded pathetically in remote places, trying manfully to handle their sticks as though they were indeed the rifles which they coveted, while keeping a sharp lookout for an Allied patrol. But Röhm knew a trick worth two of that. He stole or borrowed from the Reichswehr real rifles, and the patriots flocked to the man who had these precious toys.

Hitler, the politician, had very different ideas about the future employment of the S.A. They should be, first and foremost, propagandists, attracting the simple-minded by parades and ostentatious route-marches. At Party meetings they would provide the *claque* for Hitler and his orators and they would swiftly eject unruly members of the audience. Röhm's passion for secrecy and weapons did not appeal to the Führer, but Hitler must act swiftly if he were not to be out-manœuvred. The S.A. was falling more and more under the domination of Röhm and the Reichswehr, and its numbers were increasing so swiftly that soon Hitler might lose control over the instrument which he had created. In Captain Goering he saw the means of reasserting his authority, Röhm should become "Chief of Staff" and Goering should take active command of the S.A. Here was no divided loyalty. This admirably qualified young man was Hitler's own servant and would obey Hitler's orders only.

The spring and summer of 1923 were, for Goering, a time of unremitting work. Already by March the S.A. in Bavaria mustered three *Standarten,* or regiments, each of between 3000 and 5000 men, and every day that passed brought fresh volunteers. The Bavarian Socialists regarded this growing force with understandable alarm, particularly when, in April, Goering ordered a detachment of S.A. to occupy the Munich offices of the Party newspaper, *Völkischer Beobachter,* in order to protect a certain Herr Eckhardt, a member of the staff, from arrest. Pressure was exerted upon the Diet to outlaw the S.A. altogether, but without avail. The Brownshirts continued to drill and parade and their numbers steadily increased.

Baron and Baroness von Fock came down from Sweden that summer to visit their daughter, but of their son-in-law they saw little. Once or twice Goering was able to make a short excursion into the mountains with the family, but that was the limit of his leisure. In Berlin, as in Munich, a situation was developing which might, properly exploited, give the Nazis a magnificent chance of seizing power.

Up in Berlin the unstable Cuno Government had fallen and Gustav Stresemann took office as Chancellor, pledged to a policy of appeasement. One of the first acts of the new administration was to announce that Germany would no longer resist the French occupation of the Ruhr. German "patriots," and notably the Nazis, lost no time in expressing their disapproval of this concession, and on September 27 the Central Government proclaimed martial law throughout Germany.

The reasons which led Stresemann to take this drastic measure deserve some explanation. During 1922 France in particular had, with good reason, become increasingly dissatisfied with the manner in which the Germans were living up to their obligations under the Treaty of Versailles. Reparations payments had lagged. Disarmament had been skilfully delayed and evaded by the defeated nation. No steps had been taken to bring war-criminals to trial before German courts – thanks in part, to such noisy meetings as that at which Goering and Hitler had first met. France and Belgium, therefore, proposed to take sanctions against Germany by moving their troops into the Ruhr Valley, the cradle of German heavy industry.

They received no support in this project from Great Britain. Disillusioned by the failure of the United States to support the League of Nations and a new world order, anxious for a quiet life, the British people were in no mood to underwrite

"French chauvinism." Moreover, chivalry towards a beaten enemy seemed to imply that, although friendship between Germany and Britain might, at that moment, still be too much to ask of the victor, at least one should not "kick a man when he is down." From the United States the French Government received even less sympathy.

France, remembering her ravaged provinces, undeterred by the incomprehension shown by her former allies, occupied the Ruhr alone. M. Poincaré, her Prime Minister, demanded of Germany the "unconditional surrender" of her richest industrial area. Riots, strikes and political murders already badgered the German Government. Now Chancellor Cuno added to these burdens by acquiescing tacitly to a form of passive resistance in the Ruhr which, however effective it might have been against the Allies, was even more painful for the German people. The presses printed banknotes until the control of German currency, already unstable enough, proved to be quite beyond human ingenuity. Workers in the occupied areas were encouraged to strike and were rewarded for their patriotism by the payment of subsistence allowances which the German economy could not possibly afford; deliveries in kind to the Ruhr from the rest of Germany were suspended.

Although the German nationalists, of whom the Bavarian Nazis were among the most vociferous elements, threatened to murder any Chancellor who compromised with the French – and, with the murder of Dr. Rathenau fresh in the popular memory, that was no empty threat – Stresemann, with great courage, determined to make the best of a bad job. Rather than plunge his country into irretrievable ruin, he would come to terms with France.

The Nazis had been given the platform through which with the support of the Army and of civilian nationalist groups, they hoped to bring about a successful revolution.

Since the Nazis could muster a sizeable force only in Bavaria, the birthplace of the Party, it was fortunate for them that the Government of that State, under President Gustav von Kahr, should be bitterly opposed to Stresemann's policy of co-operation with the Allies. General von Lossow, commanding the Bavarian Military District, was, as might have been expected, of the same opinion, and it was to him that Captain Goering in the role of "Old Soldier" turned for support. Would von Lossow agree to march his troops, including the S.A. *Stan-*

darten, on Berlin, and there overthrow the traitor Stresemann's Government?

Again and again, during the days of October and early November 1923, Captain Goering put that question to the General and to von Kahr. At conference after conference, sometimes with Hitler present, sometimes in his absence, the matter was thrashed out, while von Lossow's military superiors in Berlin, thoroughly informed of what was afoot, became more and more alarmed. Finally General von Seeckt, Commander-in-Chief of the Reichswehr, ordered von Lossow to hand over his command to General Kress von Kressenstein. Von Lossow flatly refused to obey the order.

In the Party offices in Munich and in the Obermenzing villa the plotters met, all day and every night from dark to daybreak, during the first week of November. The broad plans for the *coup d'état* were laid by Hitler and Goering, but sometimes Röhm joined the discussions, for one thing at least was certain – this was the moment to use General Ludendorff. If von Seeckt and his clique of Prussian generals would not make common cause with the Nazis, at least not a man of the Reichswehr rank and file would ever consent to fire a shot against Ludendorff. The old man should be a living shield for the rebels.

On November 6, Goering, supported by von Lossow and by a certain Colonel Kriebel, who later succeeded him in command of the S.A., came close to persuading von Kahr to stage a *Putsch* against the Berlin Government. But some matters were still left unsettled, and at that meeting no firm decision was reached. Events then took matters into their own hands.

On November 8 a disturbing report reached Hitler and his confederates. General von Lossow, it seemed, was actually planning to bring about the separation of Bavaria from the Reich, and that without having notified the Nazis of his intention. The time for conferences was obviously past. The moment for action had come, unless Hitler intended to accept as an accomplished fact a *coup d'état* in which he had taken no official part. This was far from being his intention.

That evening von Kahr, flanked by the Premier of Bavaria, Dr. von Knilling, and by three other State ministers, faced 3000 citizens of Munich from the stage of the Bürgerbräukeller, an immense tavern whose very name evokes a mental picture of simple, vulgar Bavarian gaiety. The audience, sitting behind pots of beer, listened with mild enthusiasm to von Kahr's declaration that a new German National Army would arise from the ruins of that great army which had collapsed exactly five years before, to the very day. As the speaker made this announcement the swing-doors at the back of the great hall burst open and Hitler appeared, flourishing a pistol, and closely followed by Goering and Hess. The intruders forced their way to the platform, Hitler fired a shot, for no very obvious reason, since they had already managed to secure the undivided attention of the audience, and announced that 600 of his S.A. had surrounded the tavern.

Before the beer-drinkers had had time to assimilate this ominous news, Hitler went on to inform them that a national dictatorship was being established and that the unfortunate Dr. von Knilling, a bourgeois politician with no marked taste for violence, was under arrest. A new Bavarian Government had been formed under von Kahr, the speaker continued. Herr Poehner, once chief of the Munich Police, would be Premier, General von Lossow would be Minister for the Reichswehr and General Ludendorff Commander-in-Chief of the whole German Army.

"Do you approve of those appointments?" Hitler demanded.

A roar of approval answered him.

"The day for which I have waited with such longing has arrived," Hitler shouted. "I will make of Germany a glorious State!"

Von Kahr and von Lossow, who were also on the platform, said nothing, and their silence had the appearance of consent. In fact, they were as surprised as any other member of Hitler's audience.

Hermann Goering, standing behind his Führer, said nothing either, and it is permissible to suppose that even at that dramatic moment a part of his thoughts were in the little bedroom at Obermenzing, where Carin lay with a high temperature and inflammation of the lungs. That afternoon he had sat with her, holding her hot hand, until at last, as darkness was falling, he kissed her and rose to his feet:

"I must go now," Goering said. "We have a lot to do tonight. There's a big meeting in the Bürgerbräukeller and I may be home very late. Don't worry about me, though."

He left the room and Carin lay, alone, watching the snow which had begun to fall outside, waiting until Marie, the maid of all work, should bring her some supper.

There was little time for thoughts about a sick wife, however well loved. In the beer-cellar the audience, solid burghers though they were, had been alarmed by Hitler's dramatic pistol-shot and were beginning to become restive. In a little room outside Hitler was engaged in an attempt to blackmail von Kahr and von Lossow. It fell to Goering to keep order in the hall.

"*Ruhe! Ruhe!*" he shouted. "Keep quiet, do! There's nothing to fuss about. They're forming a new Government next door – that's all."

He looked around the hall and smiled.

"Anyway," he added, "what have you fellows got to worry about? You've got your beer, haven't you?"

At that there was a burst of laughter and several people ordered up fresh *Steins* of lager. The tension relaxed.

At the little conference there was endless talk. Neither von Kahr nor von Lossow wished to be hustled into a desperate adventure by the extraordinary mountebank who now confronted them. Hitler had changed a great deal during the past weeks. In October the Party's first rally had been held at Nuremberg and the success of that demonstration had apparently gone to his head – so at least von Lossow thought. At the conferences which had preceded the dramatic invasion of the Bürgerbräukeller, Hitler had taken to speaking of himself as the "Gambetta of Germany," as "another Mussolini" and even as the "Saviour of the Fatherland." He had repeatedly promised von Kahr and von Lossow that he would not on his own initiative attempt an insurrection with his Party troops, and Goering had given the same undertaking. Now the politician and the soldier realized that the fears which had hitherto restrained them from concluding a full alliance with the Nazis were only too well founded. Hitler intended to go back on his word and to raise a rebellion whether von Kahr and the Army supported him or no.

For the moment the thought uppermost in the minds of von Kahr and von Lossow was to get out of that little room at any cost. As long as they were penned up with this megalomaniac, both were powerless to act. Only if they appeared to agree to an alliance with Hitler would the Nazi leader call off his S.A. and liberate them. Von Kahr and von Lossow therefore assented to Hitler's proposals.

The behaviour of the Führer when he had secured this agreement bore out the worst apprehensions of his unwilling allies. Rushing back to the hall "with a frank, childlike expression of joy on his face" (to quote a Nazi witness of the scene), he once more pulled the pistol from his pocket. His voice rose to a shriek of ecstasy.

"Tomorrow," Hitler cried, "will either see a national Government in Germany, or it will see us dead!"

He clapped the pistol to his forehead.

"Unless I am victorious tomorrow," he shouted, "I shall be a dead man!"

Shouting and singing, the audience, now reassured and hopeful of fun on the morrow, streamed out into the snow-covered street. Von Kahr and von Lossow hurried back to their offices. Captain Goering, having watched his S.A. march off in good order, drove to the outskirts of Munich, where his *Standarten* and detachments representing other patriotic associations were forming up for a demonstrative march into the Bavarian capital on the following morning.

Dawn found Captain Goering, dressed in a long, black oilskin, Sam Browne belt and steel helmet, the *Pour le Mérite* twinkling at his throat, prowling along the bank of the River Isar. In the bitter cold he was superintending the siting of a few light field-guns, while Hitler and Ludendorff stood beside him. There had been no time to return to Obermenzing during the night. Once victory had been won he would perhaps have leisure to take care of Carin. For the present nothing mattered save the march on Munich.

Throughout the night the telephone lines between Munich and Berlin had been busy. Von Kahr had talked long and vehemently with his enemies in the Wilhelmstrasse, and for once their opinions had coincided. Von Lossow's disobedience had evidently been condoned by the *Reichswehrministerium*, for he spoke at length to General von Seeckt. That officer, upon whom President Ebert had conferred full executive powers for the whole Reich, had already sent orders by telegram that the Hitler *Putsch* must be suppressed. Von Kahr and von Lossow spent the hours of darkness in making swift, efficient preparations to that end. At first light, bill-posters went out with armfuls of placards, wet from the presses:

"WARNING!!"

"The deceit and perfidy of ambitious comrades have converted what should have been a demonstration in the interests of national re-awakening into a scene of disgusting violence. The declarations extorted from myself, General von Lossow and Colonel Seisser at pistol-point are void. The 'National Socialist German Workers' Party' and the 'Oberland' and 'Reichsflagge' fighting associations are hereby dissolved.

VON KAHR,
General State Commissioner."

News of this proclamation was brought to the Nazis as they prepared to march off, but it did nothing to alter their intention. At eleven o'clock the long column moved away, headed by General Ludendorff, his tunic ablaze with decorations, Goering, Hitler, Hess and other Nazi leaders beside him. Behind them came a detachment of S.A. carrying rifles, with bayonets fixed, and a lorry on which machine-guns were mounted. The rank and file of the marchers carried for the most part no firearms.

At the head of the Ludwigsbrücke, which spans the Isar, a platoon of State police confronted the marchers. As the procession approached, the policemen brought their rifles up to the shoulder and prepared to open fire. Although the marchers continued to advance, the muzzles of the rifles which faced them did not waver. At last the Nazi column halted and Captain Goering, stepping forward from the front rank, saluted the police officer in charge of the detachment.

"If a single man on our side is killed or wounded," he said grimly, "it'll turn into a general shooting-match!"

The policeman hesitated and then told his men to order their arms. The police drew aside and the column moved off again, over the bridge and along the Zweibrückenstrasse towards the heart of the city.

As the marchers came up to the neo-Gothic town hall, a man who had been addressing a crowd in the Marienplatz opposite broke away from his listeners and took his place with the leaders of the column. This was a certain Julius Streicher who, trained as a schoolmaster, had during his wartime service as an officer conceived a fanatical hatred of the Jewish race. Upon demobilization he had formed, with other ex-officers, an anti-Semitic society which had brought him into contact with Hitler, whose views so closely resembled his own. On hearing in Nuremberg of the happenings of the previous evening, Streicher had hurried to Munich, eager to play his part in the Nazi triumph.

At the town hall the column wheeled to the right, and was soon marching through the narrow Residenzstrasse, towards the Felderrnhalle or Hall of the Generals, a depressing mid-nineteenth-century copy of the fourteenth-century Loggia dei Lanzi at Florence. It was here that von Kahr planned to bring the Nazi rebels to a final standstill. The bottleneck was entirely blocked by a strong force of heavily armed police.

The opponents faced each other in silence. Then Hitler drew his pistol and called upon the police to surrender. Somewhere a man shouted:

"Don't fire! Excellency Ludendorff is coming!"

The column halted, hesitant. Then one of the marchers advanced towards the police, and there came a sudden crack of carbines. A man fell near Hitler, and Hitler, although unwounded, fell at the same instant, dislocating his arm. Goering, hit twice in the groin, collapsed in a spreading pool of blood, and beside him lay twelve Nazis, dead. Only grim old Ludendorff marched steadily on, thrusting aside the weapons of the police, until he reached the Odeonsplatz. A man ran towards him. It was Neubauer, the General's devoted batman. The servant had just time to throw himself in front of his master. Another volley was fired and Neubauer fell, having given his life for his General.

There was much shouting and some ragged, ill-directed musketry. A car forced its way through the crowd, its occupants crying: "Where is Hitler?" A moment later the defeated Führer, neither wounded nor, as he had promised, dead, was being driven away towards Uffling, and the hospitable villa of his friends, the Hanfstaengls. But Captain Goering still lay on the cobbles, in his own blood.

"I know, I know," said Carin, as forgetting pain, weakness and a high temperature, she struggled out of bed and began to dress herself. But only when she reached the hospital and learned that the upper part of her husband's right leg had been shot to pieces did she know the full truth.

They bandaged him quickly, while he bit his lips at the pain. There was no time to lose, for at any moment von Kahr's police might come for Goering. No matter how grave his wounds, he too, like the Führer, must get away from Munich.

The Lost Years

THE *Putsch* had been an inglorious failure. After two days spent in hiding at Uffling, Hitler was arrested, and with him Ludendorff, Röhm and other Nazi leaders. A warrant for the apprehension of Hermann Goering was issued. The Party was dispersed, its Stormtroops apparently dissipated.

The affair had not passed unnoticed abroad. From the calm eminence of Printing House Square the leader-writer of *The Times* newspaper felt bound to take the leaders of the revolt, and in particular Ludendorff, severely to task:

> "It is fortunate for Germany, and for the whole of Europe, that the insurrection engineered by General Ludendorff and Herr Hitler in Munich has been so quickly suppressed. The condition of Germany is bad enough, but it cannot be remedied by any such wild adventure as that to which a general who gained a considerable reputation in the War has lent his name and authority. In making his premature *coup,* in association with the house-decorator and demagogue Hitler, on the fifth anniversary of the German Republic, General Ludendorff committed the most foolish error of tactics."

The ripples raised by the revolt went round the world for a few days and subsided. Soon the whole business was forgotten abroad.

Hermann Goering lay, desperately wounded, in the home of friends at Garmisch-Partenkirchen, on the frontier of Austria and Bavaria. He was in constant and violent pain from his shattered leg, but the agony of his bewilderment was no less sharp. The Nazis had been betrayed, and betrayed by Germans! That, as he saw it, was the bitter, the almost incredible fact. As he lay, wrapped in bandages, his face white and drawn, Goering learned some hard lessons. "Germans can't go against Germans!" he cried again and again, yet that is just what had happened. Writing a little later to her mother, Carin said of him:

"He is so loving, patient and kind, but at heart he is in deep despair. Three weeks ago today he was wounded, not only physically but perhaps even more mentally."

With the insight which love bestows, Carin perceived at once that the events of November 9 had inflicted a double wound on her husband. The torn flesh and bone might knit together, but the more searching injury to the spirit would still remain unhealed. Perhaps she realized, even then, that she had lost for ever the cheerful, impulsive man who had loved long rambles over the Bavarian mountains and high-flown, naïve discussions about the future of Germany, about life, death, the place of man in the universe. She had said good-bye to that man in a little bedroom at Obermenzing, on the snowy evening of November 8, 1923. The husband who lay wounded at Garmisch was already on the way to becoming an embittered, ruthless politician.

Garmisch could be for the proscribed fugitives no more than a temporary refuge. The police were searching for Goering and his presence in the little mountain village could not be kept secret. Crowds of cheering sympathizers soon gathered, in misplaced zeal, outside the house where the Captain lay. Whatever the condition of the wound – and that in all conscience was bad enough – the patient must cross the frontier into Austria.

A car took them to the border, but Bavarian police were waiting there, and the Austrian police would have nothing to do with visitors so compromising. The Goerings were arrested and escorted back to Garmisch by armed constables, through knots of people who shouted "Heil Goering!" booed and hissed the guards, and on one occasion almost lynched them. Goering tried, feebly, to quieten his excited supporters and to reassure Carin. Back at Garmisch, officials confiscated Goering's passport and took both him and his wife to a hospital, which was heavily guarded.

"But despite all this," as Carin related to her mother, "we were helped, as if by a miracle. Hermann was carried out (for he can't walk a step), back into a car, dressed only in a night-shirt, covered with a fur coat and rugs and provided with a false passport, and in two hours we were 'across the frontier.' I just don't dare to describe how all this happened. I shall have to tell you when we meet.

We left Munich in such a hurry that I only had time to pack the most necessary things in a little handbag. You, dear Mamma, will understand what it was all like."

The fugitives made their way to a clinic in Innsbruck, and there Goering lay in great pain, weak from loss of blood, his tired brain ceaselessly going over the Munich fiasco. His wounds throbbed horribly, yet they seemed to be healing. Then they opened again and the doctors insisted on an X-ray examination. This disclosed that dirt and stones from the street where Goering had lain had entered the wounds and that fragments of a bullet still remained to be extracted. An operation was performed, and for three days thereafter Goering lay in high fever, shouting in his delirium about the revolt. He could not move because rubber tubes had been fixed to his leg to drain away the poisonous matter which infected it. The doctors prescribed strong injections of morphine to deaden the pain.

In Munich, von Kahr issued a warrant for Carin's arrest. Much of the story of these dramatic days has been told by Carin herself in the letters she wrote home to Sweden and which were later published in her biography by her sister, Countess von Wilamowitz-Moellendorf.

"I am sitting," Carin wrote to her mother, "in the sickroom, at the bed of my beloved Hermann, and I have to watch him suffer, both physically and mentally – and I can really do nothing to help him. You know how that feels! His wound is just one great mass of matter – the whole thigh. It hurts so much that he just lies there and bites the pillows to pieces, and I only hear inarticulate moans. You understand how this cuts into my soul. It is just a month ago today since he was shot, and in spite of daily morphine the pain has not subsided. . . . Our Munich villa is being watched, our mail is being confiscated, bank accounts have been blocked, the car impounded . . . "

Back at Obermenzing Marie, the maid, stoutly held the fort against the encroachments of vested authority. Her letters were opened, her belongings searched by the police and she was repeatedly questioned about the doings of her master and mistress. Still Marie refused to leave the villa. Carin could send her no money, yet rather than abandon the belongings of the *Herr Hauptmann* and his lady, Marie sold, bit by bit, her own few possessions and, refusing to take another post, lived on somehow in the little house.

The handy-man, who had sometimes done odd jobs about the house and helped in the small garden, proved himself no less loyal. He organized a one-man courier service across the mountains into Austria, through which passed letters and many of the Goering's personal belongings. Crossing the frontier with a false passport he brought the exiles some of their clothing, butter, and a few tins of Marmite and coffee, which Carin's mother had sent to Munich from Sweden. He was arrested for his pains and served fourteen days' imprisonment in Munich, but his loyalty remained unshaken.

As the news of Goering's presence in Innsbruck spread, Nazi sympathizers from the surrounding countryside flocked to the hospital with presents and expressions of sympathy. Among these visitors was Hitler's sister Paula, whom Carin describes as "a charming, ethereal being, with large, soulful eyes in a pale face, trembling with love for her brother."

Couriers came too, from Germany, bringing a little money and some cheerful news. In spite of the arrest of Hitler and thirty other Nazi leaders the Party was not unduly discouraged by the *débâcle* of November 9, and was determined to push ahead. Arms and ammunition had been safely hidden and the work of organisation was continuing in secret.

For almost two months Goering's condition caused great anxiety to his wife and to his doctors, but during the week which preceded Christmas they were able to perceive a real improvement. The pain was much less acute now, and two days before Christmas Eve the rubber tubes were removed from the patient's thigh. Using all his very considerable powers of persuasion, Goering induced the doctors to allow him to leave the hospital on Christmas Eve and the little family moved to the Hotel Tiroler Hof. It was a strange, sad Christmas, which Carin described in a letter to her father:

"At Hermann's urgent request the Professor allowed him to leave the hospital on Christmas Eve, and since yesterday he can walk about on crutches, hollow-faced and white as snow. I can scarcely recognize him. His whole being is different. He hardly speaks a word, depressed by this act of treachery to a degree that I would have never thought possible in his case. But I hope that his inner balance and his old energy will return when he has regained his strength."

Goering, his system full of morphine, had at that moment neither physical nor mental energy. The physical forces were, in time, to return, as Carin had hoped, but never the "inner balance." That, such as it was, had been shot away by von Kahr's police.

In the circumstances it could not be expected that the Goerings' Christmas would be a very merry one, yet Carin did what she could to make the stiff hotel bedroom, with its plush furniture and glaring lights, as gay and welcoming as possible. The Innsbruck S.A. presented their leader with a little decorated Christmas tree, each candle adorned with a black-white-red ribbon – the German nationalist colours – and this was set on a table. Carin deliberately bought no present for her husband, since she felt that to do so would make him feel more bitterly his own inability to choose one for her in return. The sick man dragged himself painfully about the room on his crutches, and at last sitting down beside his wife, took her hand and stared in silence at the flickering candles of the Christmas tree.

"It hurt me so," wrote Carin to her father, "to see Hermann a persecuted refugee – I just can't describe my feelings. About eight o'clock I just couldn't bear it any longer and I put on my coat in order to get a breath of fresh air. There was a terrible snowstorm outside, but I hardly noticed it. Suddenly I heard something most beautiful coming from a first-floor window – organ and violin playing 'Silent Night, Holy Night,' and, very strangely everything suddenly became quite calm inside me. I cried, of course, but was once more full of confidence and calm. I returned to Hermann and was able to cheer him up and encourage him – and two hours later we both slept peacefully."

The result of this excursion into the snow was, for Carin, who for two months had utterly neglected her own precarious health, a heavy cold and a high temperature, which sent her to bed for several days.

Two days after Christmas Goering made his first attempt to walk without crutches. It was only partially successful, but at least it gave the convalescent relief from the haunting fear that he might never walk again. New Year's Eve, therefore, was a gayer occasion than had been Christmas, and was, moreover enlivened by the presence of Hitler's lawyer, come straight from visiting the Führer in prison and full of the latest news. The management of the Tiroler Hof entered into the spirit of the occasion and caused the Goerings' table in the dining-room to be decorated with evergreens, red ribbon and German flags adorned with the inscription: "Heil! to our Hero!" The band struck up *"Deutschland! Deutschland! Uber alles,"* and an unknown diner came over to the Goering table and made a long, confused but flattering speech, whereupon the manager, carried away by his German emotions, offered a round of punch on the house to all who would toast Hitler and Goering in it.

Sympathizers sent more than 200 telegrams, which was gratifying, although Carin, with an anxious eye on their dwindling resources, wished that some of these expressions of goodwill had taken a more practical form. One of the most welcome of these messages, nevertheless, was from Goering's chauffeur, Schellhorn, now unemployed and penniless, having refused as a matter of conviction to take a well-paid post with a Jewish family.

By February 3, 1924, Goering was well enough to enjoy his second wedding anniversary. It was the first thoroughly happy day that he and Carin had spent together since the flight from Germany. Such days were rare indeed, for now Goering was working again, with savage energy, organizing the Nazis in Austria. Although his wound was not fully healed, he drove himself mercilessly, catching sleep in the third-class compartments of night trains in order that his days might be free and no time wasted in travel. On February 15 orders came from Hitler, in his Bavarian fortress, that Goering should go to Vienna and there visit local Party leaders. At the same time Goering did what he could to secure the release from prison of Lieutenant Rossbach, like himself a Nazi refugee from Germany, and now one of the most active Party organizers in Austria. Rossbach, who had been living in Vienna with false papers, had been arrested a few days previously and Goering, deprived of one of his most efficient supporters, did what he could to secure his release.

There had been a plan that Carin should return to Sweden on a visit in the early spring, but it came to nothing. She was again ill, the trial of Hitler, Ludendorff and their fellow conspirators was impending, and in any case there would be elections in Germany in April which, in the event of a Nazi success, might lead to an amnesty for political offenders and enable the Goerings to return to Munich. Carin decided to stay with her husband, though she was very homesick.

The couple were living comfortably now, at the Tiroler Hof. The owner of the hotel, a Nazi, allowed them to occupy a little suite at cost price, and the restaurant provided excellent meals at a 30 per cent. reduction. For some time Goering had been forced to stay at the hotel on credit, but now some money had arrived from Munich and he tried to pay off the arrears. The proprietor at first refused to accept payment and then declared that any money which Goering did pay would be handed over to the Nazi Party. Surrounded by people who thought well of her Hermann, Carin was very happy, in spite of her illness.

Goering, seeing his wife so cheerful, took care not to reveal to her the full extent of his own anxieties. To his mother-in-law he was less reticent, as his correspondence with her shows. Even to her, though, he never confessed that his wound was still very painful and that he tried to take the edge off the pain with the morphine to which he had become accustomed in hospital.

"Dearest Mamma," Goering wrote to Baroness von Fock on February 22, 1924, ". . . . It has certainly been a terribly hard time and a severe test. The load which suddenly fell on me was almost too much, almost too heavy to be borne . . . and so your dear letters were like rays of sunshine, penetrating our darkness and giving us new strength and courage to have faith and to hope. . . . You probably don't fully realize yourself how enormously you have helped us. Thanks to you it was easier for me to overcome the crisis of mental depression, for I did not care about the physical injury, because it meant nothing beside the terrible hurt to my soul. All the evil, treachery and miserable cowardice which came down upon me at that time almost robbed me of my faith in mankind and, in the first place, of my faith in my Fatherland. But now the worst is over, already truth is struggling towards the light and the traitors will be defeated by their own treachery. . . . Only we shall have to have more patience now, and everything will progress more slowly. Therefore we must count on a longer interval before we can return to Germany. I want to stay here until the trial is over, but then, if there is no prospect of being able to return for the time being, we would like to go to Sweden via Italy, as life is cheaper there in any case and much pleasanter than here, in Austria. I had already thought that we might, perhaps, sell our villa and send the furniture to Sweden, where we might rent a flat, because, after all, we can't go on living in a hotel for years and years. Perhaps I could also find some sort of job there until conditions allow me to return to Germany. For I only want to return to a Nationalist Germany, and not to this Jewish Republic. I shall always be ready to fight again for the liberty of my Fatherland. I certainly love Sweden more than anything else, for I am, first and foremost, Germanic, and the purest Germanism dwells there. Besides, I long, just as Carin does, for all of you, who are so kind and loving to us. For Carin's sake, too, I should like to live there for a while, so that at last she can be with her family and friends, especially after all the excitement and privations of the last few months. But these are all plans for the future, which we shall have to think over carefully."

The trial of Hitler, Ludendorff and their associates opened in Munich in March, and the exiles followed the proceedings anxiously, day by day. The verdict was delivered on April Fool's Day, 1924. During the weeks which had just passed, Goering had several times suggested to Hitler that he should return to Munich and stand his trial at the side of the Führer, but Hitler dismissed the proposal out of hand. Whatever sentence the Court might pass on him, Goering must remain a free man and continue to do what he could for the Party.

Now, on a mild spring day, Goering learned that Hitler had been found guilty and sentenced to a long term of confinement in a fortress. Ludendorff was acquitted. Paula Hitler hurried to them when the news of the verdict and sentences was received in Austria, and the three of them ate a somewhat tearful lunch in the open air. An application for an amnesty for Goering was sent to Munich by courier, but this was no more than a formality. There was little likelihood that von Kahr would pay the slightest attention to Goering's appeal, and so there was nothing for it but to wait, hope for the best and watch the stock of money dwindle steadily.

At least there were the German elections to discuss. A Nazi

success there might make all the difference in the world to their prospects. In April the results came through. The Nazis had done unexpectedly well in Bavaria, in securing more than half the total poll and their first seats in the Reichstag. It was expected that Goering would fill one of these, and he anxiously awaited Hitler's permission to do so. From his cell the Führer himself had announced that he would not take a seat in the German Parliament, but he might allow his faithful follower to sit. Surely for an elected Deputy there *must* be an amnesty.

Those were happy days. Goering received 157 telegrams of congratulation and flowers in such numbers that Carin rang up the hospital where her husband had been treated and asked the nuns to take them away in bunches for the patients and for their own chapel. Yet Goering's leg was still stiff and painful, and he still had secret recourse to morphine to deaden the throbbing ache which never left him.

All the high hopes upon which the Goerings had built proved to be illusions. There was no amnesty, no prospect of an early return to Munich, and money was running very short. Long, anxious discussions took place between husband and wife at the Tiroler Hof. At last even the limited power of deciding their own future which they still possessed was taken from them. The Austrian Government, tired of Goering's political agitation on their soil, alarmed, perhaps, at the picture post-cards of him and Carin which had begun to appear in the shops, not of Innsbruck only but of other towns, and at the unconcealed enthusiasm of many Austrian Nazis for their persons, ordered the couple to leave the country.

Goering's wound was still not completely healed and Carin's health was frail. A warmer climate would benefit both of them. And so, saying farewell to the hospitable Tiroler Hof and to their friends in Innsbruck, Hermann and Carin travelled southwards to Venice.

The Hotel Britannia was comfortable and cheap and Venice was enchanting. Moreover, the protecting hand of the manager of the Tiroler Hof was still extended over them.

Baedeker in hand, Goering conscientiously "did" the museums of Venice and marvelled at what he saw. His natural, untutored liking for "nice things" led him on long expeditions upon which Carin, now almost an invalid, could not always accompany him. When they went on to Rome, in the middle of May, there were more galleries to be visited, more museums to be inspected, but here, too, there was serious work for the young revolutionary, and for his wife.

Benito Mussolini, the prototype of successful Fascist dictators, had by now set his stamp firmly upon Italy and was there in Rome for inspection and emulation. Goering, setting forth each day from the unpretentious Hotel Eden, made as close a study as possible of Fascist theory and practice, and was able to have several conversations with the Duce himself. What with that study, a few business deals which brought in a little money, and visits to picture galleries and places of interest, time did not hang heavy on his hands.

Yet now he was far from Munich. Couriers from the Party could not slip easily from Bavaria to Rome, and so Carin herself became courier. Twice she travelled alone to Bavaria, to maintain Goering's contacts with his Party comrades, and once she visited Hitler, who presented her with his photograph, inscribed "To the brave wife of my loyal Comrade." She called, too, on General Ludendorff, only to find that the old man had lost all interest in the Nazi Party and was now utterly absorbed in the new pagan cult which, with his wife, he was founding. "I'm a heathen, and proud of it!" he boasted to Carin, and she was a little shocked.

The little family stayed in Italy throughout the winter of 1924, living on Captain von Kantzow's alimony, supplemented by money sent by friends and relatives in Germany and Sweden. Both were far from well. Carin, who had been attacked by an inflammation of the lungs during the hectic days of November 1923 in Munich, now was also affected seriously by heart trouble. She suffered dreadfully from the cold, dry winds of the Campagna, and Goering's wound gave him no rest, except when morphine enabled him to forget it.

At last, in the spring of 1925, friends in Sweden sent enough money for a roundabout journey to Stockholm. The direct route via the Brenner, Munich, Berlin and the Sassnitz-Trälleborg ferry was closed to the exile. Instead a long, tiresome circuit must be made through Czechoslovakia and Poland to Danzig and thence, by a small steamer, across the Baltic.

The von Fock family gave the wanderers a warm welcome. With their help a small flat was found in Odengatan, a long, dark, dreary street, some distance away from the fashionable Östermalm district where most of Carin's relations lived. The furniture which Carin had so lovingly collected for the Obermenzing villa was still in Munich, and so with money provided

71

by the von Focks a minimum of household apparatus was procured and, after a year of hotel life, the Goerings set up house again.

For Carin the homecoming had many compensations. Poor she and Hermann might be – Hermann was, in fact, obliged on more than one occasion to pawn his watch in order to pay the household bills – but at least she was home, in Sweden, and there were many friends to be visited and much gossip to be exchanged over cups of coffee and sweet cakes. Her health, though, was wretched. To consumption were now added periodical fainting fits, and she spent many long days in bed, in the gloomy little flat, while Hermann hawked articles, with very indifferent success, to any newspaper which would accept them, and tried in vain to find steady employment.

Three years' absence had changed "Stockholm's popular air-chauffeur," and the change was an extremely disagreeable one. The von Fock family noticed it with concern and alarm. Hermann was no longer the kind of young man who would be welcomed at dances and dinner-parties. A glandular deficiency, which had probably always been present in his make-up, had now made itself distressingly apparent. At the age of 32 his body, in the words of a physician who treated him at that time, "was like that of an elderly woman, with much fat and a pale, white skin." The man looked thoroughly unhealthy, but, worse than that, the effect of a steady course of drugs over a period of two years was now all too evident. The craving for morphine was firmly rooted in Goering's system, and must at all costs be satisfied. Though it might mean going without food, supplies of Eucodal, a morphine preparate, must always be kept at hand, since two or three injections, self-administered, were needed every day.

There was no hope of concealing the true state of affairs any longer. It was, of course, natural that Goering, exiled from his country, harassed by poverty and by his inability to find work, worried moreover by a law-suit over the custody of Carin's son Thomas, should no longer be the gay young man whom Carin had married. But, as the summer wore on, long spells of dismal brooding gave place to more sinister manifestations. Goering began to show signs of mania, and mania of a particularly violent kind.

The man was becoming dangerous. Even Carin, loyally though she supported her husband, began to feel increasing anxiety for him. Sometimes, without the slightest warning he would pick up any heavy instrument which lay to hand and threaten whoever happened to be with him at the moment with assault. He was liable, at the smallest provocation or at no provocation whatever, to throw glasses, crockery or any other handy object at his companions. At last a doctor was called in, and his verdict was simple and unequivocal. Captain Goering was a dangerous drug-addict. The matter was one for the police.

The doctor issued a certificate and the police lost no time in backing the certificate with an order for Goering's removal from Aspudden Hospital, where he had been under observation, to a more rigorous place of confinement. The authorities can scarcely be blamed for this decision, since Goering's behaviour during his stay at Aspudden had not inspired them with much confidence in the patient. When a nurse had refused to supply him with morphine he had thrown a knife at the girl, and on being refused the drug a second time had tried to strangle her. There was nothing for it, in the opinion of the police, but the "violent ward" of Långbro lunatic asylum.

Goering resisted his removal from Aspudden as best he might, but the police were taking no chances. Under their escort the man who, eight years before, had been one of Germany's war heroes, the man who was still one of the leaders of the National Sociialist Party, was hustled off to Långbro.

No sooner had he been led into the "violent ward" than Goering fully justified this choice of lodging. Throughout his first night in the asylum he raved and stormed, until even the experienced attendants were alarmed. In the morning one of them hurried to the hospital psychiatrist and asked him to see the patient. The doctor found Goering in a state of furious rage and self-pity:

"I'm not mad!" he shouted, again and again. "I've no business to be here!"

The doctor began to talk quietly. No doubt Captain Goering would agree that he had become a morphine addict? Yes, Captain Goering would agree to that. Did the Captain wish to be cured? The Captain did wish that.

"Well," said the psychiatrist, "why don't you pretend that you are here of your own free will? That will make things much easier for everybody, and then there will be no question of your being 'insulted' as you say you now are."

The patient reflected on this proposal for some little time, and at last agreed to it.

"There is one condition," the doctor added. "I will put you in a paying ward if you will give me your word of honour, as a German officer, that you will not attempt to escape."

That was good psychology. Goering's word of honour was given, nor, during the three months that he remained at Långbro, was it broken.

A drug-addict must, if he is to be cured, face agonizing pain during the early stages of the treatment. In order to give some relief during this dreadful period the doctors at Långbro generally prescribed for their patients sodium bromide, which, by making them drowsy, enabled them to escape the worst suffering. In the case of Captain Goering this treatment was a failure. Under the influence of the bromide his mind grew hopelessly confused and he began to suffer from delusions. The attendants from the "violent ward" were, he became convinced, coming at any moment to take him back to that horrible place by force, and he prepared to defend himself against them. Somehow – just how nobody ever knew – he obtained a heavy iron bar and hid it in his bed, ready to dash out the brain of anyone who laid forcible hands on him. The attendants found this weapon before its possessor had had time to use it, and the sodium treatment was suspended. Gradually Goering's mind cleared.

The doctor who had first rescued Goering from the "violent ward," and who was now in charge of his cure, often asked the young man up to his house in the evenings. He did not do this out of friendship, for in fact both he and his wife took a positive dislike to their patient. The doctor, a psychiatrist well versed in the twists of the human soul, came to the conclusion that the ex-officer was basically an evil person. It was possible, he thought, that the man was suffering from some disorder arising from the endocrine gland, but he detected flaws in Goering's character which, in his opinion, could not have arisen either from his upbringing and early environment nor from his wartime experiences.

Speaking long afterwards, one of Goering's physicians at this time expressed his belief that his patient was basically a bad character. During the war the rigid "corset" of military discipline had kept this side of his nature in abeyance, but by 1925 it was plain to a mental specialist, if not to every layman. A strong streak of bravado in the man's make-up was very evident. Goering loved to defy situations, but the doctor, as he sat and listened to his patient's tales of wartime adventure and of the Munich *Putsch*, came to the conclusion that the narrator was not a brave man. Ambition gnawed relentlessly, the instinct to "show off," to cut a dash, came peeping through every story he told. Those strong motives, the doctor decided, had enabled Goering, during the war and afterwards, to display courage which was not truly his.

"As a psychiatrist," the doctor said, "I saw Goering in an unvarnished condition – and it was not a pleasant sight. I should say that his character was what psychiatrists call 'hysterical' – which means that his personality did not keep together coherently. At one moment he displayed one personality and a few minutes later quite a different one. He was sentimental about his own people and utterly callous about everybody else. When one was treating Goering one was always, to some extent, afraid of him. One could not predict what he would do next. I always knew that if I made a false step he might do terrible things. Yet, having been a German officer, he was not difficult to discipline. . . . I think that explained his attitude to Hitler, too."

After three months Goering was discharged from Långbro as cured. He left promising to return there voluntarily if he found that the craving for morphine still persisted. It did persist, and soon the surreptitious injections of Eucodal were resumed.

Goering kept his promise and returned of his own free will to Långbro. This time the cure was successful, and although in later life Goering took a mild morphine derivative with some regularity, he never again became a drug-addict. His health improved rapidly, and with it his spirits and his ability to make a living. He resumed his connection with the German manufacturers of parachutes.

England was a mysterious land which had long fascinated Goering, and some business connected with his dealings in parachutes gave him at this time an excuse to visit that country. He would not have acted in character had he been content simply to transact whatever business brought him to London and to depart unostentatiously on the boat to Sweden. He did not intend that his visit should pass unnoticed, and accordingly, political exile though he was, he had no hesitation in approaching the German Embassy as soon as he reached London and in proposing that as a gesture of comradeship he, the former Commander of the Richthofen Squadron, should lay a wreath on the Royal Air Force Memorial.

Although formal diplomatic and commercial relationships between Germany and Great Britain had been resumed, the feeling between the two countries could not be described as cordial, and Count Bernstorff, the Counsellor at the German Embassy, feared that were Captain Goering allowed to carry out his project it might have an effect in England which would be precisely the reverse of that which the Captain intended. Accordingly he rang up the Air Ministry and asked their advice; the Air Ministry fully agreed that the laying of a wreath on the Memorial by Captain Goering would be disastrous. On the other hand it would not be only impolite but impolitic to rebuff a gesture which was, after all, well meant. Casting around for a solution, somebody at the Air Ministry remembered Captain Beaumont, now a regular officer of the Royal Air Force stationed near London, and recalled that he and Goering had once been friends.

Beaumont, accordingly, was astonished to receive a sudden summons to the Air Ministry and even more astonished when he learned the purpose for which he had been brought here. He was to be given three days' leave, and during those days he was not to allow his friend Goering out of his sight. He was to amuse him in every way that lay in his power – amuse him so thoroughly that he would not have a moment to think of such matters as the laying of wreaths.

Somewhat dubiously Beaumont set himself to carry out the orders, and as a first step invited Count Bernstorff and Captain Goering to lunch with him at the Savoy. The Captain, a little conspicuous from the fact that he wore a miniature of the *Orden "Pour le Mérite"* in his buttonhole, was delighted to meet his old friend, and the lunch was a very pleasant one. The three days which followed were for Beaumont, and especially for Mrs. Beaumont, far less pleasant, for Captain Goering had lavish ideas about amusement and appeared to be quite tireless.

Summoning stout-hearted brother-officers of the R.A.F. to his assistance, Goering's host carried out his orders to the letter. On one occasion he entered Goering's bedroom – which in normal times was his own dressing-room – to find his guest stretched out, still in his dinner-jacket, on the mat beside the bed. He had been so drunk when they returned home that he had been unable to undress. Violent though these tactics were, they nevertheless succeeded, and Goering, his money exhausted and business calling him back to Sweden, left British soil without laying the debatable wreath upon the Royal Air Force Memorial. In later years he very much regretted the omission.

The visit to England was a bright interlude in a bleak year. Denied the relief of drugs, Goering sought solace in religion and spent much of the time at the little "Edelweiss Chapel," where he found peace.

Life battered hard at the little household in Odengatan, but at last relief came. The amnesty for which Goering had waited so long was proclaimed in the autumn of 1927, and the exiles were free to return to Germany. Goering packed his few belongings in a fever of excitement, yet sadly, for he must leave Carin in Stockholm. She was sick, and her husband had no money with which to give her in Germany the care and treatment which she needed. He must first establish himself and create an income. Then, Carin promised, she would come to him.

The Sorrows of a Careerist

THE Berlin to which Goering returned alone wore a different face from that of the defeated city which he had left in 1918. The shops were full of goods, though at a price beyond the means of many Berliners; theatres, music-halls and cinemas did a brisk trade, restaurants were crowded. There was money again in Berlin, although by the standards of 1914 it was in strange hands.

If Goering, in 1924, had felt moved to express his hatred of the "Jewish Republic" he found nothing, three years later, which might cause him to modify his views. To any German bourgeois, brought up in the old traditions, Berlin, capital of the "freest Republic in the world," was a sorry spectacle. While the legion of unemployed in Germany mounted towards the 1,000,000 mark, Berlin, and in some degree the other great cities of the Reich, presented a picture of frenzied luxury and of unbridled licence, displaying itself cheek by jowl with poverty, squalor and hunger.

The Kurfürstendamm and the streets which led off it were,

in those days, little more than a complex of night-clubs, "dives," bars and brothels, each offering "attractions" designed to appeal to every perverted taste. The pavements of the Friedrichstrasse, the Leipzigerstrasse and the Kurfürstendamm itself were cluttered with prostitutes of both sexes – women in thigh-length boots, carrying whips, boys in women's clothing, girls in male attire, jostling one another on the pavements, made a stroll through the lamp-lit streets a matter of embarrassment and even of some danger for the respectable visitor to the German capital. Every bookseller and newspaper kiosk displayed prominently magazines, books and brochures devoted to all conceivable and inconceivable aspects of sexual perversion. "Trial marriage" was all the rage, even in those circles which the Germans term the "better people," and thousands of girls, upon leaving school, lost no time in making arrangements to ensure themselves against the birth of unwanted babies. They had been taught to do so at high school.

From the Brown House at Munich, Hitler and his Party orators thundered against "culture-Bolshevism" and their denunciations found a ready echo in the hearts of the German lower-middle classes. Julius Streicher and a young man named Goebbels could, in particular, be relied upon to provide a really spicy evening's entertainment on these lines, and respectable people flocked to their meetings to enjoy a couple of hours of vicarious sin, much as dwellers in the rural areas of the United States once thronged to the dilapidated marquee of the travelling "hot gospeller." Goebbels and Elmer Gantry would have understood one another very well indeed.

For Goering, in any case almost penniless, Berlin held no attractions, and he lost no time in journeying southwards to Munich, where, in the recesses of the "Brown House," Hitler awaited him. The two years which had elapsed since the Führer's premature release from Landsberg had been years of progress for his Party, although the National Socialists had made a poor enough showing at elections. In May 1924 they had secured thirty-two seats in the Reichstag, but by December of the same year, after the acceptance by Germany of the Dawes Plan and the stabilization of the currency, this figure had been reduced to fourteen. In May 1928, however, fresh elections were due, and Hitler had every hope that his platform of opposition to Jewry and "culture-Bolshevism" and his skilful propaganda against war-reparations would have its effect on the middle-class voters.

Goering's old post as leader of the S.A. seemed, at first sight, to be open to him. During the years of exile this appointment had been filled by a nonentity named Pfeffer, a mere stop-gap, whose duty it presumably was to keep the seat warm for Captain Goering. As time dragged on without bringing the amnesty which would allow Goering to return to Munich, Hitler had considered reappointing Captain Röhm to the position from which Goering had orginally ousted him. A particularly unsavoury sexual scandal involving Röhm's favourite, the former *Fehme*-member Heines, put a stop to this project. Heines' penchant for taking advantage of the boys who joined the S.A. became a matter of notoriety. In vain Hitler tried to assuage outraged parents by protesting that, while he did all he could to prevent such "swinishness" within the ranks of the Party, the S.A. was not a kindergarten. His powers of persuasion were not equal to the occasion. At Ludendorff's suggestion a deputation, headed by Count Reventlow, waited upon Hitler and insisted that Heines and his protector, Röhm, be expelled from the Party. Heines was duly expelled in May 1927, whereas Röhm, although still a member of the Party, refused to assume command of the S.A. and withdrew in a huff to Bolivia, there to serve as a soldier of fortune. Surely the way was open for Goering.

Yet Goering was poor, and the Nazis, now better off financially than in 1924, still had no money to spare for him. For the present Pfeffer must continue to fill the gap. In the Germany of 1927, however, the prospects of employment for an "expert" in aeronautical matters were promising. The Lufthansa Aviation Company had secured, with the support of the Deutsche Bank, a monopoly of German civil flying. Every German city with any ambition was busily establishing an airport, thus making itself a mesh in the great Lufthansa network, which already covered the Reich and most of Europe and was now being cast as far afield as Eastern Asia and South America. A certain Erhardt Milch was in effective control of the operations of this great undertaking.

For Goering, not only an experienced airman but a prominent member of a political party whose favours German industrialists might one day require, there were good pickings in that heyday of German aviation. The Bavarian Motor Works, the firm of Heinkel (whose name was to become almost a part of the English language in 1940) and the Aircraft-Motors Industry were all willing to negotiate with Goering. Money began to come in, slowly at first, and then with some regularity. Goering's spare time was spent at the Brown House, but his place was still in the shadows of the Party. While Goebbels and Streicher courted the limelight, Goering sat, a willing pupil, at Hitler's elbow, learning, tardily, the lessons which he had missed during the years of exile.

The unemployed of Germany rallied to the Party in some numbers, and they were not the flower of the population. Whenever industry felt forced to turn off men, the least efficient, the idlest workers were the first to go, and many of them turned, in their despair, to the Nazis. Here leaders well suited to such a following awaited them – Hitler and Goebbels, Streicher, Karl Ernst, Count Helldorf, and, in the background still, Hermann Goering. At the end of 1927 election prospects for the coming spring looked very bright.

By Christmas 1927 Goering's personal finances had so far recovered that he was able to travel to Sweden and to spend a few weeks there with Carin. He brought with him presents for his wife and her family and Carin was relieved and pleased to observe that her husband seemed to be fitter, both in mind and body, than he had been for some years. It was a happy time, brightened by the hope of an early reunion in Germany and by the improvement which had taken place in the fortunes of the little family.

Early in 1928 Goering moved to Berlin, where he took a large, sunny room in the Berchtesgadenerstrasse. Settled in a good, residential suburb, possessing a respectable address, he began to write for the newspapers, this time with some success, and his deals with aircraft firms became increasingly profitable. By the spring he was able to bring Carin to share his life.

Her arrival coincided with Goering's public re-entry into politics. During his stay in Berlin an acquaintanceship, made in the old Munich days with Josef Goebbels, now the Nazi "Gauleiter" for that city, had developed, until the two men were on terms of close intimacy. Now, with the approach of the elections, Goebbels and Goering barnstormed together through "Red Berlin." Family life went by the board. Carin found herself snatching hurried meals in cheap restaurants while Hermann and his secretary, Paul (or "Pilli") Koerner, talked politics endlessly. The *Kraftbrühe*, or "Strength soup," a watery extract which is the standby of German eating-houses, the pigs' trotters and the caramel cream were shovelled away to a monotonous accompaniment of denunciation – of the Treaty of Versailles, of reparations, of the Jews, of "culture-Bolshevism." Carin was almost relieved when family affairs called her back to Sweden for a short visit.

She came back to Berlin in May, on the eve of the elections. A friend and supporter had lent Goering a car for the election, and in it he careered from meeting to meeting. Wherever he was billed to speak bands of Communists paraded, seeking to break up the gathering, while detachments of S.A. protected the speakers, who called upon Berliners to register their votes "against the unworthy parliamentary swindle which destroys the nation, AGAINST THE NONSENSE OF DEMOCRATIC PARLIAMENT AND FOR THE FREEDOM OF THE WORKING MAN." One meeting, which happened to coincide with the birthday of Mr. Parker Gilbert, the Allied Reparations Agent responsible for the administration of the Dawes and Young Plans, was billed by Goebbels as: "A birthday Party for Parker Gilbert, the Reparations Agent, to thank the Fathers of our Country for all the lashes which Jewish Capitalists have given us, for our comfort and edification."

In that spirit the Nazis fought the election.

The voting, which took place on May 20, proved a sad disappointment. The Nazi representation of fourteen in the Reichstag was still further reduced. Now they commanded only twelve seats, but of those one went to Hermann Goering. Carin, characteristically oblivious of the wider implications of the election, sent an ecstatic telegram to her family:

"HERMANN ELECTED YESTERDAY STOP MOTHER YOU UNDERSTAND STOP YOUR CARIN."

Apart from the distinction of being the wife of a *Herr Abgeordnete* – an M.P. – even in a "Jewish Republic," Carin reflected with satisfaction that her Hermann would also draw henceforth a modest but steady salary of 600 marks (£30) a month.

Although his Party had not greatly distinguished themselves at the polls, Goering himself was now, as an M.P., a person of some slight influence. Important people began to seek him out, and both he and Carin revelled in this new life. On June 13 Goering took his seat in the Reichstag for the first time, and Carin, although she was then forty years of age, sent a description of the event to Stockholm which might have been written by a girl of eighteen:

81

" . . . Naturally I went to the Reichstag too. Hermann got a splendid place, next to General von Epp, from Bavaria. They sit alone together at a table right at the front. They only got this place because the number of seats had to be increased, so it was lucky! What a lot of Jews there are in all parties, except Hitler's . . . Hermann has a frightful lot to do, and I see him only occasionally. But he gives all his free time to me and we generally manage to eat together at least, though I don't think we've had a single meal alone for a long time. . . . There are a lot of people from Switzerland here at the moment – the chief of the Swiss Airlines – generals and colonels, majors and lieutenants. It would be nice if we had a home again. It is difficult always having to eat in restaurants. Things are so expensive in Berlin."

The "unworthy parliamentary swindle" was at least proving interesting and convenient to Goering. On June 17 Dr. Frick, who later became Hitler's Minister of the Interior, presided over the first constituent meeting of the Nazi deputies, at which each was allotted a special field of endeavour suited to his experience and qualifications. Goering found himself designated to be the Party's expert on communications, canals and . . . aviation.

Membership of the Reichstag brought with it other responsibilities. It was inconceivable, of course, that a Deputy should live in a single room and take his meals in cheap restaurants. Some Deputies of bourgeois parties did live in this way, it was true, but for Goering such an existence was far too sordid. At last, at long last, it might be possible to live decently – not, of course, on 600 marks a month, but there might be ways of overcoming the financial aspect of the problem. Wealthy men were apparently eager to make Goering's acquaintance. Herr Thyssen, for instance, the steel magnate, was assiduous in his attentions. Would his assiduity extend so far as to allow him to be touched for a loan? The delicate question was put to Herr Thyssen, and the great man made no difficulties. The furniture from the Munich house was recovered from repositories and pawnbrokers' shops, and on December 1, 1928, Hermann and Carin moved into No. 7 Badenschestrasse, Berlin W.

The flat, in one of the most modern blocks in the city, was a delightful place. Its windows looked down, from the fourth floor, on a pretty square of lawn, and wide balconies ran round the building. The apartment was efficiently heated, which Carin found a great blessing, and approached by a lift. There were four large rooms and a little room for the maid – altogether a most convenient residence.

Carin's illness continued to run its course. For some weeks after the move to Badenschestrasse she snatched what spare time she could to rest. But there was not much time for relaxation. The place seemed to be always full of visitors. The leading Party members made the place their headquarters, as they had once made the little villa at Obermenzing their regular meeting place. Whenever Hitler came to Berlin he made straight for the Badenschestrasse and there passed long hours in conference with his followers and with the leaders of other parties.

Old wartime friends looked in too. Bruno Loerzer was a constant visitor, so was Ernst Udet.

Although Goering ranged the country, spreading the Nazi gospel in East Prussia, in Franconia, in the Ruhr and in the Rhineland, his chief sphere of activity was Berlin. While Goebbels stormed the Red citadels of Neukölln and Moabit, now caressing the crowds with his strangely resonant voice, now lashing them with bitter invective, Goering played a role more discreet but scarcely less important. Almost every day he and Carin were invited out to luncheon or to dinner, and their hosts were people of distinction. The Kaiser's nephew, Prince August-Wilhelm, known to all Germany as "Auwi," had leanings towards the Party (he joined it in 1930), and through him Goering began to penetrate into high society.

Here, at last, was the atmosphere of luxury and comfort which Goering coveted and envied. Berlin society found the Captain pleasant enough and his wife charming. There were, of course, rumours that the man had been a drug-addict, but that, in the Berlin of 1929, was a venial indiscretion. As for Carin, society thought that she was rather simple but quite delightful and, of course, well-connected. If such people, friends of the Prince, held high positions in the Nazi Party, there must be something to be said for the Nazis, that vulgar little man Hitler notwithstanding.

In 1929 the Nazi Party, with its 800,000 votes, did not appear at first glance to be a very formidable political force. When, in March of that year, Hitler, speaking at a meeting in Munich, delivered a frontal attack on the Reichswehr, even the Party's well-wishers shook their heads at such temerity. Yet events were playing into the hands of the Führer. The economic crisis which held the whole world in its grip did not spare Germany. Unemployment figures rose steadily. "Respectable" people who had lost their livelihood turned towards the right-wing party which had been the most uncompromising in condemning the system under which they now found themselves without work. The leaders of industry were terrified, the middle classes bewildered and without a shepherd. Although the Communists gained recruits, as they always do in times of misery, their propaganda made no impression on any but the working classes, and even there they were forced to share the spoils with the Nazis.

Hitler could no longer be ignored, and towards the end of 1929 the long-standing order which had prevented him from speaking in Berlin was revoked. Making common cause for the moment with Hugenberg's Nationalists, Hitler harangued crowded meetings in the capital, demanding a national referendum on the Young plan, denouncing international capitalists, bourgeois politicians and the Jews, promising work and bread in a regenerated Germany if the Nazis came to power. Goering, proud of the nickname "Hitler's Ambassador," worked on in the salons of the Bendlerstrasse and the Lützowufer, at discreet tables in the Adlon grill-room, at Horcher's restaurant, where they did such a delicious dish of pressed duck. He too spoke at meetings, going straight from the warmth and shaded lights of the Bristol restaurant or the Eden Roof to a stuffy, ill-smelling hall or public-house in Wedding or Pankow. As a rule he took no trouble to prepare his speech, but faced the audience armed with a restaurant menu or wine-list, upon which he had scrawled a few slogans. Speaking came easily to him, and he claimed with some justice that his method of oratory suited him better than the more painstaking technique employed by most of his colleagues.

"When I just jot down a few headings on a menu," he once said, "I always do well, but if I try to prepare a speech I get tied up and the whole thing is a failure."

Goering found the role of "salon-Nazi" a pleasant one. His Reichstag salary, supplemented by the monthly alimony of Captain von Kantzow and by loans which became larger and more frequent as time went on, enabled him to compete with the society in which he now found himself, particularly since he was extremely remiss in settling the bills of the tradesmen who supplied the needs of his household. As money became more plentiful, Goering developed a streak of parsimony which grew ever more marked as his material position improved. Unwilling to deprive himself of the material comforts which he had always regarded as his just due and which were now at last coming within his reach, he nevertheless avoided paying for them whenever possible. The magnificent opportunities for blackmail of which he later took full advantage were not yet open to him, but he nevertheless became skilful in evading his debts and was thus enabled to live considerably above his means.

Carin, brought up to principles of economy, did all she could to keep the bills down. Although distinguished guests came to the flat for meals, they had to content themselves with simple fare.

The last treatment at Långbro had, apparently, been a complete success. Goering had laid aside the Eucodal and the hypodermic syringe. Another drug had replaced morphine – the drug of ambition, not now frustrated but in a fair way to being achieved.

In March 1930 the aged President von Hindenburg invited precise, conscientious Heinrich Brüning, Leader of the Catholic Centre Party, to form a Government. Brüning, beset on the right by the rising power of the Nazis and by the Nationalists, on the left by the Communists, dissolved the Reichstag and proceeded to govern by Presidential decree. The personal authority of the Field-Marshal was still very great. That and his own energetic leadership would, Brüning hoped, woo voters away from the extremist parties towards the "middle road" which he himself represented. There were 3,000,000 unemployed in Germany.

Brüning's hopes were reinforced in some degree by internal dissension in the Nazi Party. While Goering courted high society, in Berlin Hitler consorted with industrialists, bankers and such venerable ghosts of a lost war as Admiral von Tirpitz and Colonel von Xylander. The Party needed money and respectability, and Hitler intended to obtain both.

These flirtations with reaction were observed and deplored by the left wing of the Nazi Party, led by the brothers Otto and Gregor Strasser and (for as long as seemed prudent) by Josef Goebbels. Otto Strasser, as Reich Press Chief of the Party and Editor of the *Völkischer Beobachter,* was a man whose influence in Nazi circles was second only to that of Hitler. But he was a Socialist, who believed that the second word in the Party's title – National Socialist German Workers' Party –

was not merely a sop to the proletariat but a declaration of policy. The *Völkischer Beobachter* published articles critical of the very circles which Hitler was now fervently wooing, articles which reminded the Führer that very little had been heard, of late, about the Socialist aspect of the Party Programme. The Führer's new friends complained. Goebbels, seeing an opportunity of ridding himself of a rival, hastened to range himself with Hitler. Gregor Strasser, whose influences in the Party were very great, did the same. Otto was expelled from the Party, and with him went the Socialist element of National Socialism, leaving a gap which was never again filled.

Goebbels had triumphed. Now it was Goering's turn to win, if he could, a palace victory. Pfeffer, the nonentity who still commanded the S.A., stood between him and the command of a private army of almost half a million men. Röhm, Goering's only possible rival for the supreme command of the S.A., was thousands of miles away in Bolivia. To succeed as a diplomat was well enough, but to lead an army was a great deal better. Pfeffer, Goering decided, must be put out of the way, and he enlisted the support of his friend Goebbels in the project.

Events played into the hands of the plotters. Among the Berlin S.A. discontent was already rife. Recruited chiefly from the ranks of the unemployed, many S.A. men resented, in a dim, confused way, Otto Strasser's expulsion from the Party. They complained moreover that they were called upon to bear personally an unduly large share of the cost which membership of the S.A. entailed. At this inauspicious moment Pfeffer, with the support of his subordinate in Berlin, Captain Stennes, decided to launch an attack against the "homosexual clique" in the Nazi private army. The Brown House at Munich promptly stopped the pay and allowances of the Berlin leaders. Pfeffer, although discreetly egged on by Goebbels, was inclined to capitulate, but Stennes held fast, and Goebbels promptly withdrew his support from the rebel as he had hoped to do from Pfeffer himself, had Pfeffer proved conveniently obdurate. Announcing that the Berlin S.A. would refuse to perform any further duties for the Party, and appointing himself head of the S.A. for Northern Germany, Stennes issued a proclamation which declared, in part:

> "The Stormtroopers are expected not only to offer their blood, but also to pay for propaganda, travelling expenses and motor-cars, because, apparently, the Party has no funds.

Yet Herr Goebbels, at a time when our Movement has no money, buys a new Mercedes car which costs at least 15,000 or 20,000 marks!"

In Berlin the Party offices were stormed by the dissident Stormtroopers, and repelled by the S.S. (the Schutzstaffel – Party Elite Guard) and by police reinforcements, hastily summoned. Hitler decided to compromise. He levied a special tax on all Party members, the proceeds of which were to go to the S.A., and himself went to Berlin. There he hurried round from tavern to tavern, each public-house a regular S.A. headquarters. He promised his hearers a glorious future, he promised them money, he wept at them, he bullied them. The revolt fizzled out.

Pfeffer, the trimmer, was removed from office; Stennes, a dangerous man, was not. But for Goering, waiting patiently in the Badenschestrasse, no good news came. Hitler himself assumed supreme command of the S.A. The effective leadership of the organization was vested in a Chief of Staff, but no appointment to this post was made at the time. Goering wondered why. He was to wait five months for the answer.

Notwithstanding this bitter disappointment, Goering's loyalty to Hitler remained unshaken. September would bring fresh elections, and once again the Party's hopes were high, this time justifiably so. At last the failure of 1928 would be retrieved and the Nazis would be well on their way to power.

The work of establishing and improving social contacts still continued, but as 1930 wore on Goering found that more and more of his time must be given to speech making. Frail though she now was, Carin accompanied him whenever she could, and he accepted her company as a natural right. Just what such a life must have meant to a woman in the last stages of tuberculosis may be gathered from an extract from one of her letters:

"A few days ago we drove from Berlin at 5 p.m. Hermann spoke at Magdeburg at eight o'clock. We left Magdeburg at midnight, got home at half-past five in the morning, had baths and breakfast, then Hermann went straight off to his office and I went to bed! Every minute of the day is filled up – and half the nights as well!"

In the summer Carin broke down completely and was sent away to a sanatorium at Kreuth, in Bavaria. The treatment which she received there enabled her to rally sufficiently to accompany her husband to the Party Rally, held at Nuremberg in August, but the parades, the speeches and the social duties expected of the wife of one of the Party leaders were too much for her. In September she collapsed again and returned to the sanatorium, leaving Goering to fight the election battle alone.

Brüning, after a summer spent in trying to induce a recalcitrant Reichstag to accept the emergency decrees which he considered necessary for Germany's salvation, finally dissolved the Reichstag altogether. The Nazis seized their chance. At 34,000 meetings held throughout the length and breadth of Germany they proffered to a people, utterly disillusioned with the present, the hope of a bright and glorious future. "GERMANY! AWAKE!!" screamed the Nazi posters, the Nazi orators, the marching Stormtroopers. The German people, feeling that they were already in a nightmare, began to ask for nothing better than to awake from it.

By train, car and aeroplane Goering ranged the country during the election campaign, since with Hitler and Goebbels he led the team of Nazi speakers. Although at the age of 37 he was now frankly a very fat man, his girth in no way detracted from that "soldierly presence" which he deliberately cultivated. He developed, too, a strain of coarse, public-bar humour which went down very well indeed with his audiences. As he stood there, his dark uniform breeches girt with what was already one of Germany's longest Sam Browne belts, the bewildered, worried people who heard him speak were apt to feel that here, at least, was a solid man, the sort of fellow one could trust. The election campaign was a great success.

But another "soldierly presence" was about to reappear in Goering's life, a man tougher than he, though less subtle, a dangerous rival indeed. On urgent orders from Munich, orders of which Goering in Berlin, was unaware, Captain Ernst Röhm was on his way home from Bolivia.

The election, held on September 14, 1930, was a surprise to everybody, including the Nazis. Even the parties of the Left – the Communists and Social Democrats – had been ready to concede that the National Socialists were bound to show an improvement on their 1928 poll. Experienced journalists were prepared to guess that Hitler might even achieve 60 seats in the new Reichstag, but that they said was the absolute maximum. When the completed returns showed that the

Nazis had secured 107 seats and were thus, after the Social Democrats, the strongest party in the Reichstag, a shock ran through the world.

For Hermann Goering the sweetness of success was soured by the return of Röhm. Now the reasons for Hitler's refusal to give him command of the S.A. after the Berlin rebellion were painfully clear. The Führer did not think him good enough for the job. For all his war-record, his medals, and his carefully cultivated "soldierly presence," Hitler had preferred to bring back Röhm, the tough, scarred vulgarian, from the ends of the earth, rather than give to Goering the post which he coveted.

Röhm lost no time in buckling down to work. The rancorous Stennes, now Commander-in-Chief of the S.A. in Eastern Germany, refused to obey Röhm's orders. Goebbels, in his weekly paper *Der Angriff* and through the other channels available to him, sought to support his friend Goering by raising yet again a virtuous clamour against the irregular sexual habits of the S.A. Once more recalcitrant Stormtroopers barricaded themselves into their offices or, alternatively, attacked the offices of their opponents within the Party. In the shadows Goering remained very quiet.

Röhm won the day, as he was bound to do, since he had Hitler's support. Whatever Goering's qualities – and from the Führer's point of view those qualities were many and valuable – they did not include the particular kind of toughness which the Chief of Staff of the S.A. now required. The April revolt in Berlin had shown that the force was getting out of hand. Röhm, not Goering, was the man to whip it into shape. And in any case Goering was so ludicrously loyal – subservient even – when it came to dealing with his Führer that his feelings could be safely ignored.

Goebbels, supple, unprincipled, hastened to side with the winner, yet discreetly, lest he lose the friendship of Goering. Stennes was expelled from the Party and the S.A. felt the hand of a master on its neck.

Christmas 1930 was a fairly pleasant time, nevertheless, for the Goering family. On Christmas Eve Josef Goebbels and his wife came round to the Badenschestrasse for the evening. Although Carin had a temperature and was forced to lie on a sofa throughout the party, the whole affair promised to be a great success. Carin's son, Thomas von Kantzow, was there and Cilly, the maid, joined in the fun round the Christmas tree.

Among Hermann's presents was a fine set of antique silver cruets from his mother-in-law. Then, as they were all singing "Silent Night, Holy Night," the carol was interrupted. Carin had fainted and fallen off her sofa. Goering carried her to bed and the little party continued.

Next day Carin was too ill to occupy herself with the household, but since guests were expected to luncheon Goering and Cilly got to work and produced a very adequate meal. Prince August-Wilhelm, who was one of the party, was highly amused, although full of proper sympathy for his hostess, to whom, beaming all over his vacuous face, he brought a bowl of lilies and a camel-hair rug.

By the new year Carin was better, though forced to spend much of her time on the sofa. Meanwhile Röhm, energetic and to Goering intolerable, was fulfilling Hitler's hopes. The S.A. was well on the way towards becoming a really formidable force. As soon as he felt his position secure Röhm appointed the pervert Heines to the position of S.A. Leader for Eastern Germany, which had been left vacant by the expulsion of Stennes. Although, since his exclusion from the Party in 1927, Heines had served eighteen months of a sentence of five years for a *Fehme* murder committed in 1920 (he had thereafter been released on bail of 5000 marks), Röhm still clung to this tall ungainly monster with the desperate persistence of unnatural love, and Hitler made no objection to Heines' appointment.

Goering made no objection either. What suited the Führer must, of course, suit his loyal followers – but it was more than a coincidence that the editors of anti-Nazi newspapers began at this time to receive articles, anonymous indeed but evidently written by somebody who knew his subject thoroughly, which treated the private life of Ernst Röhm in great detail. The Social-Democratic editors seized gleefully upon this material which combined "spice" with a series of body-blows at the leadership of the hated S.A. Goering had taken to journalism once more.

His secret struggle against Röhm was carried on against a background of constant worry. Carin's health was now definitely broken. In the spring of 1931 she fell desperately ill and the doctors held out no hope for her recovery. As his wife lay apparently unconscious, Goering, standing by her bedside, asked the specialist to tell him the truth. The doctor shook his head.

"There is no hope," he said. "She cannot get well again."
Yet Carin heard that death-sentence and determined to falsify it. As she afterwards wrote to her sister:

"I know now what it is like to die. I could hear everything that was going on when the doctor said to Hermann that there was no hope . . . but I felt that my senses were no longer there and that I could neither move nor speak. I suddenly felt as though I was taking leave of the earth and coming into a new and indescribably marvellous world. I knew that if once I went through the gates I saw ahead of me I should never return. Then I heard Hermann's voice – and I knew that I must not leave him alone just yet."

On February 3, 1931, the 107 Nazi Deputies in the Reichstag, led by Goering and Frick and supported by the Nationalists and other right-wing groups, marched ostentatiously out of the Chamber, announcing that they refused to co-operate any longer with the Brüning Government. Yet there was to be no revolution. Hitler had publicly declared that his Party intended to achieve power by legal methods only, and this undertaking, given just before the elections in the previous September, had already had the most gratifying results. General Kurt von Schleicher, the cold, calculating soldier who, ever since Germany's defeat, had built up the Reichswehr until now the Army was the most important political force in the country, forthwith approached the "soldierly" Nazi leaders, Röhm and Goering. Provided that the Nazis did not intend to plunge the country into revolution, it might be possible to come to some arrangement with them. They had the men – 400,000 of them, who would very shortly be admirably organized and trained by Röhm. The Reichswehr had only 100,000 men, the maximum allowed by the Treaty of Versailles, but each soldier was a potential officer or senior N.C.O. – and the Reichswehr had arms. Schleicher had not forgotten von Lossow, and Hitler's breach of faith in 1923, but things were different now in 1931.

Goering longed to take the leading part in these vital negotiations, upon which the whole future of the Party might well depend, but his role was only secondary. Röhm, as Chief of Staff of the S.A., was actually in command of the *Standarten* which von Schleicher coveted. He could talk to the General on equal terms, while Goering, for all his military background, was regarded more as a politician than as a soldier, a fact which he deeply resented. He observed, however, that Röhm had by no means given up the heretical ideas which had got him into trouble with Hitler long ago in 1922 and had enabled Goering to replace him then as leader of the embryo S.A. Röhm still saw the S.A. as an army, in the full sense of the term, trained and equipped for civil war or for war against Germany's foreign enemies. That was quite clear from his conversations with von Schleicher. Hitler, as Goering knew, had clung with equal obstinacy to his own very different conception of the Party militia. For the moment Röhm must be given rope, trying though that period might be for the man who longed to take his place, but given enough rope he would hang himself and patience would be rewarded.

Meanwhile "Hitler's Ambassador" was called upon to justify his nickname. The Führer, committed to "legal methods," determined to destroy the structure of Brüning's State stone by stone. To do this effectively it was necessary to draw away from the Chancellor at least some of the Catholic voters who provided him with the solid core of support upon which his power was based. This was no easy task. The Nazis, spawned in Catholic Bavaria, had by now lost their close associations with Southern Germany, although Party Headquarters were still in Munich. Their strength lay now in the North, the country of Luther, Kant and Bismarck. Neither in the Rhineland, nor in Bavaria, nor in Upper Silesia – the solidly Catholic provinces – had Hitler achieved a plurality of votes. Somehow the Papists must be gulled into believing that National Socialism was not a pagan movement. This could only be done indirectly, since the German Catholics seemed to be singularly impervious to the blandishments of Nazi propaganda. To Goering, therefore, fell the task of squaring the Vatican. He was accordingly packed off to Rome in May 1931.

Those who in later years had the misfortune to conduct international negotiations with the Nazis might have done well to reflect upon that first contact of Hitler's Party with a foreign Power. The mission to Rome was characteristic of the mingled cunning and crass simplicity with which Hitler ever afterwards managed his foreign policy. The frontal assault on the German Catholics had so far failed. Their spiritual leaders must therefore be won over. Goering was just the man for the task. He had travelled – to Italy, England, Denmark and Sweden – whereas Hitler had never been beyond the confines of Germany and Austria. He was an ingratiating talker. He even spoke a little Italian. The fact that the man was a Protestant, and a very lax one at that, a reformed drug-addict, married to a woman whom he had taken from her husband and son, seemed to Hitler to matter very little. To the Vatican it mattered a great deal, but in any case it was folly to suppose that a leading Nazi, however irreproachable his character, could succeed in persuading the Church to yield an inch in their support of Brüning, the Catholic champion.

Nevertheless Hitler's emissary was received by the Pope and by the Cardinal Secretary of State. Photographers stood by to take his picture as he entered the Vatican, and the result of their labours was prominently displayed in the Nazi Press. Once more Germany had struck a blow for Nazi respectability, but that was the only outcome of his visit to the Vatican. His protestations that National Socialism was the friend of the Church were heard with politely concealed disbelief. Even had they been believed the result would have been the same. No orders went out to the German Bishops that they were to look with greater favour than hitherto on the Nazis. The Church, and with them Brüning's Centre Party, remained unshakably suspicious of Nazi ambitions.

That summer, while Röhm worked quietly on the Reichswehr, Hitler extended his contacts with the great industrialists of Germany. The Party treasury had provided him with a new Mercedes touring car, and Goering induced Hitler to find the money for a similar car for himself. In this splendid black monster he, Carin and "Pilli" Koerner, his secretary, set out on a motor tour. At Dresden the ubiquitous Hitler was speaking, and the holidaymakers were dragged off by the Führer to a small, grubby restaurant where they spent a long, and for Carin, extremely exhausting evening. Next day they drove on southwards to the christening of a new relative, the child of Frau Paula Huber, one of Goering's sisters. Thereafter they pottered slowly about Austria and returned by easy stages to Berlin.

Hardly had Goering and his wife settled into the Badenschestrasse again when a telegram brought the news which was to deal Carin her death blow. On September 25 she learned that her mother had died in Stockholm, and promptly collapsed. So ill was she that the doctors absolutely forbade her to travel. It was only on the day after Baroness von Fock's funeral that she and Goering reached the Swedish capital.

On the evening of her arrival Carin collapsed again, and lay unconscious for hours, while the doctors assured her husband that she could not live. But at last her eyes opened, and she whispered to Goering, who sat beside her: "I feel certain that I should soon follow mother."

Meanwhile Röhm had been at work with von Schleicher. Old Field-Marshal von Hindenburg was approached. Would the *Herr Reichspräsident* receive Herr Hitler and Captain Röhm in order that they might explain to him the aims and purposes of the National Socialist Party? The victor of Tannenberg showed no enthusiasm. Hitler was a vulgar demagogue, a foreigner, a mere private soldier. As for Röhm, whatever the man's war record, the fellow was a notorious pederast, and the Reichspräsident would in no circumstances receive *him*. Would Herr Hitler and Captain Goering be a couple more acceptable to the Field-Marshal? Hindenburg growled, grumbled and assented.

The news reached Goering in Stockholm, while Carin lay at death's door. Here was a magnificent chance to score off Röhm and to get into Hindenburg's good graces. Nothing, not even a devoted wife gasping out the last hours of her existence, must stand in the way of that vital appointment in Berlin. Besides, Hitler had ordered him to come, and Hitler's orders must be obeyed. Captain Goering left Carin weak and mortally sick, as he had left her once before on a snowy evening in Obermenzing, and hurried to Berlin.

The interview took place on October 10. The Field-Marshal received his guests without effusive politeness and listened with scarcely veiled impatience to a long harangue by Hitler. Occasionally Goering put in a word, but he took little part in what soon became a monologue. As the Nazi leaders left the Chancellery, to shouts of "GERMANY AWAKE!" put up by the claque which Goebbels had to gather in the street, Hindenburg observed to von Schleicher that the "Bohemian" was a queer fellow.

"D'you mean to say *he* wants to be Chancellor," the old man growled. "Never! Minister of Posts at the very most!"

There was no time to return to Carin now. On the day after the inauspicious interview with Hindenburg, Goering put on his brown shirt and breeches and drove with Hitler and Röhm to Bad Harzburg in the Harz Mountains. There Nazis, Nationalists and members of the "Steel Helmet" organization had gathered to denounce Brüning's second Government, which had just been formed. The list of guests at this demonstration was a tribute to the position which the Party now occupied and to the success of Hitler, Goering and Röhm in getting on with the "right people." General von Seeckt, the man who had helped to smash the 1923 *Putsch,* was there; Herr Blohm, the great Hamburg shipbuilder, and Dr. Hjalmar Schacht, who had resigned the Presidency of the Reichsbank after disagreeing with the Government over the Young Plan for reparations. The little mountain spa fairly reeked of money and influence, and Goering, as he stood with right arm raised while the Brown Shirts stamped past him, was well content.

The Harzburg demonstration was, in fact, a declaration of war on the Brüning Government. On October 16 the Reichstag was adjourned until the following February, and on that day a telegram from Stockholm told Goering that his wife was sinking fast.

Carin Goering died at 4 a.m. on October 17, 1931, after a final severe attack of *angina pectoris.* A few hours later her husband, accompanied by his brother and by "Pilli" Koerner, stood by the bedside of the dead woman. He took his last leave of her in the Edelweiss Chapel, kneeling alone by the coffin, while the little congregation sang Luther's noble hymn "Ein' Feste Burg ist unser Gott" and "Home Sweet Home," Carin's favourite song.

The flat in the Badenschestrasse seemed very empty when its master returned to it a few days later.

Lonely Victory

WITH the death of Carin the third stage of Hermann Goering's life ended. The first chapter had closed when the Commander of the Richthofen *Geschwader* shattered his empty glass on the wall of the Stiftskeller public-house at Aschaffenburg, the second when he fell in the Residenzstrasse in Munich under the fire of the Bavarian police. Now he was alone again.

For nine years a woman had shared his disordered life. She had not been an intelligent woman, nor, as middle-age approached, any longer a beautiful one, but she had given Hermann Goering what he needed – love and, above all, admiration. At times, when friends and acquaintances had been inclined to turn away from the broken ex-officer, to dismiss him as a drug-soaked failure, Carin had stood by him, filled still with faith in him and in his future. She had sewed for him, cooked for him, taken his telephone messages, entertained friends and associates. It is unlikely that her husband ever realized, during her lifetime, the effort which this service cost to a wife racked by sickness, but he appreciated the service itself.

Carin never had a rival in her husband's affections. While Goebbels indulged in a series of facile amours, while Röhm sated himself with unnatural pleasures, Goering remained true to his wife. Yet two passions dominated Goering's mind, beside which love for Carin – and his love was real enough – took second place. Ambition and loyalty to Adolf Hitler held the first places in his heart. For them he had neglected Carin's health and abandoned her on her deathbed. The morphine, taken originally to allay physical pain, had become, during the years in Sweden, a means of escape from the eternal nagging of frustrated ambition. Carin's love was only a secondary palliative.

Now, at 38 years of age, it seemed that ambition might soon be satisfied, and Carin was not there to share in the prizes of success. Goering missed his wife horribly and in his loneliness gave rein to the sentimentality with which he was wont to regard his own personal affairs and those of anybody closely connected with him. Bruno Loerzer and "Pilli" Koerner bore the chief brunt of his mourning, but he was prepared to talk about his lost wife to anybody who showed the slightest inclination to listen. The man who later loved to be called *"Der Eiserne"* ("The Iron Man") displayed no very striking degree of self-control in his bereavement. Hitler sympathized suitably, but with some reserve. He had liked Carin well enough, but looked upon her as a rival who took away from himself an undue proportion of Goering's time and attention. Goebbels and his wife Helga showed a more satisfying depth of commiseration. Kind letters and presents from the most unexpected sources were delivered at the Badenschestrasse, but they did little to console the widower, or to still the conscience which told him, implacably, that he had done ill to desert Carin in her last hours.

Work was the best antidote, and of that there was plenty. There was also Ernst Röhm.

The atmosphere in which Goering now moved was heavy with intrigue – intrigue against Brüning, against the Social-Democratic Government of Prussia, but intrigue, above all, against Party comrades. In one respect only all the Nazi leaders stood on common ground – they meant to seize power as swiftly as possible and as ruthlessly as was consistent with the "legal" methods to which Hitler had, regrettably, pledged them. Röhm, satisfied with the manner in which his contacts with Schleicher and the Reichswehr were developing, secure in the knowledge that he commanded 600,000 men who were becoming, every day, a more efficient army, aimed to come to power with Schleicher on the shoulders of the Army and the S.A., but by diplomacy rather than by force. Goering and Goebbels favoured more direct methods. The S.A. should be used, they thought, to whip up popular dissatisfaction still further, street fighting, already almost a normal feature of the German scene, should be intensified, and in the general confusion the Nazis could then snatch the reins of Government from Brüning's hands, Gregor Strasser favoured an alliance with Brüning against the Social Democrats.

Meanwhile Röhm commanded the big battalions and Goering must still be content with diplomacy, a pursuit which, in point of fact, gave him plenty to do. The inopportune discovery, for instance, of a plan by local Nazis to stage a rising in the province of Hessen led to an unpleasant interview with General Groener, Minister of the Interior and of the Army, in which Goering, the exponent of revolutionary methods, solemnly promised that "the leadership of the Party stands now, as ever, by its determination to observe strictly legal methods, a fact which has been affirmed often enough on oath." Groener was not impressed by this declaration and the guerrilla warfare between the Nazis and the Government continued unabated for a time.

In January 1932 Brüning, bedevilled by the financial crisis, which had reached chaotic proportions, by the tactics of Nazis and Communists and by dissension within his own Government, invited Hitler to visit him. Hindenburg's term of office as President was drawing to an end. Would Hitler, Brüning asked, support an extension of the "Old Gentleman's" term in the Reichstag? If he would do this, thereby ensuring that the Field-Marshal would remain at the head of the State, Brüning would in return surrender the office of Chancellor to Hitler as soon as the question of the future of reparations,

97

which was now the Government's main preoccupation, had been satisfactorily settled.

Hitler agreed in principle to this proposal, and in so doing incurred the pained reproaches of the "revolutionaries" in his Party, led by Goering and Goebbels. How, these forthright followers demanded, could they hope to drive Germany to the very brink of catastrophe, as they must if their plans for a swift seizure of power were to succeed, when Hitler deliberately went out of his way to help Brüning out of the very unpleasant mess in which, thanks partly to the efforts of the Nazis, he already found himself?

Hitler, having already accepted Brüning's suggestion in writing, was hard put to it to withdraw, although the arguments of his "Ambassador" and of his chief propagandist convinced him that he had made a mistake. However, he saved the situation by imposing an additional condition on Brüning – namely that the Chancellor should not await the outcome of the negotiations about reparations but should surrender his office to Hitler at once. Since this fresh demand was obviously inacceptable, Goering was able to congratulate himself upon having persuaded his Führer to wriggle out of Brüning's "trap," thus leaving the field clear for an extension of the incendiary activities in which he and Goebbels delighted.

On February 22, 1931, Hitler, after weeks of hesitation, decided that he himself would fight Hindenburg for the Presidency. The result of the voting, which took place in the middle of March, seemed to indicate that here, too, he had miscalculated. In spite of a whirlwind election campaign Hindenburg obtained a majority of more than 7,000,000 votes over Hitler. Technically, however, the result was a draw, since Hindenburg had failed to secure the majority required under the Constitution, and the voters must therefore do their duty again.

No sooner was the election over than General Groener struck back at the Nazis, and in particular at Captain Goering. Party headquarters in all parts of the Reich were raided by the police. On March 18 no fewer than 170 of these raids took place in Prussia alone, and the anti-Nazi Press, whooping with mingled satisfaction and alarm, announced that Goering and his colleagues had made all arrangements for a rebellion, which was to take place if Hitler failed to win the election.

On the afternoon of March 19 every foreign correspondent in Berlin received, to his surprise, an invitation to a Press conference which was to be held that day in Hitler's luxurious suite in the Hotel Kaiserhof. The journalists assembled and waited. Presently Goering appeared, smart and dapper in a grey suit, swinging his walking-stick and beaming amiably upon the company. Hitherto the Nazis had not bothered much with the foreign Press, but now it had been thought prudent to conciliate them, and the task of doing so had naturally fallen upon "Hitler's Ambassador."

He soothed his listeners. The Nazis, he assured them, intended to act within the framework of the Constitution. The very suggestion of any illegal intent was monstrous.

"It was most commendable of us to concentrate 350,000 Stormtroopers in their own quarters on election day," Goering went on. "By so doing we prevented bloodshed. As for the allegation of the police that we Nazis were preparing to surround Berlin, the whole idea is absurd. We are surely entitled to take our own measures for the evacuation from the city of our women and children so as to protect them from injury by Communist mobs, and that, in fact, is what we did. Why, Heaven help us, we have so many former officers in our ranks that if we really wanted to stage a rising we'd set about it in quite a different manner, I assure you gentlemen."

The Captain's air of injured innocence deceived only the more gullible of the foreign correspondents – and since foreign correspondents are paid not to be gulled, this represented only a comparatively small proportion of the audience. Most of them realized that this fat, bland, genial man would have asked nothing better than to loose the S.A. against his enemies. But Goering did not command the S.A. Röhm did, and he and Hitler were playing a cautious game.

Injured innocence even went so far as to bring a suit before the Leipzig Federal Court in which the National Socialist Party asked for an injunction to restrain the police from making further raids on Party premises. In reply Groener produced evidence of the Party's bellicose intentions so formidable that the case was hastily dropped.

On April 10 the second round of the presidential election was fought and resulted in Hindenburg's return with a majority of 6,000,000 over Hitler. The first act of the re-elected President was to sign a decree which made the S.A. an illegal organization.

Röhm at once got to work, with von Schleicher, to have the decree rescinded. It had been the doing of his old enemy,

99

Groener. Groener must therefore be put out of the way. This was successfully achieved through a neat intrigue by which Hindenburg was made to lose confidence in Groener as Minister of the Interior, while Schleicher saw to it that the Army expressed their dissatisfaction with his work as Reichswehr Minister. The unfortunate man, who had put up a sturdy fight against the Nazis, resigned, and Brüning's position became more precarious than ever. On May 30 he followed Groener's example and returned his seals of office to the President.

Röhm had succeeded in bringing about the downfall of Brüning. Not only was the man in command of the S.A., but had proved his ability in the field of diplomacy, which was Goering's special province. Every day made it increasingly evident that there would, eventually, be no room, even in so large a party as Hitler's, for two "soldierly presences" of such calibre. For the present, however, Captain Goering was in no hurry.

An hour after Brüning's resignation, Goering and Josef Goebbels drove northwards from Berlin into Mecklenburg, where Hitler had been lying low lest his presence in Berlin during that critical period should rouse Brüning's suspicions. Goering bore a message from the President. Hindenburg expected Hitler to call on him that very afternoon. The Führer bundled into the car and with his two lieutenants drove fast to the capital.

Among Goering's influential acquaintances was a certain Franz von Papen, an aristocrat of the old school, but one possessed of far more intelligence and subtlety than is often granted to men of that stamp – at least in Germany. His name had, for a time, become notorious throughout the Allied world during the war when it was discovered that he had operated a sabotage organization in the United States from the German Embassy in Washington. Thereafter he had retired into the background, but without losing any of his very extensive contacts or missing the opportunity of making new ones.

He had first met Goering at a little gathering which had assembled at von Papen's invitation in 1930 at the Herrenklub, the inner sanctuary of the land-owning aristocracy. The meeting had been called to discuss the formation by the various centre and right-wing parties, in collaboration with their counterparts elsewhere in Europe, of a front against

Communism, and Goering had been very favourably impressed by his host. Although the representatives of the Army, who had also been invited to the discussion, were sceptical about the possibility of friendship with France, which von Papen regarded as essential for the success of his project, Goering received the idea with enthusiasm. The acquaintanceship with von Papen had ripened and Goering had introduced his new friend to Hitler.

Now von Papen was about to succeed Brüning as Chancellor. Hitler had known that this might happen for the past two days and had already signified his willingness to co-operate with the new Chancellor. The forthcoming interview with the "Old Gentleman" was intended, presumably, to confirm this.

Hindenburg received Hitler at four o'clock. He was obviously no better pleased to see the "Bohemian" than he had been at their last meeting, and took good care to give him no chance of delivering another monologue. During the eight minutes of the interview Hitler was hardly able to get in a word. Hindenburg announced that von Papen was to be the next Chancellor. He understood that Hitler would support him and desired a further assurance to that effect. Hitler gave that assurance and mentioned again the terms on which his support would be given – the Reichstag must be dissolved, new elections held and the ban on the S.A. lifted. Those terms, said the President, would be carried out. There was no more to be said. Good afternoon. The interview was ended.

For Goering the accession of von Papen was a most gratifying event. Röhm might have his Schleicher, but he, Goering, might surely almost be said to have the Chancellor in his pocket. In any case von Papen was no more than a stopgap. Every indication pointed to a great Nazi victory at the election which would follow on the dissolution of the Reichstag.

The election campaign was a savage affair. The S.A., emerging refreshed from their brief period of illegality, went to work with gusto, and blood ran in the streets of German cities, greatly to the satisfaction of Goering, who had always favoured this type of electioneering. On July 17 alone 27 people were killed and 181 seriously wounded in street-fighting.

Voting took place on July 31, and this time the result was quite unequivocal. The Nazis secured 230 seats out of 609 and were thus by far the largest party in the Chamber. Hindenburg surely had no alternative now but to offer the Chancellorship to Hitler. Schleicher indeed assured the Führer that he practically had the seals of office in his hand. With Goering and Goebbels, the Führer, proceeded to draft plans for the new Government.

On August 9 the whole house of cards came tumbling down. Hitler's "men of confidence" brought him grim news from the Wilhelmstrasse. Schleicher, in whose influence with the President the Nazis had reposed absolute faith, had proved himself a sorry ally. Hindenburg was determined that von Papen should remain Chancellor, notwithstanding the Nazi success at the elections, and nothing would budge the obstinate "Old Gentleman." Brought up in an age when "Bohemians" did not venture to aspire to the highest positions in the German State, the President was having none of Hitler as Chancellor now. Von Papen was a gentleman by birth with whom the Field-Marshal was on extremely good terms, and he was determined that his Chancellor should continue to be *"salonfähig"* – fit to be received into good society, which, by the President's old-fashioned lights, Hitler was certainly not.

Goering lost not a minute in striking at his rival, Röhm. Was not this, he asked the Führer, proof of the utter failure of Röhm's diplomacy. The S.A. leader had induced Hitler to put all his faith in Schleicher, and just look at the result! Revolutionary methods were, as he and Goebbels had always urged, the only answer to the present situation. Hitler, as Supreme Commander of the S.A., must order the mobilization of his private army.

Hitler, disillusioned, furiously angry, gave the order, and the S.A. concentrated round Berlin, ready to massacre the "Reds." In East Prussia and Silesia the local *Standarten* did not even wait for orders, but began, in accordance with a plan obviously arranged long in advance, to murder their opponents systematically. The rising which Goering had been so ready to pooh-pooh in March has become a reality in August. So much for Hitler's promises of "legality," so much for Goering's "soldierly honour." As at Munich in 1923, so now in 1932 Hitler and Goering had broken faith.

But if Goering regarded such tactics as compatible with his "soldierly presence," General von Schleicher did not – and Schleicher was a soldier on the active list. Notwithstanding his involved flirtation with Röhm, he now summoned the leader of the Berlin S.A., Count Helldorf, and warned him roundly that unless the S.A. were called off the Army would open fire on them. Von Papen, Goering's old friend from the Herrenklub, was a disappointment too. He declared martial law and announced that execution or imprisonment awaited anyone who infringed it.

Goering and Goebbels worked hard on their indignant Führer. The situation was intolerable. Almost 14,000,000 German voters stood behind the Nazis. To yield now, to forgo the slaughter of the "Marxists," would be to betray all those trusting souls. Hitler went off to see Hindenburg, steeled to desperate measures while in Goebbels' flat Goering awaited the outcome.

Ernst Röhm this time was chosen to accompany Hitler to the President's palace, and the sight of that notorious debauchee did nothing to improve von Hindenburg's senile, but still formidable, temper. He was a real soldier who like Ludendorff before him, made the Nazi champions look remarkably small.

The President did not even invite Hitler and his companions to sit down. In his deep harsh old voice he asked Hitler whether he would co-operate with von Papen. Hitler explained that he must have absolute power, just as Mussolini had it in Italy. The President replied that he insisted upon a non-party Chancellor, and reminded Hitler that he had promised him, personally, before the elections, to support von Papen if necessary. However, if Hitler now refused to do so there was nothing more to be said. The Nazis were then shown to the door.

For a second time the soldiers had beaten Hitler, and he determined upon revenge. Death would remove Hindenburg before long without any outside assistance, but Schleicher must go, and von Papen. Goering warmly agreed with this programme and quietly added to the list another name – that of Ernst Röhm – though he did not mention that candidate for extinction to his Führer.

In the meanwhile there was still the Reichstag, of which Goering was now President-Elect. That "parliamentary swindle" might still be useful, properly manipulated. A Government defeat on a vote of confidence would bring about new elections with which to force Hindenburg's hand. Goering, the diplomat, could be trusted to manage things.

The Reichstag met on September 12, and for once Communists and Nazis made common cause. The vote of no-confidence in the Government was moved by the Communist

Deputy Torgler and, having been adopted by an enormous majority was given first place on the agenda of the session. Von Papen had prepared for this possibility. At his suggestion the President had already signed an order dissolving the Reichstag, and now, during a brief adjournment, the Chancellor fetched the red leather dispatch-box in which this document lay – the sheet of paper which could keep him in office. If the Reichstag were dissolved before the vote of confidence was taken there would be no new elections.

When the Chamber reassembled, Goering, from his rostrum, announced that the vote of the motion would be taken at once. Von Papen, clutching his dispatch-box, rose and sought to catch the President's eye, but Goering's gaze was studiously bent on the papers before him. The Chancellor demanded the right to speak, but somehow the President of the Reichstag was too preoccupied to pay any attention to him. At last von Papen strode angrily to Goering's desk and slammed before him the order dissolving the Reichstag, but so intent was the Captain on the voting, which had already begun, that, as he himself said afterwards, he never had time to look at the paper which the Chancellor had thrust at him.

The vote was counted and resulted in the defeat of von Papen's Government by a majority of 481 votes. Only then did Captain Goering realize the importance of the document which Herr von Papen had tried so hard to bring to his notice. Alas for his very regrettable fit of inattention! It was now too late to dissolve the Chamber, since the Cabinet had already been voted out of office. Parliamentary procedure, Captain Goering pointed out, must be observed at all costs. That Reichstag did not meet again.

Instead elections took place on November 6, and the Nazis lost votes. It was a sickening blow. Gregor Strasser, who had warned Hitler that an appeal to the electorate would have this very result, was quietly triumphant. Goering, who had engineered the defeat of von Papen and thus made the election inevitable, was correspondingly cast down. The Nazis must make a bargain with somebody, and they had the choice of two alternatives – the hated von Schleicher or the equally hated von Papen.

Schleicher, the Head of the new Government, now loathed both Hitler and von Papen – the former as a perjured firebrand, the latter as a tool which Schleicher had proposed to cast aside as soon as its usefulness was over and which now proved to have ambitions of its own. His aim therefore was to attract to himself, as he hoped, the "best elements" of the Nazi Party, by enlisting Gregor Strasser on his side, leaving von Papen stranded with Hitler, Goering, Goebbels and a hot-headed, venomous but, it was to be hoped, impotent following.

To counter this intrigue von Papen was forced to rely on his enemy, Hitler. Goering resumed his visits to the Herrenklub, the little dinners at Horcher's, the discreet chats in the corners of quiet drawing-rooms. He represented now not a party well on its way to power but a party which in the eyes of most experienced judges, was almost finished as an independent political force. It still enjoyed the support of 11,000,000 voters and was thus a useful ally for either Schleicher or von Papen, but the Nazis no longer had any hope of outright power – so said the experts, including von Schleicher and von Papen.

The Nazis were divided – Gregor Strasser, the Party Organizer, had deserted Hitler, and with him several prominent members. Funds were very low – so low that it was necessary to cut the salaries of Party officials, an injudicious move in an organization already threatened with disruption from within. However, since von Papen seemed willing to come to terms with Hitler, the Führer must, in the circumstances, be ready to reach an understanding with von Papen. The preliminary moves in this unnatural manœuvre were entrusted by Hitler to the man who had already proved himself conveniently unscrupulous where politics were concerned – Captain Hermann Goering.

Money was the first problem, and this was obtained. For some time Goering had been raising personal loans from Fritz Thyssen, the steel-magnate. Now he suggested that Thyssen and his associates in the coal and iron industries should dip rather more deeply into their pockets and finance the whole Nazi Party for a few months. Once Hitler was in power those who had given such practical proof of support for the Nazi cause would have no reason to regret their investment. Thyssen, Vögler and Springorum of the Steel Trust, harassed by the steady deterioration of their business, were prepared to do anything within reason which might help to fill their order-books again. Goering promised that once his party came to power there would be orders in plenty for the steel industry. The magnates paid up

On January 4, 1933, Hitler and von Papen met at a secret rendezvous in Cologne. Twice Hitler had been affronted by Hindenburg's obvious liking for the former cavalry-officer, by his even more obvious dislike of the "Bohemian private." Now he proposed to use von Papen as a channel to the President's good graces. Von Papen, on his side, sought to control the National Socialist Party. To achieve this he was perfectly prepared to allow this ridiculous fellow Hitler to become Chancellor, if that was the summit of his ambition. As Vice-Chancellor he, von Papen, the experienced politician, the smooth, polished diplomat, would be the true ruler of Germany. Both plotters were therefore reasonably satisfied with their enforced alliance.

The battle with Schleicher lasted a month, and von Papen fought it while Hitler, Goering and the other Nazi leaders stood quietly aside and awaited the issue. Schleicher and Strasser were outgeneralled from the very beginning. Von Papen had the President's ear, and, more important, that of his son, Major Oskar von Hindenburg, and of State Secretary Meissner, the "Old Gentleman's" right-hand man. Gradually von Papen brought the Field-Marshal round. This work of education was consummated by the discovery of Schleicher's alleged intention to declare martial law and to arrest not only von Papen, Hitler, Goering and the other Nazi leaders, but even the Field-Marshal himself and his son.

Schleicher had already asked the President to dissolve the Reichstag and to grant him absolute powers without which, he said, he could not rule Germany. Hindenburg had refused this request and Schleicher had resigned. Already, therefore, Germany was without a Government. Now Schleicher's hold over the Army must be broken at once. General Werner von Blomberg, commanding the Berlin Military District, passed for being a Nazi sympathizer. At least he had had some traffic with Hitler and the two men had seemed to understand each other. The General was promptly summoned and offered the post of Minister of the Army in a Government headed by Hitler and von Papen. He accepted the offer.

It fell to Goering to bring Hitler the news that Hindenburg would receive him and invite him to form a Government. On January 29, he burst in upon Hitler and Goebbels as they sat, drinking coffee, in the Hotel Kaiserhof. The scene is best described by Goebbels himself in a characteristc passage of his diary:

106

"Goering came to us suddenly and announced that everything is perfect. The Führer, he said, would be given the Chancellorship next day. . . . It is certainly Goering's happiest hour, and rightly so. He has prepared the ground for the Führer with diplomacy and skill by negotiations which have lasted for months – one might even say years. His prudence, his strong nerves, above all his strength of character and loyalty to the Leader were real, strong and admirable. His face became a mask of stone when, in the midst of the hardest struggle, his dear wife was torn from his side by a painful death. But he did not waver for an instant. Instead he went on his way, strong and earnest, a resolute shield-bearer for the Führer. . . . This upright soldier with the heart of a child has remained true to himself – and now he stands before his Führer and brings him the happiest message of his life."

For three days Goering had wrestled with von Papen. Now at last unity was achieved. On January 30 Hitler was received by Hindenburg. He was offered, and accepted, the Chancellorship, with von Papen as Vice-Chancellor. As Hindenburg set his bold, flowing signature (a strange contrast to Hitler's cramped and illegible scrawl) to the document which was, twelve years later, to bring Germany to destruction, he remembered a phrase which he had used long ago, just before the Battle of Tannenberg in which his victory had saved Germany from a Russian invasion. He blotted the fatal sheet of paper.

"Und nun, meine Herren, vorwärts mit Gott!"
"And now! Forward, gentlemen, with God's help."

The Firebrand

EVEN if Goebbels' estimate of Captain Goering's character be accepted, it is necessary to make some reservations. For a man whose heart was still that of a child, the Captain kept some strange company, nor were the reasons which lay behind these frequentations always those which would have found favour in a well-ordered nursery.

Throughout 1932 a certain Otto Diehls had paid repeated,

if somewhat surreptitious, visits to Captain Goering's flat, now no longer in the Badenschestrasse, but in the even more fashionable Kaiserdamm. This young man of 32 was a peculiar personage. Even more remarkable than his notoriously insatiable appetite for women and for beer, of which he could and did drink enormous quantities, was his well-known habit of enlivening the parties to which he was invited by crunching up and swallowing the glassware. It was not, however, on account of these accomplishments that he struck up a friendship with Hermann Goering. Diehls was a professional policeman serving in Department IA (Political) of the Prussian force, and he knew how to make the most of his opportunities.

During the months when Nazi fortunes hung in the balance young Diehls, with a sharp eye on the future, had provided Groener and the anti-Nazi leaders with confidential information about their opponents, while at the same time reinsuring by giving many useful hints to the Nazis themselves. By virtue of his position he was well equipped to do this.

If Otto Diehls was far sighted, so also was Hermann Goering. The President of the Reichstag saw in the policeman a tool who could not only be made to serve his immediate purposes but who might well prove himself a joker in the poker-hand which he was assembling against his colleague, Captain Röhm. Diehls soon made himself almost indispensable to the President of the Reichstag. He helped Goering in several little Stock Exchange deals, since the police sometimes hear more than do the brokers about the movements of the market. Diehls was also extremely useful in keeping creditors at bay, but above all his value lay in his excellent knowledge of police organization and of the dossiers dealing with the lives of all kinds of people which lay in the police headquarters at the Alexanderplatz, in Berlin.

Goering had now drawn up in broad outline his plan for the destruction of Röhm's power and influence, and after Hitler's accession to power in February 1933 he could begin, with the help of Diehls, to put it into effect. Röhm might command the S.A. and have 600,000 men at his beck and call. Goering would counter him by seizing control of the police. That ambition once achieved, he would have the whip hand, for Diehls had explained to him in detail the intricacies of the police organization. Goering was an apt pupil, and now Diehls was continually, if discreetly, at his side. The two men understood one another very well.

The moment for action, however, had not yet come. Admittedly the Nazis were in power, but they had come to power "legally." In his previous insistence upon snatching office by revolutionary methods Goering had been influenced by the splendid opportunities which public tumult gives to a resolute intriguer of grabbing the key positions in the State and of ridding himself of enemies. From that point of view the present position was most unsatisfactory. Apart from the bands, the parades of S.A. and the cheering which had accompanied Hitler's installation as Chancellor, life went on in a depressingly normal manner. As Goebbels wrote in his diary on January 31, 1933:

"In a discussion with the Führer the main lines to be followed in the struggle against the Red Terror were established. For the moment we shall refrain from direct counter-measures. The Bolshevik attempt at revolution must first *flame up*. Then, at the right moment, we shall strike."

Goering was present at that discussion, and he applied a very literal interpretation to the decisions which were reached.

He was now Minister of the Interior for Prussia and as such one of the effective rulers of Germany. The Prussian police were his and Diehls, now head of the Political Department, stood at his elbow as he worked, night after night, indefatigably, remorselessly, throughout the month of February. There was no need any more to rely upon Diehls' second-hand accounts of the contents of police records, or upon smuggled copies of this or that dossier. Now the archives of the Alexanderplatz were wide open to the Minister and he ploughed through them painstakingly. In the process he learned a great deal about his avowed enemies and his professed friends, and the information was carefully tabulated. One of Hermann Goering's most striking characteristics was an admirable memory, which many a man, henceforward, would have good reason to curse.

There was no time now for social life – not even for a meeting with charming Emmy Sonnemann, in whose occasional companionship Goering was beginning to find great comfort. He had known Fräulein Sonnemann for more than a year. The meeting had taken place at Weimar, where Fräulein Sonnemann, an actress since the age of 17 and now in her early thirties, had played Gretchen in a production of *Faust* at the State Theatre. Goering, smarting bitterly from the death of Carin, had nevertheless been struck by Fräulein Son-nemann's performance and had asked to be introduced to her.

They met in a café and at once a bond of sympathy was established. Goering spoke of his loneliness and of the gap which Carin's death had left in his life. Giving confidence for confidence, Fräulein Sonnemann told of her unhappy marriage, now dissolved, with an actor named Köstlin, and of the recent death of her mother, which had deeply grieved her.

A warm friendship was established between the politician and the actress, the warmer because Fräulein Sonnemann knew nothing whatever about politics and cared even less. Her whole life was centred in the theatre and in human beings. A warm-hearted woman, she had friends in every class of society, many of them lame ducks whom she helped over stiles as best she could. To her this fat, vigorous man, so obviously lost without the wife whom he had loved, was a pathetic figure – another lame duck to be helped along.

Goering found Fräulein Sonneman's complete disregard of politics refreshing. Carin had known very little about politics either if it came to that, but she had insisted in taking an interest in them for her husband's sake, and Goering had always found her views depressingly naïve, for Carin was a very honest woman. Emmy Sonnemann, educated in the hard school of the theatre from girlhood, had many topics of conversation, an advantage which Carin had rather conspicuously lacked. It was restful, Goering found, to forget for a little the struggle and intrigue which made up his daily life and to speak about Schiller, Shakespeare, Ibsen and Bernard Shaw. Carin had never made Goering feel the deficiencies in his own education, but Emmy Sonnemann did so, and by introducing him to a world of which he had little knowledge gave him a new interest in life, an interest subsidiary to the lust for power which now dominated him, but a real one nevertheless. Moreover Fräulein Sonnemann's views on "culture Bolshevism" were very much in accord with those of Captain Goering. For the "expressionist" drama of Toller, Unruh and Kaiser she had no time whatever. Her interests lay in the German classics and in the work of the great foreign dramatists. Captain Goering found it all very soothing.

In February 1933, however, there was no time for relaxation. The German States still had more power than the Nazis were to allow them a few months later; Prussia was the key to the Reich, and Goering was the most powerful man in Prussia.

110

Yet even after the *Machtübernahme*, as the Nazis styled their accession to office, the Prussian Diet, or Parliament, sought stubbornly, if belatedly, to insist on its democratic rights. On February 4 it rejected, by 214 votes to 196, a Nazi motion dissolving the Diet on March 4. Herr Braun, the Prime Minister of Prussia and Goering's technical superior, declared that to dissolve the Diet would only lead to public unrest and that new elections would produce a Chamber substantially similar to its predecessor. Hindenburg had already transferred the rights of the Prussian Cabinet to von Papen, as Reich Commissioner for Prussia, and democratic government came to an end. One of those who played a leading part in opposing the Nazis on this occasion was Dr. Adenaur, now Prime Minister of Western Germany.

Hitler had been raised to power because the "respectable" people of Germany saw in him the champion who would slay the Bolshevik dragon. Yet the dragon was, in those first days in 1933, inconveniently quiescent. Even those who had been frightened by the horrid visions of Red devilment presented to them by the Nazi Press and by Nazi orators began to feel that perhaps Hitler and his men had exaggerated the Bolshevik danger and that the new powers which they were now so busily assuming were unnecessary. As for the opponents of the Nazis, they made no secret of the scepticism – that was still possible in those early days – and many waverers listened to them.

Captain Goering decided that he must bring this state of affairs to an end. The "revolutionary" element of the Party leadership would, for once, act independently, without consulting "Legality Adolf," as Hitler was already called behind his back. Goebbels, a fellow "activist," must be in the plot and also, unfortunately, Röhm, since the help of his S.A. was needed. The *camarilla* which finally drew up plans for the "frame-up" against the Communists consisted, besides Captain Goering, its originator, of Goebbels, Röhm, Heines, Count Helldorf, leader of the Berlin S.A., Karl Ernst, a certain Standartenführer (regimental commander) of the S.A. named Sander and two other members of the S.A., Fiedler and von Mohrenschild.

At five minutes past 9 p.m. on February 27, 1933, Hans Floeter, a student of philosophy – tall, lanky and bespectacled – was walking home along the Sommerstrasse, which ran from the Brandenburg Gate northwards towards the River Spree. As he passed the massive hideousness of the Reichstag building he was startled, so he later asserted, to observe a man standing on a balcony apparently brandishing a flaming torch. Something was clearly wrong and Floeter's very proper impulse was to tell a policeman about it.

Constable Buvert, his grey-green greatcoat tightly buttoned against the chill of the night, the patent-leather peak of his shako pulled down over his eyes, had noticed nothing amiss. He was roused by a shout from Floeter, who announced that somebody was trying to set fire to the Reichstag and, to give point to his words, thumped the constable vigorously on the back. Buvert, thoroughly alarmed, ran off to summon assistance while Floeter, whose study of philosophy seems to have inoculated him against the sin of curiosity, walked on towards his supper.

While Buvert was ringing the fire-alarm, Captain Goering, in his office on Unter den Linden only a few hundred yards away, pored diligently over his endless dossiers. At 9.20 the news of the fire reached him and he lost not a moment. Snatching a furry, grey felt hat and throwing on a trench-coat, which for the Nazis, as earlier for the Irish Republican Army, was almost a uniform in itself, he climbed into the black, Ministerial Mercedes and was driven to the scene of the fire.

As the Minister of the Interior stepped from his car and looked upwards at the glow which now shone from the windows of the Reichstag he heard (as he afterwards declared) the word "arson" muttered by a member of the crowd. Until that moment, he later affirmed on oath, the notion of criminal incendiarism had not for a second occurred to him. This is the more remarkable since the Berlin Nazis had for some time past been themselves indulging in a little mild arson as part of a programme designed to keep the public alert and apprehensive. Small gangs of Nazis were in the habit of plastering Berlin's *Litfassäulen* – stout wooden erections on which advertisements of concerts and theatres were displayed – with an incendiary phosphorus compound, which after a few minutes' exposure to the air ignited spontaneously. This trick had kept the police and fire-brigade busy and the Prussian Minister of the Interior had certainly had it brought to his attention, yet we have his assurance that no thought of arson had entered his head until he heard that muttered word from the crowd.

Then, however, all was suddenly revealed: "A this moment," he stated later in evidence, "a veil fell from my eyes. I knew that the Communist Party was the culprit. I only wish that the rest of the world had seen this as clearly."

While this process of enlightenment was taking place Adolf Hitler was enjoying a quiet dinner at the flat of another of the conspirators, Josef Goebbels. The news of the fire arrived there by telephone, relayed by "Putzi" Hanfstaengel, the kind friend who had hidden the Führer after the 1923 *Putsch* and had remained his court-jester ever since. Goebbels, playing his part well, answered the telephone, professed to believe that Hanfstaengel was joking and replaced the receiver. Hanfstaengel rang again, shrieked the news once more at the suitably flabbergasted Dr. Goebbels, and five minutes later both host and guest were standing beside Goering while the great building, now well alight, blazed above them.

"This is a Communist outrage," Goering assured the Führer, and announced that one of the culprits had been arrested. At 9.27 p.m. a certain Marinus van der Lubbe, a young Dutchman of weak mentality and Communist antecedents, had been found in the burning building and taken into custody.

Hitler remarked that the fire was a "sign from Heaven" of the dangers which lay ahead of Germany unless the claws of the Communists were thoroughly drawn, and with that remark rose perfecly to the occasion. Fortified by his Führer's approval, Goering proceeded to draw the claws.

Van der Lubbe was later sentenced to death and executed for his share in the burning of the Reichstag, but it is only fair to remark that most of those who actually did the deed did not long survive him. In fact Karl Ernst, Gruppenführer (major-general) of the Berlin S.A., assisted by Fiedler and von Mohrenschild, extended to the Reichstag the technique which had proved so effective with *Litfassäulen*. The furnishings of the chamber were smeared with incendiary compound, curtains and carpets saturated with petrol. According to a confession allegedly written by Ernst himself, and almost certainly written by one of the conspirators, these preparations were completed by 9.5 p.m. – at the very moment, in fact, at which the incurious Floeter had first observed signs of fire.

The "Bolshevik attempt at revolution" had duly "flamed up," in accordance with Goebbels' wishes.

Goering drove back to his office and got to work. With Helldorf he had already made all arrangements for a general round-up of leading Communists and anti-Nazis in general. That night between 4000 and 5000 people were arrested in

Berlin by the police or by Helldorf's S.A., most of them local officials of the Communist Party. When Berliners went out to work next morning they found all public buildings under police guard, nor were they able, that morning or ever thereafter, to buy a Communist newspaper.

The moment had come to instil panic into the "Old Gentleman." It might be supposed that to stampede a man aged almost 86 would not have proved beyond the powers of the Nazi leaders, but the Field-Marshal was tough, and had so far resisted all Hitler's attempts at intimidation. One of the purposes of the Reichstag fire had been to break down this resistance, and the trick succeeded. On February 28 the President duly signed a decree which, in effect, gave Goering a free hand. Paragraphs 114, 115 and 117 of the Constitution, which guaranteed to all Germans their personal liberty, the inviolability of their homes and the secrecy of postal, telegraphic and telephonic communications, were erased by the tremulous signature of a very old man. Sabotage and acts of violence might be punished by death. Paragraph 123 of the Constitution, guaranteeing to citizens the right of free assembly, was set aside, as was paragraph 118, which granted freedom of expression, by word, writing or any other means, to all within the frontiers of the Republic. In a matter of a few minutes Germany had become a police State and Goering its chief policeman.

All that day police and S.A. prowled about the streets of Berlin and the list of their victims lengthened.

On the following evening Captain Goering set himself to make the flesh of his countrymen creep at the recital of the perils from which his resolute action had saved them. The Government, he declared in a broadcast, had discovered, in the raids on Communist headquarters which had followed the Reichstag fire, absolute proof that Red Revolution was impending and that the burning of the Parliament building was to have been the signal for action.

"What," Goering asked his great unseen audience, "would have happened if this Communist bestiality had been given 24 hours' grace? Who would then have been able to restore order. . . . We have no wish to see the German people torn to pieces by the Red Monster. Perhaps I may be allowed to say this to my Communist opponents: My nerves are not yet played out. I feel myself quite strong enough to stand up to your criminal activities!"

A few days later Germany again went to the polls. This time the National Socialists secured 17,000,000 votes. The Reichstag fire had achieved its principal objective. With 288 seats in the Reichstag – an increase of 92 over the results of the previous November – the power of the Nazis was absolute. Captain Goering had succeeded in stampeding the German people and they had rushed, blindly into his corral.

Nevertheless, the Berliners – a shrewd, humorous race – passed their own verdict on the Reichstag fire in a *Berliner Witz,* irreverent, like so many jokes, but characteristically pithy.

Goering, it was said, died and went to Heaven, where he was welcomed by an apologetic St. Peter.

"I'm afraid we're rather short of accommodation just now," St. Peter said. "We haven't got anything really suitable to offer you, General. In fact, for the present you'll have to share digs."

Making the best of a bad job the General indicated his willingness to put up with this inconvenience as a temporary arrangement.

"Unfortunately," St. Peter continued, "the gentleman with whom you'll be living is a Jew . . . a very distinguished Jew, of course . . . in fact, Moses himself."

Even that, Goering replied, would be preferable to no lodging at all, and so the matter was arranged.

A few days later St. Peter met the General near the Golden Gate and asked him how he was settling down with his fellow-lodger.

"Not at all badly," Goering answered, beaming. "We find that we have a good deal in common. You see, Moses has just told me – in strict confidence, of course – that he actually *did* set fire to the Burning Bush himself!"

The first months of 1933 had been, for Goering, exhilarating but a little wearing. He felt that he owed himself a holiday. As President of a Reichstag which would never meet again under the old, democratic rules and which thanks to his enter- prise, had now not even a building of its own in which to meet, his parliamentary duties were not likely to be arduous. Diehls and Helldorf could be trusted to keep the pot boiling in Berlin. Besides, Goering knew that he, as the man who had done more than any single individual to establish the absolute power of the Nazis, could expect a rich reward from a grate- ful Führer, but a reward which would entail a certain amount of hard work. He might as well take advantage of a month's leisure while he could. Accordingly Captain Goering took train to Italy.

His reward was not long delayed. In April a letter from Hitler, written in terms of effusive gratitude to his henchman, announced that Goering was to be Prime Minister of Prussia and requested his immediate return to Berlin.

Now at long last Goering possessed the power of which he had so long dreamed, for which he had fought and schemed. The police was the instrument of that power, and it was the police which first received the attention of the *Herr Minister-präsident.* Dr. Frick, the "Old Fighter" who had led the Nazis in the Reichstag ever since their first appearance in that assembly, was now Minister of the Interior for the Reich. One of his first preoccupations was the position of the Prussian Ministry of the Interior, which continued to function, *pari passu,* with his own Department and independently of it. Surely, Frick argued, it would be only logical, now that the Nazis were depriving the German States of nearly all their autonomous rights, if the Prussian Ministry were incorporated in his own.

Goering swiftly blocked that manœuvre. Although he was no upholder of States' Rights it was obvious that here an exception must be made. Otherwise he would have no police organization under his own hand, and that, for his own purposes, he must have. On no account should Germany's largest and best-organized police force go to Frick. The doctor retired defeated, and on April 26 Goering announced the creation of the *Geheime Staatspolizei,* the Secret State Police, soon to become celebrated under its abbreviated title of Gestapo. Diehls, as head of the old Political Police Department, assumed the direction of the new organization with the rank of Ministerial Counsellor.

When Goering became master of the Prussian police there had been thirty-two senior officers in the force. Twenty-two of these men were promptly dismissed and replaced by reliable members of the S.A. or S.S. Their disappearance was followed by that of hundreds of superintendents, inspectors, sergeants and constables, whose place was taken by Nazis lacking experience, perhaps, in police matters, but admirably ruthless and loyal to the Party.

Yet even this was not enough. The Prussian police force, large though it was, was still not large enough to penetrate

116

into every nook and cranny of German life, and that Goering's men must do if their master was to wield the power which he had determined to exercise. Goering decided to kill two birds with one stone. By persuading Hitler to allow him to enlist the S.A. as auxiliary police he not only secured the men he needed but dealt a telling blow at Röhm. That officer might be Chief of Staff of the S.A., but the Stormtroopers were Goering's men when they were on police duty. Another sap had been driven beneath the ground upon which Röhm's influence reposed.

From Goering's point of view this arrangement had one minor disadvantage. It brought him into personal contact with the rabble – the tough, brutal louts recruited by Röhm. Every day the ranks of the S.A. were swelled by opportunists who sought advancement by a display of belated enthusiasm for the new rulers or who wished merely to conceal a compromising political past beneath a brown shirt. Members of the Communist fighting organizations offered their services to the S.A. in large numbers and found them accepted, until Röhm's men came to be known as the "Beefsteaks" – brown outside and red within.

The S.A. took full advantage of the powers with which they were now suddenly invested. In every part of Berlin the auxiliary police established their own "Bunkers," to which "suspects" were brought and interrogated. Every S.A. man with an old grudge now had a golden opportunity of settling the score, and Berliners, hurrying past one of these establishments, often heard through thick walls the screams of prisoners under interrogation.

One or two of these "Bunkers" soon became so notorious that Goering, little as he liked mixing with the lower orders, felt obliged to take a hand himself. One evening he marched into the "Bunker" in the Hedemannstrasse, where he was confronted with the usual spectacle of licensed sadism. This sort of thing, he declared to the garrison, would not do. The goings-on in the Hedemannstrasse had become a matter of notoriety, damaging to the prestige of the Prussian police. No doubt his listeners had acted in a spirit of laudable zeal, but they had overdone things. Consequently the entire crew of the Hedemannstrasse redoubt would be enrolled, as salaried officials, in his Field Police, which operated under the Gestapo. With that Goering's audience were well content. They would still have much scope in their new appointments for the duties

117

which they had come to enjoy, even though they must now perform them with more discretion.

Not that Captain Goering imposed any very onerous restrictions upon his subordinates. He had made that quite clear not only to the police themselves but to the general public. In a speech delivered at Dortmund he assured the audience – and through press and radio the whole Reich – that he alone assumed full responsibility for the actions of the police:

"The policeman who does his duty, who obeys my orders, who goes bald-headed for the enemies of the State when attacked, who uses his weapons ruthlessly, can be assured of my protection. . . . Every round fired from that barrel of a police revolver is a round fired by me. If that is called murder then I am a murderer, for I have given the orders. I support that 'murder,' I bear the responsibility for it, and I am not ashamed of it."

These words of encouragement referred to the "Green Police" – the regular force. Of the Gestapo Goering spoke little in public, but it was the apple of his eye. There lay the real power.

The energy of this newly created organization, coupled with that of the S.A., presented one awkward though by no means insoluble problem. The number of persons in police custody of one sort or another very soon exceeded the resources of the Prison Administration. Ordinary crime did not decrease and the vigorous assault on vice of all kinds which Goering carried out on Hitler's express orders brought into the net a large assortment of panders, perverts and human wreckage of all descriptions. In addition there were the "politicals" – thousands of them, ranging from mild Social Democrats to rabid Communists, from left-wing novelists to Red propagandists. They had to be locked up somewhere, and in the prisons, there was no room. Goering decided to create new prisons.

During the Boer War, in which Hermann Goering had played an enthusiastic if necessarily remote part, the British Command found it expedient to establish, behind their lines, a number of "concentration camps." These places were designed to fulfil a double purpose – to keep Afrikaner civilians, old men, women and children, away from the area of operations and to protect them from attacks by natives, who might be expected to take advantage of the absence of all able-bodied men to plunder the farmsteads and murder those who

118

remained in them. Both on the grounds of military necessity and of humanity, there might have been something to be said for these camps, had they been well administered. They were not well administered, and very soon they came to bear an evil name. The German Press in particular was loud in its condemnation of these establishments and of their inhuman inventors, and no doubt "Hermann Goering, General of the Boers," young as he then was, picked up some idea of them which now, thirty-three years later, was to bear fruit.

The "concentration camps" set up by the Prime Minister of Prussia – he was even careful to retain the original name, which went into German very neatly as *Konzentrationslager* – had no sanction in humanity, although a half-hearted effort was made, in the early days, to pretend that the unfortunate people who found their way behind their barbed-wire were shut away lest they be molested as enemies of the State by justly incensed fellow-citizens. Inquisitive foreigners, never allowed to inspect the camps themselves, were assured that the places were educational establishments in which those who had strayed from the path of patriotism and national duty were brought to repentance. In fact they were prisons of a particularly sinister kind, though they reached the zenith of horror which for the world at large came to be typified by such names as Belsen, Auschwitz and Ravensbrück, only by degrees. The first of these institutions was opened for business by Goering in 1933. He chose as its site Oranienburg, a convenient suburb of Berlin.

It always gave Goering particular pleasure to ascribe the invention of concentration camps to British ingenuity. He did so for the last time during his trial at Nuremberg.

Self-made Man

It was a fine thing, in the summer of 1933, to be an *"Alter Kämpfer,"* an "Old Fighter" of the National Socialist Movement. Hitler was tearing the political structure of Germany to pieces that he might reassemble it according to his own design. Throughout the Reich, heads and senior officials of State Governments, burgomasters, police chiefs, civil servants were summarily dismissed, and always there was among the *Alte*

119

Kämpfer an "expert" willing and eager to fill the vacancy. Money could be picked up very easily by anybody who possessed some influence in Party circles. Many rich and prominent people who had been a little slow in sensing the direction of the prevailing political wind were now extremely anxious to join the Nazi Party and to pay liberally for the privilege. Public coffers of all kinds lay open to the "experts," and so also did police dossiers, which can be very profitable things indeed if properly used. During the first months of power many minor Party members made this discovery, as had Hermann Goering a little time before.

The Prime Minister of Prussia, one of the oldest "Fighters" of all – the number of his Party membership card was 22 – deplored this rush for spoils, and indeed issued a stern decree directed against place-seekers. He had already found his place for the present, but it was delightfully easy now to thrust a finger into a large variety of pies and to extract at every thrust a plum which satisfied one or other of his tastes and ambitions.

Goering still retained a keen thoroughly untechnical interest in aviation. Since he had ceased to make his living by the knowledge of aircraft and parachutes which he had acquired in the war, he had taken no trouble to keep abreast of the strides which man was making towards the mastery of the air. Nevertheless he was determined that Germany, standing as she did now in the forefront of civil aviation, should achieve that supremacy in military flying which was still denied to her by the Treaty of Versailles. And to Hermann Goering should go the credit for that achievement.

Already in the early days of 1933 Goering had conferred with Erhardt Milch, the creator of the great Lufthansa network. Knowing nothing himself of modern technique, he was quick to recognize in Milch the man who, above all others in Germany, did possess that knowledge, and to make use of him. The post of Reich Commissioner for Air he reserved for himself. Milch became Deputy Commissioner and did most of the work.

Goering decided that this appointment should bring with it a uniform – a proper uniform, far different from the scruffy brown shirt and breeches of the S.A. upon which it was hardly fitting, as Goering now felt, to display military decorations, and which in any case did not look its best on a man weighing nearly twenty stone. Since the post of Reich Commissioner for Air was one which had never existed before, its first incumbent was able to design the costume himself. He chose to follow the pattern already set by the Royal Air Force, and, in the early spring of 1933, Goering accordingly appeared dressed in a very plausible imitation of R.A.F. uniform, distinguished from that worn at Cranwell or Hendon only by the badges on the cap, the distinctive white gorget-patches, the Sam Browne belt and a very heavy entanglement of aiguillettes. He wore this costume when he paid another visit to the Vatican in April, during his Italian holiday, and confessed, in his carefully bluff manner, that he felt more at home in it than in any clothes which he had worn since 1918. The uniform was described as that of the organization of "German Sport Flying," the leadership of which Goering had conferred upon himself.

Goering did not wear that uniform only at the Vatican, for he visited, during his holiday, some more mundane establishments. As a result of one of these excursions a number of experienced young pilots of the Lufthansa, including à certain Adolf Galland, of whose subsequent career more will be heard before this story is ended, found themselves in May 1933 summoned under conditions of strict secrecy to an office in the Behrensstrasse, Berlin, where Goering met them. The Reich Commissioner for Air and Minister-President of Prussia told his eager listeners that a wonderful opportunity awaited them. They were to travel to Italy and there take a course in fighter tactics under officers of the *Regia Aeronautica*. He himself had made all the arrangements for their reception.

The young men travelled to Italy in plain clothes and underwent a course of instruction, which for all of them was at once a pleasant change and a serious disappointment. The Italian instructors persisted in treating these seasoned pilots as raw novices in the art of flying and taught them very little which they did not already know. The pupils felt that Captain Goering might have been rather more thorough in making arrangements for their instruction, but they did not realize that when talking to the Italian Air Force Goering had used, perforce, the language of 1918, while his hosts spoke that of 1933. At all events the first step towards the creation of the Luftwaffe had been taken.

The "German Sport Flyers" was, for its chief, more than a convenient camouflage. It enabled him to give jobs to many old comrades of the war. Bruno Loerzer and Ernst Udet both joined its ranks at salaries suitable to their position as close friends of Goering. "Pilli" Koerner was ineligible for membership since he had no experience as an airman, but the post of State Secretary for Prussia suited him well enough. Whatever his official attitude towards "place-seekers," Goering knew how to make exceptions in favour of his own friends.

Another passion which Goering's new eminence enabled him to gratify was that for shooting. As the most powerful man in the Reich, next to Hitler, and one of the best shots in Germany, he could, of course, count upon receiving as many invitations to shoot as even he could manage to accept. Yet this was not enough. He must have some titular position which would enable him not only to lord it over all the sportsmen of the Reich but also to extend his protection to the wild animals which provided them with their sport.

Goering's love of animals was very genuine. One of his first actions as Prime Minister of Prussia had been to issue a decree forbidding the practice of vivisection. Now, as *Reichsjägermeister,* Master Hunter of the Reich, he was able to take an official interest in the breeding and preservation of game, and to back that interest with the force of law. Hitler, who took not the slightest pleasure in sport, made no objection to this new whim, nor to the bizarre uniform which the Chief Hunter designed for his own use. This consisted of a white silk shirt with very full sleeves, caught at the wrists, over which was worn a sleeveless tunic of soft leather with a belt of the same material. A massive hunting-knife completed the outfit.

Finally, there was the housing problem. For the Prime Minister of Prussia a flat in the Kaiserdamm was, of course, out of the question, and in any case the position carried with it the right to inhabit an official residence in Berlin. Goering found this house quite unsuited to his tastes. It was dark and gloomy, the wallpapers and decorations old-fashioned, the furniture heavy and dull. Nothing would satisfy the new Prime Minister but that the taxpayers should build him a new residence better fitted to his position in the new Reich. Diehls' Gestapo, having operated rather self-consciously for some little time from Karl Liebknecht House, the former Communist stronghold, was now preparing to move into more suitable quarters and had requisitioned for the purpose the Folk-Lore Museum in the Prinz-Albrechtstrasse. Goering decided that his town-house should adjoin the fountain-head of his power and riches. In June 1933 workmen began to clear a site on the corner of the Prinz-Albrechtstrasse and the Stresemannstrasse. The name of this latter thoroughfare, however, was an offence to the ruler of Prussia – inconceivable that he could live in a street which bore the name of a bourgeois politician, a pacifist, the very embodiment of all that the Nazis had sworn to stamp out. The *Oberbürgermeister* of Berlin quite agreed with the *Herr Ministerpräsident* in this. The name of the street should be changed. Had the *Herr Ministerpräsident* any particular preference in the matter of a new title? The *Herr Ministerpräsident* suggested that *Hermann-Goeringstrasse* would sound very well. The *Oberbürgermeister* fully agreed with this suggestion, and the affair was thus settled to the satisfaction of everybody concerned.

In those first months of office, figures from Goering's past kept thrusting themselves not unpleasantly upon the notice of the man who had become so unexpectedly powerful. Marianne Mauser, his first love, snatched from him fourteen years ago by a father who declared that young Goering had "no certain source of livelihood," was now comfortably married to a carpet manufacturer in Czechoslovakia. It gave Goering intense pleasure to see her in Berlin, to patronize her, to display the state in which her rejected suitor now lived.

To another woman friend he was able to give more practical tokens of esteem. As Prime Minister of Prussia Goering ruled supreme over the Prussian State Theatre. Thither he brought Emmy Sonnemann, conferred upon her the title of *Staatsschauspielerin* (State Actress) and a handsome salary and was able once more to enjoy her company and conversation.

Yet Carin and his Swedish relatives were never forgotten. In June, Carin's niece, Birgitta von Rosen, was married at Rockelsta Castle and Uncle Hermann joined the family party which gathered there to celebrate the occasion. It has not been given to many men to enjoy such intimate triumph as that journey to Sweden brought to Hermann Goering. The Prime Minister's Dornier-Wal amphibian put down on the very lake where, twelve years before, "Stockholm's popular air-chauffeur" had brought his old Fokker to a standstill on the ice and helped Birgitta's father, half-frozen, to alight. Then he had been a hired airman, a nobody, deeply impressed by the comforts of Rockelsta. Now, as he entered the great hall, where the stuffed bear still guarded the staircase upon which he had first seen Carin, he was welcomed as a great man, the lion of the party.

Carin's absence from the gathering took some of the edge

off Goering's satisfaction, and after the wedding the widower visited Lövö cemetery and ordered a new headstone for her grave. He flew back to Berlin, after a forced landing at Kalmar, determined soon to return to Sweden, there to bask again in the approval of a noble family to which, he felt, he had done credit.

In Berlin trouble was brewing. Relations between Goering and Röhm, between the police and the S.A., were going from bad to worse, and the time to strike at Röhm had not yet come. The Chief of Staff of the S.A. clung tenaciously to the ambitions which he had nursed since the earliest days of the Nazi Movement. He saw himself as the commander of a great Brown Army which would swallow up the Reichswehr. Hitler might be the twentieth-century Bismarck, but he, Röhm, would wield the sword which should make Germany great. Moreover Röhm was a radical who did not hide his contempt for the luxury which to Goering was now essential.

Against these ambitions Goering pitted his Prussian police and the Gestapo, and he now concluded that these forces, impressive though they were, might still be insufficient to smash the plans of an enemy whose writ ran to every S.A. *Standarte* from the Austrian border to the Baltic and from the Polish Marches to the Rhine. He needed an ally; nor was he long in choosing one.

Heinrich Himmler came, like Goering himself, from a bourgeois family. His father had been a senior official in the Bavarian administration and Heinrich had been destined for an academic career. The war put an end to these aspirations, and after it the young man studied agriculture at the University of Munich, worked in a glue factory and joined the Nazi Party in its earliest days. He had been present at the *Putsch* of 1923 – had indeed carried the swastika banner on that ill-fated occasion – and in 1929 he had been appointed to the command of the S.S. – the black-uniformed élite of the Nazi private army.

With Hitler's accession to power this slim, bespectacled, ugly man set himself the task of cornering police authority in Germany. In Prussia Goering had been first in the field, but Prussia was not all Germany. Himmler became Police President of Munich in March 1933, and of the political police throughout Bavaria in April. The complete reorganization of the German State Governments which followed gave Himmler his chance. He intended to make himself the master of every police force outside Prussia.

Goering, aware of this ambition, took Himmler into his confidence. Both men hated Röhm. Himmler, therefore, with Goering's support, would obtain control of the provincial police, while Goering retained his hold on the police of Prussia. Already Himmler commanded the S.S. Between them the two schemers would dispose of a force which could at any time be ranged against Röhm's S.A. with every prospect of victory. As leader of the S.S. Himmler was technically Röhm's subordinate, but that was a matter of small moment.

An incident which occurred in October gave point to the new alliance. In the opening of the Prussian State Council, which was to take place that month, Goering saw the opportunity for one of the grandiose displays which he loved. The Prime Minister would ride in state in a gala coach from the Wilhelmstrasse to the State Opera House, where the Council was to meet, and would there review the Berlin S.A. and S.S. as they marched past him.

This project was too much for Röhm, and indeed for the men he commanded. Neither he nor they had any stomach for the kind of ostentatious circus which Goering planned. They regarded him as a traitor to the Socialist principles upon which the Party had been founded. At a time when there were 5,000,000 unemployed in Germany, Hermann Goering had no right to flaunt about the streets of the capital in a state coach, to spend public money on a new palace for his own use, to give fat jobs to personal friends who had little or no previous connection with the Party, when many deserving *Alte Kämpfer* in the S.A. had still not received adequate rewards for their past devotion to the Cause. Röhm decided to teach the "Fat Louse," as he called Goering, a lesson.

From the National Headquarters of the S.A. orders went out that no Group Leaders of the organisation were to appear at Goering's parade. Karl Ernst, commanding the Berlin group, let it be known to his subordinates that no very high standard of marching or turn-out need be required from the troops on that occasion, and that a thoroughly sloppy march-past would, in fact, be not only condoned, just for this once, but even approved. The Gestapo brought news of the plan to their master, who forthwith fell into a heavy fit of the sulks. The state coach was countermanded, the triumphal procession cancelled, and Goering intimated to Himmler that he and Röhm were welcome to share whatever limelight there might be on the day which had been reserved for his own triumph. But he did not forget the incident. Himmler, who disliked publicity as much as Goering loved it, stood by Röhm's side, to all appearance a loyal subordinate, as his S.S. marched past. He did not forget either.

Sweden would provide balm for wounded pride, and to Sweden Goering accordingly went, soon after this fiasco, but here too fate was against him. Again he visited Carin's grave, surmounted now by the new tombstone on which the swastika was cut, and laid upon it in tribute the same emblem reproduced in flowers. The Princess zu Wied, she who had sometimes lent Carin her cook to help out when there was a party at the Badenschestrasse, accompanied the visitor to the cemetery. Goering had repaid past friendship by securing for her husband the appointment of German Minister to Sweden.

That evening there was an unpleasant little incident at Oskars Theatre, in Stockholm. As the Prime Minister of Prussia sat in his box, a young student shouted "Down with Goering, the murderer of the workers," and had to be removed. Next day, moreover, *Svenska Dagbladet,* Sweden's most influential newspaper, deplored the bad taste which had led the distinguished guest to lay a swastika token on his wife's grave, and a few days later certain Swedish citizens expressed their disapproval in a more forthright manner. The floral swastika was removed from the tomb and its fellow on the headstone covered by a sheet of paper which bore this message:

"We a group of Swedes, regard ourselves as offended by the vandalism committed by the German, Goering, on this grave. Let his former wife rest in peace, but spare us from German propaganda on her tomb!"

Goering was furious. The Prince zu Wied protested to the Swedish Government on his instructions and the Swedish Government politely expressed their regret at the incident. Goering was not appeased, nor did the flowers which Swedish friends and supporters placed on the grave or the sympathetic tone of most of the Swedish Press moderate his anger. He would bring Carin's body to Germany, where it might rest, safe from further desecration. A splendid pewter coffin was ordered forthwith, and Hermann Goering left the country which, as he saw it, had turned against him. He returned to Sweden only once again. There was no balm there any more.

As 1933 drew to a close Himmler extended his power far

126

over Germany. In October he had gained control of the political police in Hamburg, the second city of the Reich and a State in its own right. Thereafter the States fell like a shower of ripe plums into his lap, while Goering shook the tree. Mecklenburg, the Hanseatic city of Lübeck, Württemberg, Baden, Hessen, Thuringia, Anhalt – by the end of December Himmler was the effective master of them all. In January Oldenburg, Bremen and Saxony, the least "reliable" of all the States from the Nazi point of view, were added to Himmler's empire. The net had been woven around Röhm. It remained only to draw it tight.

In the meanwhile Goering had assumed new dignities. A Ministry of Aviation – of civil aviation, as was carefully explained to Germany's former enemies – was formed and Goering became its Minister. By now the burden of office had become too heavy to be borne by a mere honorary Captain (war-substantive lieutenant). No man of lesser rank than a General of the Reichswehr could be expected adequately to perform the many and varied duties which had somehow fallen to Hermann Goering's lot. A special Gazette therefore promoted him to be full General.

By the end of the year the half-wit Van der Lubbe had been tried and condemned for having set fire to the Reichstag, yet the trial had not proved as satisfactory a platform for General Goering as might have been hoped. He had made the mistake of indicting, together with Van der Lubbe and Torgler, the German Communist leader, three Bulgarian Communists, Popoff and Taneff and the formidable Georgi Dimitroff, one of the ablest and most fearless members of the international Communist hierarchy, who took it upon himself to conduct the defence from the dock.

The President of the Court, Dr. Bünger, had already been suitably overawed by the time General Goering chose to give evidence, his associate justices and counsel on both sides fully understood what was expected of them, yet Dimitroff, whose truculence had already caused him to be expelled from the courtroom several times, was quite unimpressed by the bulky figure who had spent the better part of a day in ranting at the court. He began to question the General:

"Is it not true that the allegations published by you that Communists fired the Reichstag were calculated to influence the police and to give their investigations a bias in one direction only?"

"If so," Goering retorted, "it was a bias in the right direction. It was a political crime and it was quite obvious to me that the criminals belonged to your Party."

"Does the witness know that this criminal Party rules the sixth part of the earth, that the Soviet Union has diplomatic, political and economic relations with Germany and that its orders to German industry give bread to thousands of German workers?"

At that General Goering rounded on the prisoner, shaking his fist at him, his voice rising to a scream:

"I don't care what happens in Russia. I care about the Communist Party in Germany and about foreign crooks who come here to set fire to the Reichstag. . . . I only know what the whole German people knows – that you came here to fire the Reichstag. As far as I'm concerned you're a crook, and the gallows is the right place for you!"

As the Prime Minister of Prussia lost his temper, Dimitroff became increasingly calm:

"Are you afraid of these questions, *Herr Ministerpräsident?*" he asked gently.

The General's self-control, never very strong, broke at that.

"I'm not in the least afraid of you," he shouted. "You . . . you criminal, you! I'm not going to stand here to be questioned by you! You'll be sorry for this if I catch you when you come out of gaol!"

The inconvenient prisoner was then hustled down to the cells while General Goering leaned against a chair, somewhat exhausted. It was generally agreed that he had not had the best of the exchange.

Nor did he catch Dimitroff when he came out of prison, which he did a few weeks later. Van der Lubbe alone paid for the Reichstag fire with his life – he was executed in January 1934. But Van der Lubbe was a nobody, without friends, mentally feeble. Torgler, Dimitroff, Popoff and Taneff were acquitted. A few months later Dimitroff was head of the Comintern and far beyond the vengeance even of Hermann Goering.

In January it became clear to Goering that however great his own energy – and at this time he was working very hard indeed – he could not hope to retain all the powers which were now vested in him. The establishment of the Air Force had by now become an obsession. By inventing a perfectly fictitious raid over Berlin by "unidentified foreign aircraft"

THE FAMILY MAN

With his first wife, Carin.
Paul Popper

With Emmy and their
daughter. *Paul Popper*

1918: World War I fighter ace. Hermann Goering, commanding the famous Richthofen Squadron, holds the 'Richthofen stick'. *Conway*

1923: The Storm Trooper. *Conway*

On parade. *Paul Popper*

The sportsman. *Keystone*

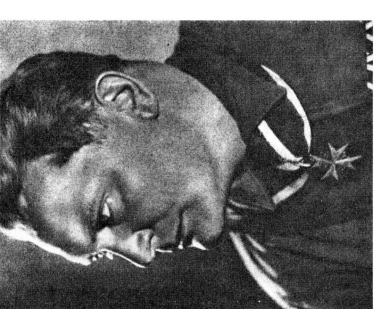

1933: President of the Reichstag in Brown Shirt
uniform, German

1937: The chief of the Storm Troopers at a birthday
feast at a Kneipe

THE TRIUMVIRATE

1937: with Joseph Goebbels at a Party congress. *Conway*

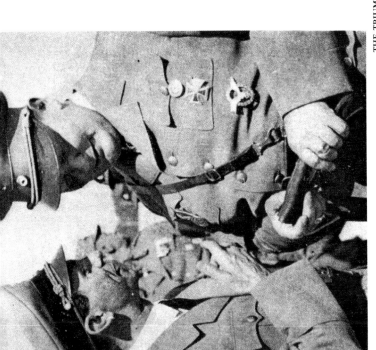

1938: with Adolf Hitler at the May Day celebrations.
Conway

1938: On manoeuvres, talking to Major General Ernst Udet. *Conway*

The Field Marshal inspects his troops. *Keystone*

Watching target practice at a training centre. *Keystone*

WARTIME COMMANDER

Interrogating a pilot just returned from a raid on England. *Paul Popper*

In his cell at Nuremburg. *Keystone*

THE FALL FROM POWER

Listening to the sentence at the War Crimes Trial. *Keystone*

which, according to the story that Goering circulated to the Press, had dropped leaflets insulting to Germany and to her Government, the Reich Minister for Aviation had already effectively drawn public attention to the fact that the country possessed no military aircraft. "Today," his story of the "ghost raid" ended, "it is leaflets. Tomorrow it may be gas-bombs, bringing death and destruction." Nobody ever saw a leaflet, or naturally, the aircraft which did not drop them.

Dr. Frick, the Minister of the Interior, benefited from this new enthusiasm. At last he achieved his ambition, of which he had been cheated a year before. Most of the functions of the Prussian Ministry of the Interior were transferred to him, but not the Gestapo. That General Goering would retain as his own. Frick, however, was forced a little later to make a concession himself. In 1933 Goering had established an organization styled the "Air Defence League," and had appointed as its chief an energetic General on the retired list, Hugo Grimme. For the sake of appearances the League had been made subordinate to Frick's Ministry of the Interior. By April 1934, however, the Reich Ministry of Aviation felt itself strong enough to assume responsibility for its affairs and Goering became its official head. The League had by then branches in all parts of Germany. It was the backbone of that air force which was even then being built in secret.

For technical details Goering cared nothing. Colonel Milch, Colonel Walther Wever – later the Luftwaffe's first Chief of Staff – and constructors like Willi Messerschmitt, Professor Heinkel and Professor Tank might deal with those rather boring matters. For all his enthusiasm Goering, in those early days, saw Milch on an average only once in three months. He signed the necessary decrees to provide men, equipment and raw materials for the factories which the experts required and left them to their work. For the present other matters claimed much of his attention.

By April 1934 Heinrich Himmler's police empire rested on secure foundations. Save only in Prussia, he was now master of all regular and political police throughout Germany. The time had come to extend his influence to Prussia also.

Himmler achieved his aim by a process of discreet blackmail. He spoke to Goering of Röhm's overweening ambition. The S.A. now numbered no fewer than 2,000,000 men. For fifteen years Röhm had schemed to build up a private army which would eventually supersede the regular Reichswehr.

Now Germany was about to announce to the world that she intended at last to defy the provisions of the Versailles Treaty by creating a standing Army of whatever strength she chose. At that moment the S.A. would, automatically, become the dominant influence in the Army, however much General von Blomberg, the Reichswehr Minister, might dislike the prospect, and Röhm would be the most powerful man in the Reich.

Although his friend Goering was a full General of the Reichswehr while Röhm's rank was no more than Lieutenant-Colonel – and of the Bolivian Army at that – this happy state of affairs could not, Himmler pointed out, be expected to last once Röhm had given 2,000,000 trained men to the Reichswehr. With Röhm out of the way, on the other hand, surely Goering might aspire to become a General of the Reichswehr in something more than name only. They had always intended to pay off old scores against Röhm. Now, Himmler urged, action must be taken soon, lest it be too late, and would it not be better if the police and S.S. were on that occasion under a single unified command? Unless Himmler could control the Prussian Gestapo he would not answer for the success of the undertaking. Some weeks of painstaking preparation would be required before the net could be finally closed upon Röhm, his associates in the S.A. and a number of other people whose names stood on the list which Goering and Himmler had drawn up. Diehls had done well enough as an organizer, but he was not, in Himmler's opinion, the man to lead such a *coup* as was now intended. Day after day Himmler worked on the ambitions and the thirst for revenge which animated Goering, and at last he carried his point. On April 1, 1934, Diehls was appointed Police President of Cologne and Heinrich Himmler assumed control of the Secret State Police.

He brought with him to the former Folk-Lore Museum a slim, dapper young man who was destined to play an important part in the shadows of Hermann Goering's life. Reinhardt Heydrich was a latecomer to the Party. Until 1931 he had been a naval officer, but in that year his career had been cut short by a financial scandal and he had been dismissed from the Service. A broken man at the age of 31, Heydrich had found a very suitable outlet for his talents and energies in Himmler's S.S. Indubitably Aryan – one glance at the smooth fair hair, the long, thin nose, the close-set blue eyes was sufficient guarantee of that – the man was extremely intelligent and utterly ruthless. Yet he was no rough diamond. He possessed all the airs and graces of the regular officer of good family, he was a sportsman, an excellent shot, one of the finest fencers in Germany, an accomplished horseman. In the most exclusive society Reinhardt Heydrich would, but for the stain on his past, not have been out of place. The man was Rupert of Hentzau to the life.

Snugly installed in the Prinz-Albrechtstrasse, Himmler and his assistant set to work with a will, while Goering began to prepare Hitler's mind for the bloody business which lay ahead. In this endeavour he was, as it turned out, to be greatly assisted by the mistakes of his enemies.

Meanwhile a private matter had claimed the General's attention. In 1933 the eye of the Master Hunter of the Reich had fallen upon a shooting-box situated forty miles from Berlin in the Schorfheide, a magnificent stretch of unspoiled forest and heathland which lies to the north-east of the capital. Situated between two small lakes, the house was a simple place, built on one storey of rough logs, save where a single gable in the deep thatched roof covered an upper room and the balcony which fronted it. It was a comfortable, manly house, a place built for long sessions of drinking and the swapping of sportsman's tales before the great open fireplace in the hall, for deep sleep after a hard day's shooting.

Here, Goering decided, was the place where the second man of Germany could worthily express his personality. The tract of woodland which surrounded the house should become a vast game-preserve and the house itself should be rebuilt so that it might be worthy of its new master. He would call it Carinhall.

An army of workmen descended on the Schorfheide and the old wooden house vanished. In its place an enormous low building, built partly of hewn stone, partly plastered, and in places half-timbered, began to grow at mushroom speed. Money was no object now. Already the Prime Minister's Palace in Berlin was almost completed, and beside it the new Air Ministry was rising. Was there not still unemployment in Germany, and did not the satisfaction of General Goering's *amour propre* provide work for many hundreds of men? To rebuild the old shooting-box was little less than an act of Socialism by the second man in the National Socialist Party.

Opposite the house a small gang of workmen built a tomb, a vault of brick deep beneath the sandy soil of the Schorfheide, approached by a flight of sunken steps.

The time had come to avenge the insult to Carin's grave which had been perpetrated by her own countrymen at Lövö cemetery. The Stockholm firm of Svenskt Tenn had completed the order which they had received in the previous October, and at the beginning of 1934 an enormous pewter coffin was ready for delivery – enormous because it had been designed to receive not only Carin's poor remains but, eventually, the body of her husband.

On January 19, 1934, Carin left Sweden. At the grave which had been in his eyes profaned, Goering stood in the snow, with Prince and Princess zu Wied, his own A.D.C.s and members of Carin's family. As the new coffin was carried to a German railway-coach, detachments of Swedish Nazis lowered their banners and the assembly sang Luther's "Ein' Feste Burg ist unser Gott," as it had been sung at that first modest funeral, less than three years before. A wreath of white roses lay upon the coffin, its centre a heart, shaped in blood-red blooms. The card on this tribute was in Goering's handwriting. It read: "To my only Carin."

The funeral train crossed the Baltic, from Trälleborg to Sassnitz, and ran slowly on to Eberswalde. Thence the coffin was carried in an open cart, along roads lined with Party troops, to Carinhall, where Hitler joined the party. Torches blazed outside the new vault, six candles burned within. A military band played solemn music.

Suddenly a car appeared, driving rather faster than might have been thought proper on so mournful an occasion, and from it stepped Heinrich Himmler, pale and agitated. He went straight to Hitler and Goering and drew them aside, while the rest of the company stood in perplexed bewilderment. Himmler, it seemed, had narrowly escaped assassination during the drive to Carinhall. The windscreen of his car bore the mark of the bullet, which had, however, somehow failed to penetrate it. Nor had Himmler or his fellow-passengers in the car actually seen the would-be murderers or heard a shot, but there was the star of cracked glass, for all to perceive.

Goering pacified his ally and the burial proceeded. Gauleiter Kube delivered a ponderous address in praise of "Germany's noblest lady," and to the strains of Siegfried's Funeral March from *Götterdämmerung* the great coffin was carried into the tomb, followed only by Goering and Hitler. The two men stayed alone before Carin's mortal remains for a few minutes and then came slowly up the steps together.

A few days later two S.A. officers were shot, privately and without trial, for having organized an attempt upon the life of the *Reichsführer S.S.* Once again the tomb of poor, simple, loving Carin had been desecrated, and this time by human blood.

The Long Knives

By April 1934, when Himmler and Heydrich began their ominous partnership at the Prinz-Albrechtstrasse headquarters of the Gestapo, it was quite evident, even to those who had no particular reason to dislike Ernst Röhm, that the man had overreached himself. The arrogance not only of the Chief of Staff himself but of his subordinate officers had become intolerable, nor, despite their sneers at the luxurious tastes of General Goering, did Röhm or the clique about him set a very inspiring example of simple living and Socialist austerity.

Money came easily to the S.A. in those days and was as easily spent by its leaders. If funds ran short it was a simple matter to levy a special toll from every one of the 2,000,000 Stormtroopers or even from the general public, who did not dare to withhold their contribution to the money-boxes which were suggestively rattled before them by uniformed members of the Party forces. A public collection taken up at the Berlin Zoo yielded £2500 in a single evening. Karl Ernst, S.A. Group Leader for Berlin, who had once been a waiter in a second-class restaurant, managed to amass over £7000 on his own account during the first two years of Nazi power, and many of his colleagues did a great deal better for themselves than he.

The S.A. leaders who gathered about Röhm liked to look upon themselves as "men's men" – hearty, hard drinking, hard fighting fellows who had no need for feminine society and no time for the kind of elegance with which such people as Goering surrounded themselves. They made no secret of their contempt for the paintings, tapestries and sculpture which the Prime Minister for Prussia had now begun assiduously to collect, or for their collector. Their money was spent in other ways, and Himmler's provincial police kept their master informed of the manner of its spending.

They told him that Röhm and his Staff had been consistently[*] drunk during a tour of Pomerania undertaken early in 1934. Two or three times a day the Chief of Staff of the S.A. and his entourage had reeled and belched before audiences of gaping countrymen. Wherever he went in Germany, drunkenness, gross immorality and a spirit of anarchy accompanied Colonel Röhm.

Himmler and Goering knew how to use the weapons which the enemy had placed in their hands. Hitler was anxious at this time to placate the world beyond Germany's frontiers, to prove to the democratic Powers that National Socialism was a "respectable" creed. How, Goering and Himmler asked, could he hope to do this while Röhm and his most senior subordinates in the S.A. persisted in dragging what good name the Party had through the mud? Cuttings from foreign newspapers, carefully selected, were laid before the Führer, each of necessity accompanied by a translation. The fact that General Goering came in for fully as many strictures in foreign newspapers as did Röhm and his S.A. was not revealed to the Führer.

Röhm penetrated the universities, establishing in each an S.A. "University Office" from which the Colonel's gospel was promulgated, with the assistance of Alfred Rosenberg, the "philosopher" of the National Socialist Party. The level of this philosophy, which in 1934 was directed particularly against the Roman Catholic Church, may be gathered from a single verse of a little song officially taught to the students of the University of Munich at that time:

Hoch die Hohenzollern am Laternenpfahl!
Lasst die Hunde baumeln
Bis sie 'runterfallen!
In die Synagoge hängt ein schwarzes Schwein
Schmeisst die Handgranaten in die Kirchen 'rein.

(Hoist the Hohenzollerns on a lamp post!
Let the dogs dangle till they drop!
Hang a black swine [of a priest] in the synagogue,
And chuck hand-grenades into the Churches!)

It was obviously a little difficult, as Goering explained to the Führer, to persuade foreigners that the Party was a perfectly respectable organization when Röhm was free to propagate such doctrines as this through the S.A., the Party's largest organization.

Fate now played into Goering's hands. By May 1934 it became quite evident that President von Hindenburg could not expect to live much longer, and Hitler determined that he must succeed the "Old Gentleman" as Head of State. To achieve this ambition he must be assured of the support of the Reichswehr, and Röhm had chosen that very moment to pick a serious quarrel with General von Blomberg, the Reichswehr Minister. The German General had rejected, with contempt, the offer of 2,000,000 Stormtroopers made by the Bolivian Lieutenant-Colonel. The Army would, he said, on no account agree to embody whole formations of the S.A. into the official fighting forces of the Reich. Each recruit to the regenerated Reichswehr must be enlisted in the normal manner and secure promotion on his own merits as a soldier. The Army did not propose to allow itself to be overrun by Röhm's rabble.

Röhm ran to Hitler and denounced von Blomberg, but he faced a Führer who had never in any case agreed with his conception of the role of the S.A. and whose mind had moreover been carefully conditioned by Goering. Hitler opted for the support of the Army and virtually rejected that of the S.A. Furious, Röhm withdrew, to seek consolation from Goebbels, whom he believed to be his ally.

On June 17 Vice-Chancellor von Papen delivered a speech at the little university town of Marburg, in central Germany. It was a forthright address which carried in it a sharp cut for most of the Nazi leaders. "The nation knows," von Papen said, "that heavy sacrifice is demanded, and this it will bear, following the Führer, Adolf Hitler, in unshakable loyalty. But it is useless to construe as malevolent every word of criticism which is uttered, or to brand perplexed patriots as enemies of the State . . . . Freedom and equality before the Law are not liberalistic conceptions, but German and Christian conceptions."

The speaker went on to rebuke Goebbels by implication for seeking to keep the German people in "perpetual tutelage" and to remind Goering, whom he did not name, that "those who speak of Prussianism should hold fast in the first place to the ideal of silent, impersonal service, and last of all – or, better still, not at all – to the ideal of personal reward and recognition."

General Goering, who lost no opportunity of reminding his compatriots that, as Prime Minister of Prussia, he intended to ensure that the whole Reich "marched in Prussian time," did not miss the allusion.

Three days later Goering attacked Röhm in a speech delivered before the Prussian State Council. He admitted that many Germans were grumbling against the regime and implied that most of the grumblers were to be found in the ranks of the Party extremists.

"It is not our business," Goering said, "to decide whether there must be a second revolution. The first revolution was ordered by the Führer and ended by the Führer. If the Führer wants a second revolution we shall be ready, in the streets, tomorrow. If he does not want it we shall be ready to suppress anybody who tries to rebel against the Führer's will."

A week later, in Hamburg, Goering saw fit to assume the mantle of the egalitarian. The man who had built himself palaces in Berlin and in the country, who had lost no opportunity of abrogating to himself any office whose prestige or profit attracted him, who had promoted himself from honorary Captain to full General, now roundly attacked class-distinctions before an audience of appreciative, if unreflective, Hamburgers:

"In Germany," he said, "the distinction between 'proletarians' and 'gentlefolk' must vanish. We must do away with all those silly notices which say: 'Tradesmen's Entrance' and 'Visitors Only.' "

Next day Dr Edgar Jung, a freelance writer closely associated with von Papen and the author of the Marburg speech, vanished from his home. The word "Gestapo" scrawled on the wall of his bathroom, where he had gone to wash his hands after the arrival of visitors in his flat, indicated his fate. He was never seen again. The twilight which preceded the "Night of the Long Knives" was almost ended.

After his disagreement with Hitler, Röhm had gone on leave, and at the end of June was staying, with a band of admirers, at the little resort of Weissee in Bavaria. Now vengeance moved southwards in pursuit. Hitler flew off to Essen on a visit of inspection to the Krupps works there, and to the Rhineland Goering followed him. At Bad Godesburg, destined four years later to be the scene of an even more ominous meeting, the two men laid their last plans. On the afternoon of Friday, June 29, General Goering flew back to Berlin charged with the duty of annihilating Röhm's principal followers throughout northern Germany. Hitler, with Goebbels, would deal with Röhm himself.

That evening Goering conferred with General von Blomberg, with Heinrich Himmler and with the senior officers of his own green-uniformed "Field Police."

The shooting began in Bavaria at dawn on June 30. In Berlin Goering's victims were allowed time to breakfast in peace. Only at 10.30 a.m. did the General order his men into action.

General von Schleicher, Röhm's one-time friend and supporter, was one of the first to fall. He was shot dead in the drawing-room of his suburban villa at Neu-Babelsberg by Goering's personal police, and with him fell his wife. Their bodies were found by their little daughter when she returned from school at lunchtime.

Von Papen was more fortunate. Although his office was raided and his private secretary, a man of many secrets, shot dead at his desk, the Vice-Chancellor was allowed to leave the building and to go home. There he remained under house arrest for ten days. Hindenburg was not yet dead, the Herrenklub was still powerful. Von Papen owed his life that day to his excellent connections.

For the rank and file of his victims Goering chose a particularly appropriate place of execution. All that day police vans rolled up to the former Military Academy at Gross-Lichterfelde, the institution at which young Hermann Goering had first imbibed the doctrines of Prussian "soldierliness" of which he was ever afterwards so proud. All that day volleys of musketry rang out behind its high, red-brick walls on the orders of a distinguished old boy of the institution. Yet was not General Goering acting on behalf of the Army in thus lopping the head of the S.A., which he had himself once commanded? So, at least, he may have thought.

Karl Ernst, the man who had fired the Reichstag, fell at Lichterfelde under Goering's bullets. So did his accomplices Sander, von Mohrenschild and Fiedler. So also did Standartenführer Gehrt, like his executioner a former Captain of the Imperial German Air Force, like him the holder of the coveted *Pour le Mérite*. It was said that Goering tried to save his old comrade at the last moment and that the reprieve came too late. That is not unlikely, since soon the shooting got beyond Goering's control and many people died whose names had not stood on the General's death-warrant. Yet one man died that day in payment of a very old reckoning. Von Kahr, the

Bavarian Premier who had smashed the "Beercellar *Putsch*" of 1923, paid eleven years later for that temerity with his life. The old man's body was later found in a swamp near Dachau, a name of evil omen.

Down in Bavaria Hitler himself directed operations. Röhm, Heines and most of the senior leaders of the S.A., whom Röhm had summoned to a conference at Weissee, fell into the Führer's trap and were dead by the evening of June 30.

In the Propaganda Ministry in Berlin, Goering that afternoon faced the correspondents of foreign newspapers and news-agencies. He warned his hearers not to distort what he was about to say or the events of that day. A revolution, he said, had been planned by the S.A., but it had been forestalled. Röhm had been arrested and awaited punishment. (He was, in fact, already dead.) General von Schleicher had offered resistance to arrest and had, most regrettably, been shot. All other important S.A. commanders had been arrested and would be tried. Some had offered resistance and were dead. Others, seized with remorse, had committed suicide.

"You know me well enough, gentlemen," the speaker went on, "to realize that I shall crush all resistance remorselessly, whether it comes from Left or Right. Whoever conspires against the Third Reich will lose his head! . . . All Germany is again in the hands of the Führer. The Reichswehr is loyal. As soon as the excitement has subsided the Führer will address the nation."

General Goering smiled grimly.

"I have given orders, gentlemen," he added, "that all telephone lines out of Germany are to be closed for a short time. Later you will be allowed to send out the truth to your newspapers, but there must be no exaggeration. You have no need to go out and look for a story, gentlemen – the story is already there for you!"

In Berlin the number of General Goering's victims on that blazing June day amounted to at least 100. Hitler's score in Munich was higher. Between them the two men took full responsibility for all that had happened, including the death of people whose death had never been intended. In such circumstances, as Goering later explained, it was very difficult to keep a perfectly accurate tally.

In the years which have passed since June 30, 1934, the world has shuddered at greater massacres. Dachau, Buchenwald, Belsen, Auschwitz, Ravensbrück, the Ghetto of Warsaw,

Lidice, Katyn, Oradour-sur-Glane – the list could be extended almost indefinitely. Each of these horrors followed a pattern established on that hot summer day by Goering, Hitler and Heinrich Himmler. Civilization in those days was not yet accustomed to mass-murder, and the world was deeply shocked. But life in Germany went on, apparently unchanged.

Years later, when the "Thousand Year Reich" had collapsed in utter and ignominious ruin, Goering was asked by an inquisitive interrogator why he had assented to the murder of Ernst Röhm. The question seemed to surprise Goering:

"But – the man was in my way," he replied.

At last Goering could afford to relax. He felt that he needed a rest. Not only had the past eighteen months been a severe strain – for if he had not settled with Röhm and the S.A. they would certainly sooner or later have settled accounts with him – but he found the comfort and luxury with which he was now surrounded so pleasant that he longed for more time in which to enjoy it. Now he reigned, after Hitler, supreme in Germany, and none would dare again to challenge him. He could afford to let things slide a little, to give his natural indolence the upper hand for a while. He never again mastered that side of his character.

Playtime

EVERY morning, whether in the new palace in Berlin or in Carinhall, Robert Kropp, General Goering's "gentleman's gentleman," brought coffee into his master's dressing-room. In the bathroom beyond, the shower hissed, and presently the General came out wrapped in a brocade dressing-gown, one of an immense assortment of such garments. A pile of newspapers lay beside the breakfast table, and the General, as he took his first cup of coffee standing, would glance through them. Thanks to the labours of Dr. Goebbels, the German papers were now politically impeccable but intolerably boring – one knew in advance just what they would print, so that it was hardly worth reading the things. For the *National-Zeitung* of Essen General Goering showed greater interest, for this journal was becoming more and more his own personal mouthpiece.

The foreign Press was more amusing. General Goering spoke very little English, but he could read the language easily enough and the cartoons were sometimes entertaining. David Low, who drew for the *Evening Standard,* regularly produced caricatures of the General which either drove that officer into a furious temper or caused him to slap his great thighs, as was his habit when highly amused. With the French language the General had only an indifferent acquaintance, nor did the slap-dash, almost "Bolshevik," style of French cartoonists appeal to him. He devoted some time to the study of the Swedish Press, since here was a language which he knew comparatively well, and then drew up an arm-chair and settled down with a book.

Robert Kropp meanwhile had observed his master closely. Now he went to a cabinet of gramophone records and made his choice for the morning. If the General had got out of bed on the wrong side – and it was not very difficult to perceive when he had done so – the programme of music generally opened with the March of the Heroes from *Götterdämmerung,* whose martial cadences never failed to restore the General's self-esteem. If breakfast and the perusal of the newspapers had gone off smoothly, Kropp chose one of the less strident favourites – something out of *Fra Diavolo* or *Arabella* was always welcomed, or Tchaikovski's Fourth Symphony, or Beethoven's Third. As he watched his master sunk in a deep armchair, Kropp, taking his cue from the General's extremely mobile face, knew just what record would suit the mood of the moment.

Goering was in the jargon of psychology a complete extrovert. Men called him later *"Der Eiserne"* – the "Iron Man" – and he loved to be so styled. On public platforms he loomed grim and bulky or humorous and down-to-earth, according to the role for which he had cast himself, and his features were arranged to suit the part. At home, beneath the discreet eyes of Robert Kropp or of faithful Cilly, now promoted to be a housekeeper at Carinhall, Goering allowed each passing emotion to be reflected faithfully in his face. In the words of a woman who knew Goering well for many years and who has never faltered in her liking and admiration for him:

"Hermann Goering had a very expressive face – one could see in it his great capacity for suffering as much as his great capacity for enjoyment. . . . I do not say joy or happiness, for he only knew them for so short a time."

At all events he knew them now, as he sat in his armchair while the gramophone played. The book which he read might deal with the life of Genghis Khan, for Goering had conceived a positive passion for everything which concerned that man of blood. His private library contained every book which had been written on the Asiatic conquerer, and all were well thumbed. Although the General liked to describe himself as a man of the Renaissance born after his time, a personage equally at home on the battlefield or in the world of art, the terrible story of Genghis fascinated him. He was at heart a satrap rather than a *condottiere*.

Detective stories fascinated him too, and these he read as a policeman, critically. One of the effects of the Nazi revolution and of Goering's interest in police matters had been to debase this form of literature in Germany. The classic formula – blundering policeman, brilliant private detective, discomfiture of police, triumph of amateur – had no place in a State in which the police were all-seeing, all-knowing, all-powerful. If Sir Arthur Conan Doyle had introduced a German Inspector Lestrade into the Reich of 1935, or Miss Agatha Christie an *Oberkriminalinspektor* Japp, they might have found themselves arraigned on the grave charge of *Beamtenbeleidigung* – insult to official personages. The ban applied only to un-flattering portrayals of German policemen. The works of foreign writers sold briskly in translation, and Goering and Himmler were well content that this should be so, since these books did something to persuade the German reader that "democratic" policemen, like all other democrats, were stupid and effete. As for German writers of detective stories, they were obliged to choose foreign settings for their plots, and some very strange portrayals of the British and American scene they produced in consequence.

Goering read them all – translations of Agatha Christie, Dashiell Hammett and Dorothy Sayers, as well as the some-what handicapped productions of his own compatriots. Books on wild animals, shooting and the fine arts made up the rest of his reading.

He tried his own hand at literature. Hitler's *Mein Kampf* was now required to be read in Germany and brought enor-mous royalties to its author. The firm of Franz Eher, which as official publishers to the Nazi Party was coining money, suggested that a book by Hermann Goering would be ex-

141

tremely successful – the entire resources of the Party could be used to push sales, schools would be "advised" to include the work in their curriculum and to give it as a prize to deserving pupils. There was a great deal of money to be made.

In one of those bursts of energy which were typical of him, Goering dictated *Aufbau Einer Nation* ("The Building of a Nation") in a matter of hours. He afterwards claimed that the book earned him 1,000,000 marks (£50,000).

The remainder of each day brought with it an increasing variety of duties. The time had now almost come when the world might be officially told what the world already strongly suspected – that Germany again possessed a military air force. No doubt Milch and Wever and their technicians were doing their jobs properly – Goering had ordered them to produce the best air force in the world, and with him, now, to order was to be obeyed. Very soon he would place himself at the head of a striking-force which would paralyse the enemies of the Reich with terror. He had ordered his subordinates to concentrate on bombers – offensive aircraft – and to make the development of fighters a secondary consideration. In 1933 Goering had declared in an interview that the defence of Germany was his sole preoccupation.

"I shall do everything in my power," he had then said to the Berlin Correspondent of the United Press of America, "to get other nations to agree to at least a minimum of air defence for Germany. I would be ready to do without bombers or other types of aggressive aircraft."

Nevertheless, by 1934 the first bombers were built, and in the next year the Dornier Do 17 and the Heinkel He 111 were rolling off the assembly lines. Goering assumed that these were excellent aircraft – everybody assured him that they were admirable and he had no means of judging for himself. In any case Goering avoided meetings with his technical experts as much as possible. Milch and Wever were always grumbling, always clamouring for more of this and that, adducing in support of their claims arguments which were extremely boring, and for a man whose aeronautical education had ended in 1922 largely incomprehensible.

The General did his best to conceal his ignorance, but he never tried to correct it. The best course was to avoid such discussions as far as possible, while assuring the Führer, who constantly asked for news of his fledgling Air Force, that everything was going splendidly. It was quite easy to persuade

142

Hitler, at any rate, of his competence in all matters concerning the air.

Goering loved to look towards the wide horizons. He had a profound contempt for detail, although his excellent intelligence enabled him to master it when it was absolutely necessary to do so. Then with a sudden burst of energy he got through an amazing amount of intricate work in a very short time. But as the mental indolence which was natural to him encroached more and more upon his whole character, these bursts of energy became increasingly rare.

To his friends Goering would speak with almost mystical fervour of the Air Force which he – and apparently he alone – was building. For the Army he expressed lofty pity. The unfortunate foot-sloggers were completely out of date. The Navy was utterly negligible, but the Luftwaffe – ah, to his Luftwaffe nothing was impossible.

With the assistance of Goebbels, who now had the German cinema and radio firmly under his control, Goering wooed the youth of Germany and found them very ready to listen. Propaganda against the restrictions of the Versailles Treaty and in favour of the airman's life flickered from every cinema screen.

Flieger, grüss mir die Sonne, grüss mir die Sterne, und
grüss mir den Mond!
Piloten ist nichts verboten, solange die Erde bewohnt.

(Flyer, carry my greeting to the sun, the stars,
   the moon,
Nothing's beyond the pilot, while there's life
   on Earth.)

Berlin's Tinpan-Alley ground out such songs as these – General Goering even tried his hand at one or two himself – and young Germans responded eagerly.

The whole question of a uniform for the Luftwaffe gave the General many pleasurable hours. Every button, every gorget patch and badge of rank he designed himself. In planning service-dress he had yielded to the German liking for high boots and breeches, but walking-out dress, both for officers and other ranks, followed that of the R.A.F. fairly closely, and the mess-kit prescribed for officers was almost identical with that worn by their opposite numbers in Great Britain. In February 1935 General Goering acted as his own mannequin when he proudly displayed the new uniform on his own person to young pilots in training at Schleissheim.

In the second week of March the Air Attachés of Great Britain, France and Italy were summoned by General Goering and were informed that the Luftwaffe would officially come into existence on April 1 – All Fool's Day. They were not unduly surprised by the news, nor by the fact that Goering now added to his titles that of *General der Flieger,* or General of the Airmen, and *Oberbefehlshaber der Luftwaffe* (Commander-in-Chief of the Air Force). He snatched from the Reichswehr the command of all anti-aircraft artillery, and announced the formation of the *Reichsluftschutzbund,* or A.R.P. Organization, of which he also assumed the supreme direction.

This latter function enabled the General to stage, on March 19, an extremely realistic air-raid exercise in Berlin. For two hours the city was completely blacked out, and its people had their first lesson of the meaning, to civilians, of air power. Next day the exercise continued, particularly in the Kreuzberg district, where no theatrical expedient was neglected which might heighten the illusion that the area had been devastated by bombs. Ten years later residents of Kreuzberg had an even more convincing demonstration, for then the district was in fact bombed flat, but in 1935 the exercise seemed terrifying enough as General Goering strode through "ruins" from which men and women, realistically smeared with red paint, were carried to the ambulances while pungent smoke belched from buildings which had been technically hit by incendiary bombs. Overhead bombers and fighters swooped and dived in a clear sky. The General pronounced the whole affair to have been eminently satisfactory.

The theatre, too, absorbed much of Goering's time. Thanks to Emmy Sonnemann, who was now his constant companion, he took a really intelligent interest in theatrical matters and had, moreover, every opportunity to gratify his tastes. Although Goebbels was the official dictator of the German stage, Goering, as Prime Minister of Prussia, controlled the Berlin State Opera and the two State theatres in the Capital. Actors, singers, scenic designers began to frequent his palace in Berlin, now an integral part of the vast new Air Ministry, and for all of them there was a welcome.

Goering's friendship with Emmy Sonnemann was a matter of general remark. It was at that time entirely platonic – the genuine companionship of a man and woman who liked one another very much indeed. Yet people talked, as people must, until some of the chatter reached the ears of the Führer. Hitler's own discretion in his relations with women was as morbid as was his dislike of any "scandal." He suggested to his friend that it might be as well if he and Fräulein Sonnemann were married.

Until that moment Goering had not seriously considered the possibility of a second marriage. The wound which Carin's death had inflicted on him was not healed, and he was rather proud of his loyalty to her memory. Yet if the Führer really wished him to do something, the Führer's wishes must be obeyed – that had always been Goering's guiding principle, the principle indeed which had taken him from Carin's deathbed. Therefore he must marry Emmy. He was very fond of her and she of him. Perhaps Carin, wherever she was, would understand, and, understanding, forgive.

The news of the engagement was given to the world on March 9, 1935, after one premature announcement followed by a suitable denial. Already it had become customary and even advisable for all who wished the General and themselves well to give him magnificent presents at Christmas and on his birthday, and the finer the present the greater, it was soon discovered, was the General's benevolence thereafter towards its giver. It may be imagined, therefore, that Goering did not lack tributes each December and January. Now, with the announcement of his engagement, the gifts came pouring in again.

Hitler sent an enormous portrait of Bismarck, the "Iron Chancellor," Dr. Schacht a painting of one of the lion cubs which Goering had recently adopted as pets. From loyal Ernst Udet came a picture of an aeroplane flying over a range of mountains. Models of aircraft, in fact, tended to dominate the display. There were aircraft in gold, silver and base metals, in gingerbread and cedarwood, and even a canary-cage shaped in the semblance of an aeroplane with a canary chirping inside it. Hundreds of bottles of wine were sent by admirers in all parts of Germany, and hamper after hamper of delicacies. One admiring housewife contributed a chocolate cake of her own baking, shaped as a heart and decorated with the word "HERMANN" in white sugar. Somebody else sent a set of fifty beer tankards; Werner Kraus the actor produced two immense chocolate Easter-eggs and, practical man, a fine array of coathangers for the General's uniforms, which were now extremely numerous.

145

Goering was delighted with this prodigal display, and justifiably so. Not all the gifts had come from sycophants and place-seekers, nor even from friends and acquaintances. Simple, commonplace Germans in their hundreds had sent presents to a man whom they liked and admired. On the day after the wedding he could not resist sharing his pleasure with a few foreign journalists. Surely this fine show of wedding-gifts would convince them of his own popularity, of the fact that he was something more than the obese butcher of the foreign cartoonists

He met the favoured journalists in the huge white drawing-room of his Berlin mansion, its air heavy with the scent of the roses, lilac, carnations, jasmine, which had been sent to the bride.

"I've invited you here," he said, genially, to his guests, "so that you can see for yourselves how much the German people love me, and not me only, but the regime. Really, I've been quite overwhelmed by all these splendid presents. Look! There's hardly a bit of rubbish among the whole lot!"

The General pointed to Dr. Schacht's gift – the portrait of the lion cub:

"Isn't that fine? It's just like him too. I think it's tremendously artistic!"

He patted his smiling wife on the cheek.

"And do you know," he chuckled, "I find that I've just about paid for the tiara which I gave my wife as a wedding-present out of the money which I've saved on my Bachelor's Tax this year!"

The wedding itself, which took place on April 10, had been a splendid affair indeed. It began on the previous evening with a lavish display of decorations in the streets – Unter den Linden burst out into a little forest of fir-trees interspersed with flag-staffs. Seventy-five of Goering's fighters – the largest formation Berliners had ever seen – zoomed low over the city, while the betrothed couple, accompanied by the cream of the Nazi Party, enjoyed a gala performance of *Lohengrin* at the State Opera and afterwards took the salute at a torchlight parade and tattoo carried out by the *S.S. Leibstandarte "Adolf Hitler,"* the Führer's personal bodyguard.

At noon on the wedding-day the bridegroom, in a car festooned with narcissus and pink tulips, drove through cheering crowds to the bride's house in the Bendlerstrasse, followed by Erhardt Milch, now a Lieutenant-General of the Luftwaffe.

146

At the Chancellery Hitler joined the party which drove to the Town Hall, while the engines of the "Richthofen Squadron" roared overhead. Four heralds in tabard and hose sounded a fanfare as the cavalcade of long black cars drew up.

After the civil ceremony Reich Bishop Müller awaited bride and bridegroom in the cathedral. The prelate had, only two years before, been an obscure Army chaplain. It had been he, however, who had brought General von Blomberg to Hitler's notice and he had done much, in a quiet way, to reconcile the Reichswehr to National Socialism. Now he too had his reward as he preached from the text of Corinthians: "Though I speak with the tongues of men and of angels, and have not charity, I am become as sounding brass, or a tinkling cymbal. . . .

"It is significant," said the Reich Bishop, addressing the bride and bridegroom, "that you were both given the same verse of the Bible when you were confirmed in the Protestant Church: 'Be faithful unto death, and I shall give you the crown of life.' Our life is usually a battle and filled with sorrow. The Crown of Life consists in remaining loyal and in keeping faith with God."

Three hundred and sixteen guests assembled for the wedding breakfast at the Hotel Kaiserhof, there to eat lobster, turtle soup, turbot, pâté de foie gras, roast chicken, ices and Welsh rarebit; while the band of Hitler's bodyguard played gay music chosen by the bridegroom. The Führer was in his most amiable mood.

"Have you any particular wishes for the future?" he asked the bride.

"Yes," Frau Goering answered. "I wish my husband had nothing to do with politics – I wish he was an actor."

She had, in fact, married a talented actor, but his career lay on the political stage. He had come a long way since that first humble wedding breakfast at the Park Hotel in Munich, thirteen years before, though many of the old faces which had then beamed at Hermann and Carin as they began their married life could now be seen around the long tables at the Kaiserhof. Bodenschatz was there, and Udet, and Carin's sister, Countess Wilamowitz-Moellendorf, besides other members of Carin's family who had come from Sweden to set the seal of their approval on "Uncle Hermann's" new union.

Even on that happy day Carin was not forgotten by the man who had been her husband. After the wedding breakfast a small party of intimate friends accompanied the bride and bridegroom to Carinhall. In the great hall a fire was blazing and drinks and refreshments were set out. The guests stood about a little uncomfortably, for the host was not there. Although Frau Goering displayed all her talent as a hostess and as an actress, the General's absence from her side seemed a little strange. At last, after a full hour, the General rejoined the party. He had spent that hour in Carin's tomb on his knees beside her coffin.

The newly wedded pair spent a few days at Wiesbaden, days which were somewhat marred by the persistent enthusiasm of the population. Tiresome though doubtless well-meaning children were a particular pest. They pursued the honeymooners vociferously until the bridegroom was forced to issue a formal order that this nuisance must cease. The loyal Rhinelanders were told to show their regard for General Goering by ignoring him. "In particular," added the General bluntly, "the incessant shouting of '*Heil!* by children is to be stopped forthwith!"

The over-loyal Rhineland was soon to be left behind, and a month later the Goerings set out on a proper honeymoon. With "Pilli" Koerner, Erhardt Milch and the Prussian Minister of Justice, Hans Kerrl, and his wife, they flew to Budapest and thence to Belgrade and on to Ragusa, where a villa had been rented from a local doctor. For a fortnight they rested and bathed in the blue Adriatic, and Berlin was almost forgotten.

The year 1935 passed on pleasantly enough. By methods with which General Goering was by now thoroughly conversant, £6000 was raised to provide a magnificent motor-yacht in which the Goerings and their friends sometimes cruised about the chain of lakes which lies near Berlin. The Master Hunter of the Reich had also acquired, at Rominten in East Prussia, an official shooting-box, where many weeks were spent in the autumn. Around Carinhall itself the Schorfheide had been transformed into a vast game preserve. Through the forest a fence ran for miles, its few gates protected by photo-electric cells which warned the guardrooms, situated at intervals along the barrier, of the unauthorized passage of any living creature, human or animal.

Good, loyal Bodenschatz moved into a comfortable suite of apartments in Carinhall, as head of his old friend's military household, an organisation which expanded continually.

And as always there were plums to be picked from the pie.

In 1935 people began to speak seriously of television, and General Goering decided that the development of that invention in Germany had better take place under his patronage. It was not difficult to secure Hitler's consent to this arrangement, although Goebbels resented it bitterly. That, however, was all to the good, since Goering's friendship with the "Little Doctor" was no longer as close as it had been during the early days of struggle. Moreover, the new post was well paid, as were most of the appointments which fell into the General's lap, and that was most welcome.

The year 1935 brought Goering one visitor in particular on whom he lavished all his charm and hospitality. Colonel Charles A. Lindbergh, hero of the first solo flight across the Atlantic, at that time the most popular and celebrated if not the greatest figure in international aviation, was the General's guest at Carinhall, and him the General delighted to honour.

The two men understood one another well enough. Even Goering's vanity was flattered by the visit of this truly distinguished airman, who accepted a decoration from his hands and listened with gratifying attention to all that his host had to tell him, and Goering kept nothing back from the quiet young American.

Together Goering and Lindbergh discussed Germany's rearmament in the air and the evidence of progress which General Goering was able to display to his guest deeply impressed the Colonel. The British Air Force, he knew, had aircraft of excellent quality but in depressingly small numbers. The Air Force of France was small, antiquated and apparently stagnant. Lindbergh observed this to Goering.

"Oh," the General said, magnificently, "if the French need aircraft I can sell them 1000 at once."

The American and to a lesser extent the British Press bitterly attacked Colonel Lindbergh for "truckling to the Nazis" in visiting Goering and allowing the General to patronize him. To those attacks the Colonel never replied, though a single statement from him could have silenced them. For in fact the United States Government had requested him to pay the visit in the service of his country.

Showing an understanding of Goering's psychology which the Governments of other nations might have done well to emulate, the War Department in Washington decided to exploit General Goering's self-esteem for its own purposes. The American Service attachés in Berlin, able and conscientious as they were, could not furnish the full picture of the rise of the Luftwaffe which Washington urgently required. Perhaps, the War Department thought, a private visit to the creator of the German Air Force by America's distinguished airman would provide the information which normal diplomatic channels seemed unable to elicit. This hope proved to be fully justified: Colonel Lindbergh returned to Washington with an extremely full report on the Luftwaffe for which he was rewarded by the enthusiastic thanks of the American Air Staff. He has yet to receive the thanks of the rest of his countrymen, or credit for the silence which he maintained during the subsequent years.

Marriage to an actress had brought with it a considerable increase in the queue of suppliants who for one reason or another sought Goering's favour. Goebbels was still busy purging the artistic life of Germany from any non-Aryan taint, and many artists of Jewish descent, or with a drop of Jewish blood in their veins, turned desperately to Frau Goering for succour. It was known that her husband was no fanatical hater of the Jews – had he not brushed aside an official report that General Milch was not of completely Aryan origin with the retort: *"I'll* decide who is a Jew and who isn't!"* As for Emmy, who in her years in the theatre had had so many Jewish friends, she was a kind woman and a "good trouper." She would not refuse to intercede for those who were now threatened with unemployment, who were already in prison or might soon find their way there. She did not refuse.

Goering hated this part of his life. Although he could be utterly merciless, his ruthlessness took the form of actions committed by himself in hot blood or by others in cold blood on his behalf. Having founded concentration camps, he wished to hear as little about them as possible – it was an extremely unpleasant subject, and Goering disliked unpleasantness more and more. Now Emmy came to him with tales of individual tragedies, of this or that old friend who by reason of his ancestry found himself in desperate straits, of acquaintances who were now in concentration camps – actual people with children dependent on them. As long as the process of "Aryanization" could be kept on a broad anonymous footing, well and good. To deal harshly with "the Jews" was no doubt right and necessary, but when Emmy kept thrusting a specific Herr Kohn, an individual Frau Wolff upon her husband's notice, the thing became awkward.

To take a stand in favour of the Jews was out of the ques-

150

tion. Goering's moral cowardice would never have allowed him to do that, for to do so would be to endanger everything – position, riches, luxury. Besides, such conduct would amount to a betrayal of the Führer, whose whole domestic policy rested on the persecution of the Jewish race. Yet here and there Goering did intervene, very discreetly, making sure that his weakness would not be discovered, and a few Jews were able to thank him, and still more his wife, for their salvation.

More and more work went by the board. Life was comfortable, everything lay ready to hand. Did the General require a jewelled sword, a yacht, a castle, a special train built for his own use? For so powerful a man nothing was out of reach.

More and more the streak of buffoonery which ran through Hermann Goering's twisted nature became apparent, and the German people, it seemed positively enjoyed its manifestations. Rearmament, a great programme of public works and the financial policies of Dr. Schacht had virtually banished unemployment from the Reich. Whatever might be done in secret by the Government, however dark the deeds of the regime and their implications, most of the people of Germany neither knew very much nor wished to know anything at all about them. Was there not money and work once more, and hope, and an intoxicating sense of Germany's reviving power? "Uncle Hermann" could afford to relax a little, and that in itself was an encouraging sign.

When, to celebrate his 43rd birthday, General Goering issued invitations to a splendid party at the State Opera House at £4 a ticket, everybody who was anybody in Berlin made up their minds to be present, and most people who were nobody read of the preparations for the affair with good-natured approval. More than 2000 revellers danced that night away as the paying-guests of the Prussian Prime Minister. A single plate of cold meat at the buffet cost 9s., a bottle of *Sekt*, the "champagne" of Germany, £1.

Such a party had not been seen in Berlin since Kaiser Wilhelm fled to Doorn, and was not the Crown Prince himself there, in full-dress uniform of the Death's Head Hussars – just like the old days – and were not Princess Mafalda of Italy and her husband, Prince Philip of Hesse, sitting with General Goering and his wife, not to mention King Boris of Bulgaria. Frau Goering, handsome in ice-blue satin, behaved in the most gracious and unaffected manner towards all her old friends from the theatre and displayed just the right degree of reverence for the Royal personages. As for the General himself, he looked both genial and imposing in the full-dress uniform of the Luftwaffe. Berlin society decided that evening that the Goerings were really quite pets.

The Luftwaffe had now been superseded in the forefront of Goering's working mind by another interest – economics. By the spring of 1935 Dr. Schacht, the President of the Reichsbank and Minister for Economics, had fallen foul of quite a number of his colleagues. Germany's reserves of foreign currency were dwindling fast, yet the demands for foreign exchange became daily more numerous and pressing. The armed services needed sterling and dollars for rearmament, the Ministry of Agriculture needed pesos for meat and fertilizers. Dr. Goebbels required foreign money of all kinds for his propaganda activities. Each Department was convinced that its own claim upon Dr. Schacht's modest resources was far more urgent than any other, and the tall, austere banker was hard put to it to strike a balance between the conflicting demands.

Goering kept himself fully informed of this situation through his nephew, Dr. Herbert Goering, who was a senior official of the Reichsbank and a close collaborator of Dr. Schacht. From him the General took a series of lessons in elementary economics whose broad principles, his alert brain, which he now chose to exert to its limit, had no difficulty in grasping. Then he had a long talk with the Führer and with Dr. Schacht.

The results of this conversation became apparent on April 27, 1936. On that day Hitler signed a decree appointing General Goering to control and co-ordinate the activities of all the Ministries concerned with the economic life of Germany. In future he, not Dr. Schacht, would allot priorities for foreign exchange, the import and allocation of raw materials would be his province. At a stroke of the Führer's pen General Goering had become the dictator of Germany's economic existence.

All through the summer Goering worked hard at the new and unfamiliar task, though he found time to display himself frequently at the Olympic Games in the summer and to give a lavish party on that occasion in the State Opera House which few of the foreign athletes who were invited to it are likely to have forgotten.

By the beginning of September the General had charted the course which he intended to follow. He demanded fresh powers from the Führer and got them. On September 9 Hitler announced, in a speech at Nuremberg, the beginning of a "Four Year Plan" which would make the Reich almost entirely independent of foreign countries for essential raw materials. By hard work, ingenuity and determination, Germany was to be given an economy as nearly self-contained as possible. General Goering would be the Führer's Commissioner for the Four Year Plan.

That announcement made Hermann Goering the world's most powerful industrialist.

In a speech delivered before an audience of 20,000 Berliners in the Deutschlandhalle, Goering set himself to explain his plans to the people in language which they could understand. The purpose of the Four Year Plan, he said, was to "safeguard Germany's honour and livelihood. . . . Never again must a foreign hand grip us by the throat. We shall break the fingers of that hand, finger by finger, until the German throat is free again. . . . We must help ourselves. . . . If we had one-quarter of Great Britain's colonial possessions there would be no shortage of food and raw materials in Germany. . . . Our Plan must succeed – say that over and over to yourselves as you get up in the mornings. . . . He who increases his prices is a thief and we shall set him alongside other thieves and swindlers. I shall suppress all parasites by Draconic measures – no matter how barbaric they may have to be. Hoarders will be treated as swindlers. We shall not only take from them their hoards, but also their very means of livelihood. . . . A great age demands a great nation. We believe in the gigantic mission of the German people. May God Almighty bless the Führer, his people and his work!"

That speech struck home to the heart of simple, patriotic Germans everywhere. Next morning thousands of letters bringing congratulations and offers of support poured into Goering's office. A minor Nazi functionary appeared bearing 637 golden wedding-rings which he had collected from Party Members as a contribution to the Four Year Plan. Professional economists might shake their heads at Goering's scheme, but at least it had the merit, which is possessed by few economic programmes, of making ordinary people "feel good inside." When a few weeks later Goering stood at a Berlin street corner rattling a collecting-box for the "Winter Help" Campaign, good-humoured crowds shouted: "Hermann needs money!" and Goering joined in the laughter.

Inventors began to beat a track to Goering's door with devices which might or might not help to fulfil the aims of the Four Year Plan, and all were welcome, even Jews.

"I don't care whether the man who brings me an invention is a Christian, a heathen or a Jew," said Goering at this time to a foreign journalist. "Inventions don't have Jewish grandmothers!"

Again the General displayed his ability to choose men who would serve him efficiently and above all loyally. On this quality he always laid great emphasis.

"Tell me, *Herr Ministerpräsident,*" said a lady to Goering at a Christmas party in 1936, "would you rather have a clever man or a loyal man to work for you?"

"Oh," replied Goering smoothly, "a loyal man every time. You see, I'm clever myself."

The men whom Goering chose to work for him on the Four Year Plan were both loyal and able. Six years of war were to put their work to a gruelling test.

Before the Tempest

THROUGHOUT 1937 the Luftwaffe was in action. In Spain Germany's new aircraft types were tested in battle and the results seemed to be satisfactory. They fought in an undeclared war. When, in the summer of 1936, the first batch of pilots selected for the "Spanish Legion" paraded at Döberitz, they heard General Wilberg, one of the real creators of the Luftwaffe, read aloud a curt order from Hitler, drawn up with telegraphic brevity, which explained the terms on which they were to assist General Franco:

"Führer decided support people now in direst human distress and rescue them from Bolshevism. Therefore German help. Owing international commitments no open assistance possible, therefore secret supporting action."

The airmen left Germany in the steamer *Usaramo* on a cruise ostensibly organized by the "Strength through Joy" organization, to all appearances a party of deserving workers embarking on a summer holiday through the good offices of

Dr. Robert Ley's "Labour Front." Thus did Goering's Luftwaffe slink into its first war.

The Four Year Plan took up much of Goering's time. In July of 1937 his economic powers were still further extended. The iron and steel industry, which had once provided the Nazi Party with funds and Goering himself with private loans, was now brought completely under the direction of its former bondsman. With the assistance of foreign firms, some of them British, new deposits of low-grade iron-ore were developed by the newly created "Hermann Goering-Werke." The nickname "Iron Hermann" or "The Iron Man" now tripped easily off every German's tongue, and Goering was content.

The shooting-parties, the receptions, the long speaking-tours were interspersed with short but intense periods of office work, most of it concerned with the Four Year Plan. Distinguished foreigners came to Germany and were royally entertained. The friendship of foreign diplomats was assiduously cultivated. Sir Nevile Henderson, the British Ambassador, spent a happy week-end shooting at Rominten, and was flattered to be formally admitted to the *Reichsjägerschaft* – the Hunter's Guild – by the Master Hunter of the Reich. During a picnic on another sporting occasion Goering played an effective little trick which duly impressed Sir Nevile. The party was drinking bottled beer with its luncheon and the Ambassador pulled off the metal cap from his bottle and let it lie on the ground at his feet. Bending forward, General Goering picked up the little disc and slipped it into his pocket.

"Mustn't waste these," he explained to the Ambassador. "Do you know we feed 500,000 pigs a year from the proceeds of the collection of these bottle-caps?"

The Ambassador was deeply struck by this lesson in practical economics.

"You can't beat people like that, you know," he said, telling the story later to one of his own countrymen.

These fruitful contacts, however, took up much time. So for that matter did General Goering's other interest. For the Luftwaffe he had less and less time to spare. Milch and his senior staff-officers and technicians now found that it was almost impossible to have any access whatever to their Commander-in-Chief, and in desperation Milch turned to Hitler himself. Here he found an enthusiastic listener. The Führer's quick brain, seemingly tireless, swift to master detail, was not

155

bored by technicalities as was Goering's. Milch came away from these interviews deeply encouraged.

In the highest places of the National Socialist hierarchy people began to gossip. Goering, it seemed, was no longer Commander-in-Chief of the Luftwaffe in any effective sense. General Milch was doing all the work – he even had direct access to the Führer. Hermann had obviously bitten off a great deal more than he could chew.

Goering reacted swiftly to this chatter. The long friendship with Milch was forgotten, forgotten the honeymoon trip to Ragusa, the early days when, as the chief executive of Lufthansa, Milch had been able to put work in Captain Goering's way. General Milch was systematically stripped of his powers as Deputy Commander-in-Chief. One by one the controls which governed the Air-Staff were taken from him and entrusted by Goering to more pliant officers. By removing the technical branch from Milch's jurisdiction the Commander-in-Chief put an end to those discussions with the Führer which had so deeply offended his self-esteem. Yet the responsibility remained on Milch's shoulders.

At last Milch rebelled. He secured an audience with Goering – for that, by now, was what it amounted to – and tried to resign. He was tired, he said, of carrying responsibility without possessing the powers necessary to discharge it. He wished to return to civil aviation. Lufthansa would be glad to take him back as their chief executive.

Goering rounded on his old friend. He could not afford to lose Milch's outstanding abilities, yet it was not on those grounds that he refused to accept his resignation.

"You'll stay where you are, Milch," he declared, "and let's have no nonsense about going sick either. If you want to commit suicide, well and good. Otherwise you'll carry on."

Milch carried on with a heavy heart.

Although Goering had resigned all control of the police to Himmler, who had by now established for the first time a federal police system in Germany embracing the whole Reich, the alliance between the two men remained unbroken. It was an alliance founded purely upon mutual self-interest – quiet, self-effacing Heinrich Himmler had little in common with his boisterous colleague – yet it held firmly. Reinhardt Heydrich, now in direct command of the Gestapo, had other ambitions. He had not forgotten that, on his first appointment as Himmler's deputy, Goering had protested against the choice for so

156

senior a post of an officer dismissed from the Navy for disgraceful conduct. Goering, Heydrich decided, was growing too big for his already ample boots. He proceeded to build up a private dossier against the General.

Heydrich found plenty of material for his files. If Goering had objected to his own appointment because of some petty financial misdemeanour, how much more might not the Führer object to the General's extremely doubtful behaviour in matters of money. Heydrich, burrowing back into the past, ferreted out a whole series of equivocal transactions of which General Goering would not like to be reminded. Blackmail was a double-edged sword. Very discreetly General Goering was informed of the existence of this highly confidential dossier, and with that Heydrich felt pleasantly secure. Goering, seriously frightened, lost no time in placating the man who, by turning against him the very weapon which he himself had forged, might now hold his future in his hands.

Ambition still drove Goering on, and to ambition was now added injured pride. For the Army, as has already been said, he felt a pitying contempt, and it was maddening to find that this contempt was returned with interest. General von Blomberg, the Minister for Defence, and General Baron Werner von Fritsch, since 1935 the Army's Commander-in-Chief, typified the class of senior officer with whom a war-substantive lieutenant, virtually self-promoted to the rank of General, cut very little ice indeed. They had devoted their entire lives to soldiering, they lived only for their Service. They were aristocrats. The spectacle of Goering, the exuberant bourgeois, decked out in his self designed uniform, for ever invoking those "Prussian soldierly qualities" of which they themselves were the true heirs, sickened the Generals. In the well-guarded privacy of the Kasinogesellschaft, the most exclusive of German military clubs, they made no secret of their feelings.

Goering was aware of these thinly disguised undercurrents and they infuriated him. He himself would make a better Minister of Defence than Blomberg if it came to that. He had supported the Reichswehr against the ambitions of Röhm, and his reward had been the contempt of its leaders. He might well oust them and lead the Reichswehr himself.

For a week or two, at the beginning of 1938, it seemed that Goering might achieve his ambition, for von Blomberg played straight into his hands. The Minister had just married a girl very much younger than himself, a certain Fräulein Erna

Grün, with whom he was completely infatuated. Fräulein Grün's origins were humble, but Hitler, the man of the people, had graced the wedding with his presence. It seemed an admirable example of that *Volksgemeinschaft,* the "Community of the People," which the Nazis were never tired of invoking.

Then Himmler's indefatigable police made a number of interesting discoveries, reflecting both on the newly wedded Frau von Blomberg and on her mother. Count Helldorf, now Police President of Berlin, brought the dossier of the Grün family to General Goering towards the end of January 1938 and asked for instructions.

That week-end Goering, Himmler and Heydrich conferred at Carinhall, and Goering then summoned General von Blomberg. The opportunity of humiliating one of the leaders of a caste which despised him was too good to miss. Von Blomberg listened furiously to a lecture on "soldierly honour." The Führers Ministers, General Goering explained, must, like Caesar's wife, conduct their private lives with the most impeccable correctness. It was doubtful whether in the circumstances General von Blomberg could hope to remain a member of the Cabinet, but the Führer himself would decide that.

The Führer, his mind suitably prepared, gave his decision. General von Blomberg was placed on the retired list. For a moment it looked as though Goering might achieve his ambition of setting his heel on the neck of the Army as Minister of Defence. He was forestalled by the only man against whom he had never plotted. Adolf Hitler himself took the Portfolio of Defence. As a consolation prize he promoted General Goering, on February 3, to the rank of *Generalfeldmarschall.* He was now Germany's senior officer.

Himmler next attacked General von Fritsch by resurrecting a file, already three years old, which contained charges against him of sexual perversion. That the accusations were utterly false, preferred by a male prostitute and gaol-bird, was perfectly well known to the Gestapo, particularly since they themselves had been at great pains to persuade the accuser, by a mixture of threats and cajolery, that it was indeed General Baron von Fritsch who had "picked him up" at Wannsee railway station, near Berlin, on a dark winter's night in 1935.

As the highest ranking officer of Germany it gave Field-Marshal Goering enormous pleasure to preside over the "Court of Honour" which von Fritsch now demanded in order that his name might be cleared. When the charges against him had first been mentioned to Hitler in 1935, the Führer had refused to listen to them or to read the dossier on the case. Now Goering made him listen, in his dual capacity of Führer and Minister of Defence, and the Court of Honour was the result. The Court had no alternative but to acquit the General of charges which were clearly, to any fair-minded man, both false and malicious, yet Goering had had the satisfaction of seeing the most upright of the Generals who despised him humiliated in a hearing over which he had presided. Von Fritsch retired to a manor house at Achterberg, placed at his disposal by sympathetic brother-officers, and the more accommodating General Walther von Brauchitsch took his place as Commander-in-Chief of the Army.

One important event interrupted the sittings of the Court of Honour. On March 12 German forces entered Austria and occupied the country without firing a shot. Goering was delighted. To him, whose childhood had been spent either in Southern Germany or in Austria, who felt as much at home in Innsbruck or Salzburg as he did in Munich or Berlin, the *Anschluss* seemed perfectly right and natural, as indeed it did to most Germans. The Luftwaffe had played no more than a symbolic part in the occupation, but Goering's aircraft nevertheless now sat on Austrian aerodromes. Austrian industry, and in particular the Linz steelworks, were welcome allies in the Four Year Plan. Now Goering could return to Austria, no longer as a refugee but as the ruler, after Hitler, of the whole country. The Tiroler Hof in Innsbruck, gave him a great welcome. Its faith in Hermann Goering had not been misplaced.

Surely even the second man in Hitler's Reich might hope for a little peace and quiet. The Four Year Plan, which fascinated Goering and was still his main interest, was going well enough, although butter was scarce in the shops and meat even scarcer. The iron-ore from the Salzgitter fields was beginning, thanks in part to British technicians, to reach German industry, non-essential imports had been heavily reduced, plants for the manufacture of *Buna* – artificial rubber – were coming into production and the output of the armaments industry improved with each day that passed.

Already it seemed that things might not work out as comfortably as the Marshal hoped. On the very night of the German entry into Austria a great part of Goering's pleasure in a magnificent ball held at the Air Ministry had been spoiled by the ill-timed anxiety of the Czechoslovak Minister in Berlin, M. Mastny. The ball had been a troublesome affair in any case, since it had been arranged long before the date for the invasion of Austria had been decided by the Führer. Now half the young men invited – officers of the Luftwaffe – should by rights be with their squadrons, standing-to in case the Austrians were foolish enough to resist the Reichswehr. Goering, remembering his own youth, realizing the disappointment which a cancellation of the party would entail and wishing above all, to prove that the sudden annexation of a neighbouring country was a perfectly normal matter of routine, refused to alter his plans.

Yet now the troops were already on the move towards the frontier, and officer after officer left the party on urgent orders to rejoin his unit. Mastny, nervous and full of anxiety, made his way across the half-empty ballroom to the spot where Marshal Goering stood, the centre of a cheerful group. He drew the Marshal aside. Did the invasion of Austria, he asked, imply that Germany had any aggressive intentions against his country? Goering laughed reassuringly.

"On my word of honour, Herr Mastny," he said, "I assure you that we have no designs whatever on Czechoslovakia. You may tell your Government so, from me."

Within a few weeks of that undertaking, carelessly but spontaneously given, it seemed that the Marshal's word of honour might have been too lightly pledged. The big guns of Goebbels' propaganda had swung round now and were laid on Prague. In May a flurry of alarm ran through Czechoslovakia, the Army mobilized and for a day or two it seemed that war might come – and Goering was alarmed.

It really seemed that the Führer and Ribbentrop between them were bent on fighting Czechoslovakia. Goering himself found it difficult, as the summer went on, to have access to the Führer, but the tone of the newspapers was quite sufficient in itself to show which way things were going. If war did come, who in all Germany had more to lose by defeat than Field-Marshal Goering? Not that Czechoslovakia could not be beaten – that would be a comparatively simple matter. But Czechoslovakia was the ally of France, and in some degree of the Soviet Union. Even Great Britain might conceivably support France if she felt bound to come to the succour of the Czechs. Against such a combination Germany could not hope to prevail, and with her defeat would vanish all those good things which at long last had fallen to Hermann Goering's lot.

Yet for the present it was unpleasant to think about such possibilities, and Goering had by now acquired the habit of avoiding, as far as possible, all consideration of unpleasant matters. More and more the little court which surrounded him fostered an atmosphere of unreality, a soft cushioned atmosphere.

For the Luftwaffe there seemed to be little time to spare. Even when Milch and Udet came back from London, deeply impressed by what they had seen at the Hendon Air Pageant and by the talks which they had had with prominent Englishmen, the Commander-in-Chief of the Luftwaffe was quite uninterested in their report. Hitler, however, was not. In particular he was struck by the report which Milch made during a dinner-party to Mr. Winston Churchill, who sat on his right hand.

"You're very interested in gliding over in Germany, I believe," Mr. Churchill had said.

Milch agreed that this was so.

"It's a pity," said Mr. Churchill, "that you don't take the engines out of all your aircraft and confine yourself to gliding, since it interests you so much."

"We should be glad to do that, sir," Milch replied, "if the Royal Navy would return to sail."

Hitler thought this an excellent joke. Goering was not amused. The world in which he now lived was moving further and further away from the world of Milch, of Udet, even of Hitler himself. The Marshal's world was becoming utterly unreal. His rank was no more than a gaudy sham. Since 1918 he had given no serious study to military matters, and in 1918 he had been no more than a lieutenant in his middle twenties. He had secured his appointment as Commissioner for the Four Year Plan because his popularity with the German people enabled him to ask from them sacrifices which they would have begrudged to any other Nazi leader, save only Hitler himself. Of economics and finance Goering knew only what he had been able to pick up, almost casually, during the past few months. He controlled the development of Germany's television, yet knew no more about the new technique than does the average householder who happens to own a television set. In matters connected with shooting and wild life Goering was well versed, but a hundred men in Germany knew more about such things than he did, for all that he was the Master Hunter of the Reich. Of police matters Goering knew a great deal, since this knowledge had been essential to his own advancement, but now not a single policeman stood under his command. In creating a federal police system in 1936 Himmler had taken even the Prussian force from him.

In a vast attic under the rafters of Carinhall a model railway ran past miniature farms and forests, through papier-mâché hills. At one end of the room an imposing mountain rose to a height of six feet or so, and from its summit a tiny castle looked down upon the miniature village which clustered round the railway tracks. Under the eaves lurked a squadron of little bombers, ready at the pressure of a button to come gliding down, each on a taut wire, and release their bombs at a train – not a German train, but a model of the French "Blue Train" specially reserved as a target.

Goering loved to play with this elaborate toy, which in some ways seemed to sum up the whole of his present existence. He had not built the railway himself – a party of experts from Nuremberg had seen to that and had explained the elaborate control-panel to their distinguished customer. What went on behind that panel Goering neither knew nor cared – an electrician could always mend the thing if it went out of order. As long as the little trains stopped and started at his command, as long as the signal-lamps changed duly from red to green and green to red at the pressure of a button, the master of Carinhall was satisfied. Here was a tiny make-believe kingdom of which he was the absolute ruler, provided always that the electrical circuits functioned properly. It was the business of other people to see that they did so function. Outside Carinhall lay the great German Reich, at whose control-panel Goering also sat. From time to time experts suggested that he might press this or that button, and here too trains seemed to move at his will, lights blazed up or were extinguished, bombers flew, bombs fell. Apart from Hitler, Goering was the only man in Germany entitled to take decisions on his own responsibility. The sense of effortless power was intoxicating and enervating.

The tense summer of 1938 dragged on and Goering's uneasiness grew. Germany was not ready for a general war, nor could Marshal Goering contemplate with equanimity the prospect of losing, in defeat, all that he had now gained. Yet openly to oppose the Führer's policy would be unthinkable –

162

and very dangerous. Ribbentrop, moreover, took good care that Goering should be kept out of the realm of foreign politics. The Marshal might have been "Hitler's Diplomat" in the old days of the struggle for power, but Ribbentrop now occupied that position, and he was jealous of it.

At no time had the Marshal been friendly with Ribbentrop. The man had always tried to elbow him aside. There had been the occasion of the coronation of King George VI and Queen Elizabeth in London, for instance. Goering had set his heart on representing Germany at a ceremony of the kind which he loved best – a blending of pomp and tradition. Yet Ribbentrop, from the Embassy in Carlton House Terrace, had sent Hitler the translation of a speech made in the House of Commons by Miss Ellen Wilkinson, in which wounding references were made to Goering's blood-stained boots which must never be allowed to pollute British soil. Ribbentrop suggested that Goering's presence at the Coronation might lead to unfortunate incidents, and Hitler, yielding, appointed General von Blomberg to represent him in London. Ribbentrop was never forgiven for this piece of official meddling. But for him Hitler would never have noticed Miss Wilkinson's remarks.

Goering, who to the end of his days was firmly convinced that he possessed a peculiar ability to deal with foreigners, resented his isolation bitterly, yet was powerless to end it. Neither the Army nor the German people wanted war – that was clear enough. Yet war might come.

The Party Congress, held as usual at Nuremberg at the beginning of September, was a tense, unhappy business. The German upper classes found themselves pilloried in the speeches of the Nazi leaders as little better than the Czechs themselves – potential traitors to a man. Prudently Goering broke off a very discreet flirtation with such potentially mutinous Army leaders as General von Witzleben, commanding the Berlin District, General von Brockdorff, his opposite number at Potsdam, and – most important of the three – General Beck, Chief of the General Staff. He formed up dutifully behind the Führer. Although in a private conversation with foreign diplomats at Nuremberg – a conversation which Ribbentrop had not been able to prevent – the Marshal had declared that a peace conference must be called and the quarrel with Czechoslovakia resolved without resort to war, yet in public Goering was, as always, the "Führer's Faithful Paladin," as Nazi journalists loved to call him.

Speaking at Nuremberg on September 10, Goering gave little sign of the doubts and hesitations which worried him. He made bitter reference to the "atrocities" which, according to Goebbels' propaganda, were being committed by the Czechs on the persons of innocent, peaceful Sudeten-Germans:

"A petty segment of Europe," Goering declared, "is making life unbearable for humanity. The Czechs, that miserable, pygmy race, without culture – nobody even knows where they came from – are oppressing a cultured race, and behind them is Moscow and the eternal mask of the Jewish devil!"

From a would-be peacemaker these were strange words, yet Goering, as he stood by the microphones before a cheering audience of loyal Nazis, certainly believed them. As the Swedish psychiatrist had observed, years before, his personality "did not hang together coherently. At one moment he displayed one personality, and a few minutes later quite a different one."

To recapitulate the events which led to the Munich Agreement would be wearisome. The "moderates" – Goering, Schwerin-Krosigk, the Minister of Finance, Baron von Neurath, Chairman of the completely ineffectual Cabinet Council – sought, timidly, to bring their views to Hitler's notice, but Ribbentrop stood always at the Führer's elbow. On September 28 these three men even succeeded in penetrating the barriers with which the Führer was surrounded. As Commissioner for the Four Year Plan, Goering, with the support of his companions, represented to Hitler that Germany was financially incapable of fighting a war against first-class Powers. Hitler brushed these representations aside, and as he was speaking the telephone rang. Benito Mussolini was on the line from Rome with a new plan for peace. To him Hitler conceded what he was prepared to deny to his own advisers. He would meet Mussolini, Chamberlain and Daladier in Munich. There would be no war . . . yet.

July 1938 had brought Goering great personal happiness. He had become a father. Carin, already aged 34 at the time of her marriage to Goering, had been prevented by ill-health from having a child by him. Now Emmy, although no longer a very young woman, gave him what he had always wanted. Of course the child would be a boy – that was understood. In the Berlin nursing-home which Emmy had chosen for her confinement, notices posted in the corridors informed visitors and staff that "Frau Goering requests the utmost quiet before, during and after the birth of her son!" Yet the baby was a girl, and the parents christened her Edda, after Mussolini's daughter.

Goering's enemies, even those in the highest ranks of the Party, seized upon the occasion of his daughter's birth to cast doubt upon the child's paternity. Julius Streicher, now the Jew-baiting Gauleiter of Franconia, publisher of the obscenely pornographic *Stürmer,* was particularly assiduous in spreading these reports, and to that assiduity he owed in part his expulsion from the Party some months later. The whisper went round that Goering had been impotent since that wound in the groin, fifteen years before. Another version alleged that he was homosexual. It is sufficient to say that no medical evidence has ever been produced which would indicate that Goering might be impotent – at Nuremberg seven years later the military doctors agreed on this. The man's whole life was itself a denial of the charges of homosexuality. Finally a single glance at the pretty little girl who for some time after the War lived quietly with her mother near Nuremberg shows her to be Hermann Goering's child.

Hardly had the German people, and not least Marshal Goering, heaved a sigh of relief at the Munich "settlement" than a fresh crisis came to trouble the autumn shooting-party. For Goering the sport had been interrupted, as it was every year, by the gathering of "Old Fighters," held each year in Munich on November 9 to commemorate the *Putsch* of 1923. On the following morning he returned to Berlin and there drove through streets littered with glass from shattered shop-windows, past mobs of looters engaged in smashing and pillaging shops, through the acrid smoke of fires. The Marshal soon learned what was afoot. As a reprisal for the murder in Paris of a minor German diplomat by a Jew, Goebbels, virtually on his own responsibility, had loosed the S.A. and Hitler Youth, and thereby the mob on Jewish shops and businesses throughout the Reich.

Goering was furious. Not as a humane man who abhorred the suffering which this "cold pogrom" must involve, but as the Commissioner for the Four Year Plan, fearful of the effects of this insensate mob-violence upon the German economy. The Marshal sought out Goebbels at the Propaganda Ministry and there expressed his views so vigorously that the "Little Doctor" hurried to Hitler and complained. At the Chancellery the two opponents met, while Hitler ordered them to compose their differences. "This is the last dirty business to which I'll lend my name!" Goering finally declared. Nevertheless, he sat down with Goebbels and other Ministers on November 12, to draw up decrees which were to settle, once and for all, the position of such Jews as still remained at large in the Third Reich.

That meeting, the minutes of which were captured by the Allies in 1945, gives some idea of the light-hearted manner in which Goering approached political matters and of his general attitude towards the whole Jewish question. Goebbels, the fanatic, proposed a series of measures which would make the life of a Jew in Germany even more intolerable than it already was. The Minister of Transport, he suggested, should issue a decree allowing Jews to travel only in a special compartment in each train, and then only if all Germans in the train were already seated.

"I think," said Goering, "that it would be far more sensible to give the Jews their own compartment in any case. If that is full of Jews, then any other Jews who want to travel will have to stay at home. . . . I'd give the Jews a special coach or compartment to themselves. If the train were ever overcrowded with Germans there wouldn't be any need for a law. The Jews would simply be thrown out, even if it meant that they had to sit on the engine for the whole trip!"

Might it not be as well, Goebbels went on to propose, to forbid Jews access to German woodlands. At the moment they walked about the Grunewald forest near Berlin in an extremely provocative manner, to the indignation of all good Germans.

"All right," said Goering, "we'll give the Jews a special bit of Grunewald to themselves, and Alpers (Chief Forester of Prussia) will stock it with the various animals which look so damned like Jews – elks, for instance – they have great hooked noses. They'd soon settle down!"

Goering ended this conference with the following words:

"I shall say in the decree that the Jews in Germany, as a whole, are to pay a fine of 100,000,000 marks for their monstrous crimes and so on and so forth. That will hit them hard! The swine won't commit another murder in a hurry! I must say, though, I wouldn't care to be a Jew in Germany. If the Reich goes to war with a foreign Power in any foreseeable future, one of the first things we Germans will have to think about is a big settlement of accounts with the Jews. The

Führer is in any case going to approach the countries which are most agitated about the Jewish question about a solution to the question of Madagascar. He told me so on November 9. He'll say to the other countries: 'What, are you still chattering about the Jews? Take them then!' There's another possibility too. The rich Jews might buy a big strip of territory for their co-religionists in the United States or Canada or somewhere like that."

As always, Marshal Goering took a broad view of the problems with which he was confronted.

The "Peacemaker"

AT the outset of a year destined to see the beginning of a war which was to end in ruin for Goering, as for his country, it may be well to consider for a moment the personal position of the man who, only six years before, had been a comparatively unknown politician, living largely upon loans provided by friends and supporters. As he supervised the Christmas celebrations at Carinhall in 1938, even he might have felt reasonably satisfied with the material situation in which he found himself.

Carinhall itself, decked out now with Christmas greenery, was, with its silk and silver hangings, its crystal chandeliers, the gold-plated bath, the picture gallery, the private cinema, the swimming-bath, the bowling-alley and taproom, a palace such as few European monarchs possessed and which, for that matter, few of them would have cared to own. Carinhall was built within ten months according to Goering's own designs by two young architects, Hetzelt and Tuch. Every detail from roof to door-handle was Goering's own design. The gardens around the castle were laid out as Goering wished them. He selected the furniture, the inner decorations, tapestry, carpets and lamps, as well as almost all paintings and other objects of art. An avenue of about two miles led to Carinhall's inner court and the main building, flanked by two long buildings which contained kitchens and storage rooms in one wing and servants' flats in the other wing. In the centre of the inner court stood, in a large water basin, a rock crowned by a sitting wild boar.

This vast house and the game preserve which surrounded it were maintained by the Prussian Finance Ministry out of State funds. Its interior decorations, which had cost millions of marks, had been financed to a large degree by industrialists who felt that in contributing to Marshal Goering's comfort they would, in the long run, be contributing to their own. In 1933, for example, Herr Reemtsma of Hamburg, Germany's largest cigarette manufacturer, gave Goering, with Hitler's full approval, the sum of 3,000,000 marks (£150,000) and a further 1,000,000 marks each year thereafter until the outbreak of the war. "Pilli" Koerner and Goering's principal private secretary, Dr. Erich Gritzbach, never hesitated to ask prominent industrialists for gifts whenever their master happened to require money for any particular purpose, nor were the gifts ever refused. In a trial in Hamburg after the war, Herr Reemtsma admitted having given to Goering in actual cash or gifts a total of 12,250,000 marks. But he declared that the sums were not voluntary gifts, but were "extorted by threats."

Nor were the other great industrialists behindhand in the race for Goering's favour, a race which became more and more hectic and more and more costly to the competitors as the Marshal's power and popularity increased. The special accounts kept by the Thyssen Bank (an appropriate tribute to the man who had first lent Goering money to any considerable extent) and the Deutsche Bank grew fat on these gifts, and to a lesser extent on literary royalties. Not only did Goering do well, as has already been mentioned, out of his own book, but he had the best of reasons to welcome the success of *Hermann Goering – the Man and his Work,* written by Erich Gritzbach. This biography is remarkable more particularly for the fact that its subject insisted in sharing the profits from it with its author; the profits, thanks to Nazi advertising and sales promotion, were exceedingly large.

A great deal of money was needed and a great deal of money was found. The hunting-box at Rominten in East Prussia, for instance, which Hitler had lent to Goering in the early days of National Socialist power, proved to be an expensive affair. The place had been Royal property, and after the departure of the Hohenzollerns the property of the German State. But what had been good enough for Germany's Emperors and for bourgeois politicians was not, as has already been seen in the case of the Prime Minister of Prussia's residence in Berlin, good enough for Hermann Goering. The old castle at Rominten was transformed. Walls were knocked down and rebuilt, great reception rooms thrown out worthy of the parties which the Master Hunter of the Reich was to give in them, electric heating was installed throughout the castle and the interior decoration completely renewed in accordance with the Marshal's lavish tastes. After dark, on the nights when Goering and his guests returned from their hunting, the court-yard of Rominten was illuminated by great flaming torches. Goering always liked to assert that the cost of these alterations had been borne by his "Special Account," but in fact a large part of it was financed by the generosity of the late Sir Henry Deterding, the creator of the Shell Oil Group, who had known Goering in the latter's early days, long before he rose to a celebrity, and had always liked him. Among Sir Henry's other gifts to his friend were a number of pictures, including a Rembrandt valued at 500,000 marks (£25,000).

At Berchtesgaden the Marshal owned a modest little house – modest because it must not clash with Hitler's neighbouring Berghof – which by Goering's standards was almost austere in its simplicity. There will be mention of other estates belonging to Marshal Goering before this narrative is ended.

Two other bank accounts, divided like the "Special Account" between the Thyssen Bank and the Deutsche Bank, ministered to the Marshal's needs. Goering's "Private Account" received his personal revenues derived from his salary as Field-Marshal, his salary as Prime Minister of Prussia and the various other "normal" sources of revenue upon which he drew. This account was used for his day-to-day personal expenses and for those of his family. The "Military Account" defrayed expenses in connection with Goering's duties as Commander-in-Chief of the Luftwaffe, and was regularly replenished from State funds. 1939 was to bring two further accounts into being.

The most diligent investigation has never been able to compute exactly how much money Goering had at his disposal at any single point in his career. The fact is that he always had as much money as he wanted. When funds ran short there was always a new source of revenue to be tapped, a new benefactor who would be only too willing to help the Marshal to finance any project which lay close to his heart. Goering could face 1939 with confidence.

Yet the shadow of Hitler's displeasure lay for the first time on Carinhall during that Christmas of 1938. Although gifts

169

poured in to the master of the house, to his wife, and for the first time to little Edda, the Christmas fun in the great mansion was no more than half-hearted. As usual the whole staff assembled on Christmas Eve, and for each man or woman there were parcels beneath the huge Christmas tree and much food and drink and singing. Yet for Goering the pleasure had gone out of the festival, for the bitterness of Ribbentrop's triumph took all the savour from the joys of Christmas.

At least Goering could reflect, he had not joined those Generals who, believing at the time of Munich that a European war must lead to the defeat and destruction of Germany, had made half-hearted bids for his support. Rather than allow Germany to be launched upon a war in which she could not succeed, these Generals were in principle prepared to overthrow Hitler's Government. For this purpose they needed the support of at least one National Socialist leader, and before Munich they had put out timid feelers in Goering's direction. These overtures had not been very decisive, since Goering's lack of moral courage was well known and his record for loyalty (save only to Hitler) was none too brilliant. Nor were these shy approaches enthusiastically received, for although Goering was sincerely opposed to war – at least at that moment – he was even more sincerely terrified of Hitler and of Heydrich. In the event Ribbentrop had triumphed and Czechoslovakia had fallen into Hitler's lap without the firing of a shot. General Beck, the Chief of the General Staff, and General von Rundstedt, the protagonists in the plan to overthrow Hitler, had resigned their appointments. Goering still sat in Carinhall, the second man of the German Reich and the "Paladin of the Führer." Yet even the feeble support that he had given to a peaceful solution of the Czechoslovak problem at the time of Munich had earned him Hitler's displeasure. Thank God, at any rate, that he had not compromised himself further.

When Hitler, dropping the mask of legality with which he had hitherto sought to conceal his acts of perfidy, marched his troops into what remained of Czechoslovakia on March 14, 1939, and thus finally destroyed that Republic, as he had always intended to do, no word came from the palace in the Schorfheide. This time there was no risk of war – the Western Democracies had been lulled into a sense of false security by the Munich Agreement – but the whole affair was unwelcome to Goering because it further vindicated Ribbentrop's policy. Perhaps, as the German tanks rattled through the snow-clad streets of Prague while his own bombers roared above them, he may have recalled the word of honour given by him to the Czechoslovak Minister only a year before. If he did remember it, it was hastily put away into a back attic of the mind which already contained an assortment of similar lumber.

The year 1939 brought with it a more pleasant reminder of the past. On his death some years before Ritter von Eppenstein had left his castle at Mauterndorf to his widow, that Fräulein von Schandrowitz whose marriage to the old man during the first war had so gravely inconvenienced the Goering family as a whole and Hermann Goering in particular. Feeling that he could now afford to be generous, Goering had resumed friendly relations with the widow and had even awarded her the Hubertus Order, created by himself for bestowal upon the most deserving of German sportsmen. Now Frau von Eppenstein too died and had left the castle to the man who had spent his boyhood there. At long last Goering had come into his inheritance, and the fact that he now no longer required the castle and a great estate took nothing from the relish of ambition achieved.

Yet pleasure was short lived, for as the spring of 1939 gave place to a warm and glorious summer fears of war again revived. Poland this time was the target, first, as usual, for the cannons of Doctor Goebbels' propaganda, but later it seemed more and more likely, as the weeks went by, for the guns with which the German arsenals became every day better stocked. Once again all that Goering had, all that he was, might at any time be placed in jeopardy, and now the Generals made no overtures for his assistance. The time had come to make another move – a very discreet move – for peace.

In 1934 Goering had made the acquaintance of a distinguished Swedish business-man, Mr. Birger Dahlerus. The circumstances of the meeting were unusual. Mr. Dahlerus was engaged at that time to a German lady but found it almost impossible to marry her, so many and complicated were the obstacles thrown in his path by National Socialist law in the matter of his fiancée's considerable property in Germany. Accustomed to the democratic methods of Sweden, Mr. Dahlerus decided to go straight to the man at the top and to state his case to him.

The preliminaries of the interview, which took place in Goering's office, were daunting enough. Through the closed double doors, outside which Mr. Dahlerus waited, came the sound of the Marshal's voice raised in furious anger. Presently Dr. Furtwängler, the conductor of the Berlin Philharmonic Orchestra, emerged from the room looking flustered and miserable. He had been pleading with Marshal Goering against the dismissal of his Jewish orchestra leader, and the Marshal, less pliant in such matters when officially approached than when asked to do favours for Jews by his wife, had refused to intervene. Undaunted by this unpromising prelude, Mr. Dahlerus walked boldly into the office and stated his case. "The Nazis," he said, "won't let me marry the lady I love! Do you think Swedes ought to be treated like this in the Third Reich!"

Goering, his temper already frayed, was inclined to take issue with his visitor, but in the end he promised to investigate the whole affair and to remove the difficulties of which Mr. Dahlerus complained, if in fact he found them to exist. They did exist, and Goering instructed the Hamburg courts to set them aside. Mr. Dahlerus was impressed by this evidence of Goering's good faith, and told the Marshal so. In thanking him, he inquired whether he could do anything to help Thomas von Kantzow, Carin's son by her first marriage who was then beginning his business career in Sweden. The offer went straight to Goering's heart. He took the hand of his Swedish visitor and said, his voice trembling with emotion, "You couldn't have said anything nicer than that!" Two years later, in response to a request telephoned to Stockholm by Goering, Dahlerus found Thomas von Kantzow a job.

Thereafter Mr. Dahlerus, whose affairs quite often brought him to Berlin, saw Goering at least once a year, and at each meeting brought him news of the outside world. He found the Marshal very ready to listen and eager to express his own views, particularly in matters of foreign affairs. Although the two men were not close friends, they liked one another well enough.

In June 1939 Mr. Dahlerus visited London on business and was deeply impressed by the determination to resist any further German aggression which he heard expressed on every side. Since his journey led him from London to Berlin, on the way back to Sweden, he took the occasion of visiting Goering on July 5 and of explaining to him the British point of view as he had heard it expounded by his friends in England. At any cost, he said, the British would make a German attack on Poland a *casus belli*, and although they might not be able to bring any direct help to that country in the first days of her resistance, an attack by Germany on her neighbour would precipitate a war with England whose consequences would be unpredictable.

At first Goering sought to brush aside these traveller's tales, but Dahlerus persisted doggedly in his assertions. If, he said, the

German Government did not realize how serious the situation was, it was time that some leading members of it came together with a few influential Englishmen who would present the British point of view more authoritatively than he himself had been able to do. He added that three English businessmen, whose views had particularly impressed him when he had met them in London, were now in Copenhagen, and he suggested that they should come to Berlin and there give a reasoned answer to the question which, above all others, seemed to occupy Goering:

Was Great Britain bluffing or not?

Goering agreed to this suggestion, the Englishmen came, and Dahlerus carried their reply to Carinhall. In the meanwhile Goering had asked Hitler whether he would have any objection to a meeting between himself and a party of British businessmen somewhere in Sweden, and Hitler replied that he would not, provided that all precautions were taken to ensure that the gathering remained secret.

A month passed before the meeting actually took place, a month during which Dahlerus laboured tirelessly for its success, travelling between London, Stockholm and Berlin. At last, on August 7, the parties met, not in Sweden but at Mrs. Dahlerus' German estate at Sönke Nissen Koog in North Friesland, close to the Danish frontier.

The Polish crisis was then, if not at its height, at least nearing boiling-point. As Goering's cars drove up to the modest country house over which the Swedish flag flew, giving an air of neutrality to the proceedings, seven British business-men, none of them in any way connected with politics, waited to receive the formidable Marshal and to present to him, as best they could, their country's standpoint.

The meeting was friendly, but both sides were determined. Firmly the Englishmen stated their case and Goering as firmly replied to it. He complained of the "chilly" attitude adopted by Great Britain towards the National Socialist Government, of the frequent criticisms of that Government's actions in the British Press and the proofs which Great Britain had often given of her unworthy distrust of Germany's actions and of the motives which lay behind them. In the crucial matter of Hitler's treachery in invading Czechoslovakia Goering could produce no better arguments than those which the German Foreign Office had given at the time of the invasion. It seemed to those who heard him that on this point he spoke without conviction and, indeed, against his own beliefs.

Yet he did not hesitate to give those with whom he spoke his "sacred assurance as a statesman and an officer" that the German demands for Danzig, which were the ostensible reason for her quarrel with Poland, and for a revision of the conditions existing in the Polish corridor, implied no intention of encircling Poland, and once granted would not be followed by any further demands upon that country. Had a Czech been present at the meeting this assurance in itself would have seemed to be ominous.

At the luncheon which followed the morning's meeting Goering proposed a toast to the English delegates and a further general toast to peace. There was no insincerity in this action. For the British Goering had always had a very genuine liking, little though he knew them, and as for peace – that he most earnestly desired, provided it would be achieved without any risk of disloyalty to Hitler on his part or even of the slightest appearance of disloyalty. The meeting ended that evening with a proposal from the British delegation that a four-Power conference should take place, and this proposal Goering undertook to convey to Hitler, giving it as his opinion that it might very well be possible to hold such a conference.

The rest of the story has been told by Mr. Dahlerus himself in his book *The Last Attempt*, and in the evidence which he gave before the Nuremberg tribunal. He told of his meeting with Hitler, at which the fawning and obsequious behaviour of Goering towards his Führer astonished and disgusted him. He spoke of his contacts with the British Foreign Office and with the British Embassy in Berlin, of meetings with Goering in the railway train, lying just outside Berlin, which became his headquarters as war drew nearer. At every meeting Goering expressed to his Swedish visitor his desire for peace. Yet he knew, none better, the preparations for Poland's destruction which were already complete. As he was negotiating with Dahlerus, and through him in a sense with Great Britain, Goering knew and had personally approved of Hitler's plans for war on Poland and Great Britain. Yet he wanted peace – provided there could be no question that any risk to himself might be involved in its attainment. To his sister, Olga Rigele, he said at this time, putting his arms about her shoulders and with tears in his eyes, "Well, you see, everybody is for war! Only I, the soldier and Field-Marshal, am not!"

But war it was to be, and while he haggled on the one hand with his Swedish acquaintance and on the other approved of the plans for Poland's destruction which Hitler and his Generals had made, Goering played to admiration his role on the larger stage which had the whole German people for its audience. In an interview which occupied almost the entire front page of every German newspaper, he declared that no enemy bomber could possibly hope even to cross the frontier of Germany. "If a single enemy bomb falls on German soil," he announced, "then my name is Meier!" These comforting assurances put heart in people now by no means as fearful of war as they had been a year before. The bold headlines containing Goering's declaration were flourished triumphantly in the face of any visiting Englishman who might be recognized as such, and any protest which he made at the obvious absurdity of Marshal Goering's claim was cheerfully laughed off. The popularity of Hitler's "Paladin" was paying good dividends in preparing Germany for war, even though the "Paladin" himself might wish for peace.

That Goering did – for whatever motives – at that time wish for peace is shown by an incident which occurred soon after the outbreak of war, but which it may be well to record here. The indefatigable Mr. Dahlerus was surprised to receive on September 22, 1939, a telephone call from Mr. Victor Mallet, the British Minister in Stockholm. The Minister asked whether Mr. Dahlerus would be prepared to go at once to Oslo, and Dahlerus readily assented. Next day, in the British Legation in Oslo, he was surprised to meet Sir George Ogilvie-Forbes, whom he had last seen a few weeks before as Counsellor of the British Embassy in Berlin. Sir George handed the Swedish intermediary a memorandum from the British Government in which the Prime Minister, Mr. Neville Chamberlain, after stating his personal belief that no possibility existed of bringing the war to an end by negotiation, went on to say that if there were any such possibility, discussions could only take place, as far as His Majesty's Government was concerned, provided that not only the future of Poland but also that of Austria and Czechoslovakia were discussed, and that the wrongs already done to Poland by Germany were rectified before any peace negotiations began.

Dahlerus immediately left Oslo for Berlin and saw Hitler there on September 26. He found the Führer in an uncompromising mood, although there seemed to be some hope that he might be ready to discuss the future status of Austria and Czechoslovakia with his enemies. As for withdrawing German troops from Poland, that, Hitler said, was out of the question.

With a heavy heart Dahlerus flew on to London, where on September 30 he met the Prime Minister and the Foreign Secretary, Lord Halifax, and dined with Sir Alexander Cadogan, leaving again for Germany on the following day after a second meeting with Mr. Chamberlain. He carried with him to Berlin the British Prime Minister's assurance that he would never, in any circumstances, negotiate with the National Socialist Government of Germany, but that he was prepared to discuss a settlement with the "German nation" – that is to say with a new German Government. Moreover, Mr. Chamberlain added, the world must be provided with solid guarantees against any renewal of such German aggression as had kept Europe on tenterhooks for the past two years and had now thrust her into war.

On October 1 Dahlerus was again in Berlin and he drove straight to Carinhall. Goering greeted him genially.

"Well, Mr. Dahlerus, tell me all about your visit to London," he said. "How did it go?"

The Swede told his host that he thought the position extremely serious, whereupon Goering cast an anxious look about his study. Even there, Heydrich might have installed his microphones.

"Come out into the garden," Goering said, and led Dahlerus to the middle of a large lawn.

"Now," said Goering, "tell me all about it."

"Marshal Goering," Dahlerus replied. "Do you work for your country or for Hitler? Because if you work only for Hitler there is no hope."

For some seconds Goering stood sunk in thought. Then he looked up sharply.

"Can you come back tomorrow at 11 o'clock?" he asked.

Dahlerus agreed. Goering, he thought, was perhaps too busy for any lengthy conversation at the moment, and that in the circumstances did not seem unreasonable. But Goering led him back to the house, and there for two hours detained him in a long talk which dealt only with trivialities. At last the Swede left Carinhall thoroughly bemused.

Punctually at 11 o'clock on the morning of October 2 Dahlerus was back at the mansion in the Schorfheide. As he sat in Goering's great study, awaiting the arrival of the Field-Marshal, he was surprised to encounter a thin haggard man, whose dark bushy eyebrows contrasted strangely with the grey of his hair. There was an awkward pause before the stranger spoke: "May I introduce myself? I am Admiral Canaris."

Dahlerus, a business-man, knew little enough of the intricacies

176

of the German hierarchy. Had he been, for instance, a diplomat the name of this unexpected visitor would have meant much to him, for Admiral Canaris was the head of the German Intelligence Service – the *Abwehr* – and was known to a few people, including Goering, as an opponent of Hitler's regime, a point of view for which he paid at last in the Flossenburg concentration camp, where he was executed by his own countrymen in 1945. In 1939, however, he was a member of the small oppositional group which at the time of Munich had flirted tentatively with the Field-Marshal, only to renounce, in the face of his indecisive attitude, all hope of collaborating with him in the overthrow of Hitler.

In introducing Dahlerus to Canaris it had been Goering's hope that the Swede would speak frankly to his visitor of the political situation in the outside world as he saw it, and that the Opposition might thus be nerved to take action against Hitler – action in which Goering himself would not be directly involved. This plan failed because Dahlerus had no idea of the identity of the man to whom he spoke, and took him for a spy either of the Foreign Office or of the Gestapo. For twenty minutes Canaris plied him with questions to which the Swede replied with the utmost circumspection. At last the meeting was ended by a summons from Goering, who was now ready to see Dahlerus. That interview was short and unproductive. Goering promised to think over what Dahlerus had said and promised nothing further.

At Christmas time that year Dahlerus received from Goering a gold cigarette-case on which were inscribed the donor's personal thanks for his friend's efforts on behalf of peace. Further the Marshal would not go.

Unexpected Ally

MEANWHILE war had come and its first days seemed to justify all Goering's facile optimism. For years he had assured Hitler that the Air Force was invincible and that it alone could win Germany's wars for him. The outcome of the Polish campaign seemed to justify his faith. Goering's bombers swept ahead of the advancing Army, battering a path for them across the

Polish plain to Warsaw. The Polish Air Force – small, outdated and inefficient – was for the most part destroyed on the ground. There was no opposition as the bombs of the Luftwaffe tore into Polish homes and Polish earth. It did indeed seem as if the Army, lumbering along in the wake of Goering's squadrons, played only a secondary part in the whole adventure. The film "Baptism of Fire," which Goering ordered to be made for his own glorification and that of his Service in those early days of a long war, portrayed well enough the savage spirit of those first intoxicating days of victory.

Within three weeks of the first assault upon her, Poland lay prostrate at the feet of the Nazis and of their Russian accomplices who had been swift to claim their share of the corpse. The victorious squadrons were withdrawn to the West, where there was little enough for the present that they could do. Occasionally an antiquated Blenheim engaged on hazardous photo-reconnaissance along the Belgian-German frontier fell a prey to one of Goering's Messerschmitts. A few British bombs did in fact fall on German soil during the winter of 1939 to 1940, but the damage which was done by these raids was so trifling that it hardly invalidated Goering's promises to the German people.

Christmas 1939, therefore, was a far more cheerful affair at Carinhall than had been its predecessor. During the early part of the new year, however, Goering made a decision which was to have disastrous consequences not only for himself but for Germany. The results of the Polish campaign seemed to prove that the Luftwaffe, as it stood, was good enough to meet any force which might be thrown against it. The Ju 87 and 88, the Me 109 and 110 had all proved themselves more than adequate in the war against Poland. Germany seemed to require, for what remained of the war, not new types of aircraft but large numbers of the types which had already been proved efficient in battle. On February 7, 1940, Goering accordingly issued an order that all work on new types of aircraft should now be suspended in favour of the mass-production of types already existing. The designers of such aircraft as the Me 210, 309 and 262, the Ta 152, the He 177 and the Ju 188 were forced to put aside their blueprints, while the labour which had been assigned to the construction of these aircraft was diverted to the production of more and more machines of existing types. Not for three years was the deadly effect of this order to become fully apparent.

The campaign in Norway did nothing to shake Goering's confidence in the machines which stood under his command.

The Norwegian Air Force hardly existed, and the few aircraft the British were able to send to Norway were no match for the overwhelming numerical superiority of the German Air Force. Goering felt that he could await the coming campaign in the West with confidence.

One unhappy incident marred the period of waiting for the Field-Marshal. In February 1940 an incautious major of the Luftwaffe, making an unauthorized flight over Belgium, was forced to land in that country. He carried with him, as it happened, the complete German plans for the attack in the West, which were now no longer a secret to the Belgians nor, as the German General Staff was forced (correctly) to presume, from the Allies. Furiously Hitler upbraided Goering for the inefficiency and carelessness of his subordinates, and the Field-Marshal tried, feebly as always, to defend his own Service. The incident was to be but the first of many such, had Goering only known it. Nevertheless by May 9, 1940, all was again ready for the assault upon the Western Powers.

Once again, it seemed, Goering's faith in his men and in the machines which they flew was vindicated. In a month the French Republic was beaten to her knees and the British Army, small although not insignificant, driven from the Continent. All Europe, virtually speaking, lay in the German grip, and Goering felt with some justice that in that success his Air Force had played the major part.

One enemy still remained – an enemy embattled on his island which lay like an aircraft carrier off the coast of continental Europe. His army, disarmed though it now was, had been rescued in spite of all the fury of the Luftwaffe. For the first time Goering's flyers had encountered, in the men of the Royal Air Force, adversaries worthy of their steel, and the result of that meeting had not been too gratifying from the German point of view. The French Air Force had not been ready for action, and bravely as its men had fought, its part in the Battle of France had been a relatively small one. It was the British Fighter Squadrons based on England, battling in the last days of the campaign miles behind the British lines to save their Army, which took a heavy toll of the Luftwaffe. Nevertheless, victory lay with Goering, and with that he was content.

General Milch, his chief adviser, was less satisfied. More closely in touch with the ebb and flow of battle than Goering, he knew that beyond the cliffs which could be seen shimmering in the summer sunshine from the French coast lay reserves of

179

latent power which must be destroyed quickly if they were to be destroyed at all. The evacuation of the British Army from Dunkirk, he explained to his Field-Marshal, had been something of a triumph for the enemy, and this point of view he maintained in spite of Goering's indignation at such blasphemy. As the two men stood together at the German Air Force headquarters at Cap Blanc Nez near Calais, looking out across a few miles of water at the island which still defied them, Milch urged that an immediate attack upon Great Britain must be made. Even as the last weary, grateful men from Dunkirk were setting foot upon English soil, which most of them had never thought to see again, Milch was urging Goering to assault them without delay. Within four days, he said, two Air Fleets commanded by Generals Kesselring and Sperrle could move forward and be made ready for the final tussle. Let the Luftwaffe strike now, while the iron was hot.

Goering as usual hesitated, and in hesitating he lost, perhaps, the battle. Not for two months after the Germans entered Dunkirk did Air Fleets 2 and 3 move into position for their assault upon the British islands.

Goering spent little time at his headquarters. The delights of Paris were his to command, and he did not resist the temptations they offered. France, moreover, reserved for the victorious Marshal pleasures more subtle than those which even the wealthiest tourists can normally enjoy. On June 21, in the little clearing in the Forest of Compiègne, where on November 11, 1918, the Armistice which ended the First World War was signed, Hitler delivered his own armistice terms to France, and Goering was at his side. Here at last, at long last, was his revenge for the humiliation of defeat which he had felt so bitterly twenty-two years before. Here now he stood, his sky-blue uniform ablaze with decorations, in the very restaurant-car in which the German delegates had been forced to set their signature to capitulation which he had always regarded as shameful. Outside that railway coach stood a granite block bearing an inscription in French. Hitler and Goering walked over and read it:

"Here on the 11th November, 1918, the criminal pride of the German Empire succumbed, defeated by the free peoples which it tried to enslave."

It was very satisfying to read that, as the second leader of a newly victorious Germany, to enjoy the warmth of the June sunshine and to know that the shame of defeat had been wiped out.

With the impersonal politeness which is reserved in the best hotels for guests whose distinction makes it impossible to exclude them, but who are nevertheless not particularly welcome, the Hotel Ritz in Paris received the Marshal. Goering surrendered himself to the indolence of his nature, and that surrender communicated itself to his whole Command. Every man in the Luftwaffe, from Milch himself to the humblest aircraftman, knew that for the present at least their Commander-in-Chief cared less about the final stages of a war which he and they regarded as virtually won than for the treasures which the victories already achieved could now shower upon him.

The Ritz, admirable hotel though it is, was not, as might have been foreseen, good enough for Marshal Goering and he cast his eye around Paris for a house in which he could live during his future visits there in manner which befitted his position. One residence seemed to be particularly suitable for his purpose – the British Embassy in the Rue du Faubourg St. Honoré – a large handsome building standing well back from the street, fronted by a gravelled courtyard and cut off from the gaze of the vulgar when necessary by heavy gates. The Embassy was almost deserted. Its staff had long since left to follow the French Government to Bordeaux and had returned thence sadly to England. One man only remained on guard – Mr. Christie, once a cavalryman and now the sole custodian of the building.

One morning the bell on the *porte-cochère* rang. Mr. Christie, looking cautiously through the postern gate, saw outside the German Ambassador, Otto Abetz, whom he had known by sight in pre-war days, and behind him a bulky figure whose identity could not be mistaken. The German Ambassador exuded charm. He had come, he said, with Marshal Goering to inspect the Embassy, which the Marshal believed might make a suitable Paris residence for himself. The Marshal, Abetz added, would be glad to inspect the Embassy at once. Mr. Christie's reply to this suggestion was curt:

"Over my dead body, your Excellency!" he said, and slammed the postern.

Twenty minutes later, in response to a strictly illicit call from Mr. Christie to the American Embassy, who had undertaken the protection of British interests in Paris, the unwelcome visitors went away and never returned. Mr. Christie still guards the gates of His Britannic Majesty's Embassy in Paris.

Unaccustomed as he was to having doors slammed in his face, Field-Marshal Goering took his defeat with tolerably good grace.

Of his other doings in Paris at that time it will be more convenient to speak in a later chapter.

At last the preparations for the assault which was to pulverize British resistance were complete and Goering went north to the headquarters of the Luftwaffe. The experiences of the Polish war, of the battle in Norway and of the defeat of France had indicated that to attack enemy aircraft on the ground is a particularly effective method of destroying them. So at least it had always been, and so Goering assumed it would be in the case of the Royal Air Force. Officers with greater professional knowledge than the Commander-in-Chief himself possessed disagreed with these conclusions, but their doubts were disregarded. For several years Goering's decisions had had the power of law in Germany, and what was the Royal Air Force that it should now invalidate one of them? He decided that the British fighters could be destroyed on the ground by the bombing of their stations, nor could the advice of his experts, and particularly of his chief fighter pilots, deflect him from his purpose.

Accordingly Goering's bombers took off, wave after wave of them, for the fighter stations of southern England, and returned often severely mauled but reporting that they had dropped their bombs upon the objectives which had been assigned them. Goering, standing in the headquarters of General Kesselring, received these reports with delight, and as each one came in he crossed off from the Order of Battle map the British squadrons which were based upon the fighter station concerned – all the squadrons. Experienced pilots such as Galland, of whom some mention has already been made and who was now a Lt.-Colonel, protested that the mere fact that a British fighter station had been bombed did not necessarily imply the complete destruction of all the aircraft based on it. Goering refused to listen to such defeatist talk. The stations had been bombed – therefore they were wiped out. All the experience of the Polish campaign went to prove that that must be the case. But this time Goering was not launching his squadrons against Poland, and it was not long before events proved the extent of his miscalculation.

At last Goering, who was now taking a keen interest in the campaign, satisfied himself that any British fighter opposition which remained must be negligible. That the Luftwaffe Operations Staff did not share this view was for him a matter of supreme indifference. He gave orders for the daylight bombing of London.

The orders given by Goering to the bombers which were to

carry out the assault on the British capital were deceptively simple. They were to fly with fighter escorts at heights ranging from 21,000 to 23,000 feet, deliver their load upon the recalcitrant British and return to their French bases. Assuming as Goering did, that no considerable force of British fighters was now left to oppose his squadrons, the orders were reasonable enough, but the bomber pilots soon discovered that his assumption was false.

Spitfires and Hurricanes took off in inconveniently large numbers to intercept the invaders, and it seemed, for some reason which the German pilots did not then appreciate, impossible to evade the enemy. The unwelcome appearance of the British defenders might have been more tolerable for the men who managed the bombers had it been possible for the German fighters to stay at all times close to the slower aircraft which they were protecting. That, however, was not possible. The fast, handy Messerschmitts were quite unable to adjust their pace to that of the lumbering bombers, and were forced to peel away from the formation, circle and return to it in order to keep pace with their charges.

It was precisely at these moments that the British fighters chose to deliver their attacks, and the bomber crews became increasingly nervous. They complained to Goering, and the Field-Marshal, with his customary decision, found a simple solution for their problem. The German fighters, he decreed, were in future to fly a straight course and to keep up with the bombers at all times. That this was not only technically impossible but that it also deprived the fighters of their chief asset – that of speed and manoeuvrability – did not apparently occur to Goering. At all events the fighter pilots protested bitterly against this order, and Colonel Galland was particularly loud in his expostulations. How, Galland inquired, could a Me 109 possibly be expected to comply with Goering's orders? In fury the Marshal rounded upon him:

"Well, in God's name, what kind of fighters *would* you like, Galland?" he asked.

The young officer's reply came quickly:

"A *Staffel* of Spitfires, sir!" he replied, and his retort went ringing round the Luftwaffe, which was already beginning to have serious doubts about the competence of its Commander-in-Chief.

The daylight raids on London failed and the Luftwaffe was perforce driven back to a policy of night bombing. Goering lost interest in the whole business. There was nothing particularly dashing about the despatch of bombers to an enemy city under cover of darkness. The pulverization of London would be a slow and boring business, and such business had no appeal for the Field-Marshal. It was widely reported in Germany and Great Britain, and is still believed by many people in both countries, that Goering himself flew over London. He never did, and he took no personal hand in the "Blitz." He was interested only in quick spectacular triumphs.

At a later stage in the war Goering expressed his own views of the Battle of Britain. He complained, rather querulously, that the Royal Air Force, which in 1940 was mainly designed for defence, had not in the Battle of France displayed itself in sufficient numbers, and that he had thus been misled as to its true strength.

"The British had decided to give a defensive character to their Air Force," Goering said, "and they had built on that assumption. In particular they had established an exemplary system for locating enemy aircraft. They were very considerably in advance of any other Power in the matter of radar. German aircraft were located without any difficulty and the British fighters could be directed with ease and precision and commanded and directed from the ground."

It can be argued – and it has been argued since Germany's defeat by many of Goering's senior subordinates – that had the Field-Marshal displayed resolution immediately after the evacuation of Dunkirk and ordered an attack upon Great Britain at that time the Battle of Britain would not have been lost by Germany. Again, it is said, the fortune of war might have been reversed but for Goering's insistence that by bombing of fighter stations alone the fighter strength of the Royal Air Force could be destroyed. There seems to be substance in both these arguments and it is not unreasonable to say that, in the summer and autumn of 1940, Goering proved himself a better ally to Great Britain than he realized.

Whatever Goering himself may have felt in his inmost heart, he reacted characteristically to the failure of his airmen. A new and magnificent flying-decoration was instituted by the Field-Marshal – the "Golden Pilot's Badge with Diamonds," a distinction which he awarded first to himself and then to a very small number of deserving fighter pilots.

Much has already been said about Goering's homes – Carinhall, the palace in Berlin (now very little used) and Rominten.

Another palace must now be added to the list, a moving palace in which Goering spent much of his time.

Of all things, Goering loved to travel, to show himself, to receive the applause of as many people as possible in as many different places as possible, to gather the proof that he was loved and respected for which he never ceased to crave. As his bulk increased – he now weighed twenty stone – flying became more and more disagreeable, and in any case Hitler had given orders that he was to fly only when absolutely necessary. Yet travel he must, and just as no ordinary house could be considered good enough to lodge him, so was no ordinary train worthy to carry him where he wished to go. A special train had therefore been built, and its code name was "Asia."

"Asia," in fact, consisted of two trains – a pilot train made up of ordinary coaches, including two which had previously formed part of the celebrated French "Blue Train." It included, however, special wagons for the transport of cars and a coach with shower baths for the troops who accompanied the caravan. Goering's own special train, hauled by two of the heaviest locomotives which the German State Railways could provide, was headed by an open wagon upon which anti-aircraft guns were mounted, while a similar wagon formed the tail of the train. The whole train was specially designed, but the two coaches specially built for Goering's own use were particularly remarkable.

These massive vehicles, specially ballasted with lead in order that their distinguished occupant might feel as little as possible the jolting which is inseparable from railway travel, contained in the first place Goering's immense wardrobe, the greater part of which accompanied him wherever he went. The proper disposition of the Field-Marshal's uniforms took up a good deal of space, so that in the remainder of the coach there was room only for two bedrooms – one for himself and one for Frau Goering – for elaborate toilet arrangements, and for a little panelled study adjoining Goering's sleeping-room.

The second coach was designed as a single large saloon, furnished with heavy mahogany and equipped moreover with a film projector, which when Goering was on the train was used almost every evening for a showing of the latest pictures. The next coach contained Goering's map room and command post, then came a dining-car, and bringing up the rear of the train specially designed coaches to house the Marshal's distinguished guests and senior members of his staff. No fewer than 171 people were permanently assigned to man this train, and its cost was borne on the "Military Account" – whose funds were provided by the State. As the war went on expenditure on the upkeep of "Asia" far exceeded any other item of the Marshal's military expenses.

In October 1940, as German bombers stood ready to deliver their first daylight attacks upon London, the two trains rolled away from Berlin towards the West. In this, the first of many "Royal" progresses which he made in the special train during the war, Goering was accompanied by the two old friends who formed what was ironically called his "Brains Trust." Bruno Loerzer, his friend since the early days of Infantry Regiment 112, had seen in Poland the only active service which the Second World War was to bring him. Now, with the rank of General, his duties were no more arduous than those of being Goering's constant companion. When the Marshal conferred decorations Loerzer stood behind him with the cardboard boxes containing the Iron Crosses. When the General went shopping in Paris or visited the Jeu de Paume, there to inspect the art treasures which his agents had displayed for his selection, there was General Loerzer, always beside his Marshal.

There, too, was "Pilli" Koerner, at the great man's elbow offering advice and flattery which, since it always suited, Goering's prevailing mood, was readily accepted. Colonel von Brauchitsch, son of the Field-Marshal of that name and later Goering's principal A.D.C., concealed his dislike of Loerzer and Koerner as best he could, but worked unremittingly to displace them from the Marshal's side. He never succeeded.

The owner of the special train, incidentally, was now a unique person in a new sense. On July 19, 1940, Hitler, flushed with victory, had created twelve new Field-Marshals, thus depriving Goering of the distinction of being the only man in the German fighting forces to hold that exalted rank. That others – mere professional soldiers – should presume to approach his solitary eminence was unthinkable, and so Hitler had created a new rank, one which had never existed before in German history. As the special train pulled out of Berlin it carried with it Hermann Goering, Reichsmarschall – Marshal of the Great German Reich – once more a unique military figure. The wardrobe in his special sleeping-coach carried now a new set of uniforms, their epaulettes more gorgeous than any that Goering had as yet worn, while in a safe lay the Reichsmarschall's baton, diamond-studded and glorious in its bed of white velvet.

The train's route lay through Brussels and thence into northern

France. It had been carefully studied in advance so that at each likely stopping-place there might be a convenient tunnel in which "Asia" could hide from air observation. Near Calais this forethought was justified for the first time. The trains were shunted into a tunnel and Goering, clambering into his great Mercedes which had been unloaded from the pilot train, drove off to the headquarters at Cap Blanc Nez. He did not propose to tarry there long since other matters claimed his attention, but the presence of a wireless reporter with a recording van gave him an opportunity of displaying himself to the German people as the avenger who was personally directing the first of the great daylight bombing raids on London.

The fact that the R.A.F. had recently dropped a few bombs on Berlin gave point to his remarks. Goering said to the wireless audience: "This moment is a historic one. As a result of the provocative British attacks on Berlin on recent nights the Führer has decided to order a mighty blow to be struck in revenge against the capital of the British Empire. I personally have assumed the leadership of this attack, and today I have heard above me the roaring of the victorious German squadrons which now, for the first time, are driving towards the heart of the enemy in full daylight, accompanied by countless fighter squadrons. Enemy defences were as we expected beaten down and the target reached, and I am certain that our successes have been as massive as the boldness of our plan of attack and the fighting spirit of our crews deserve. In any event this is a historic hour, in which for the first time the German Luftwaffe has struck at the heart of the enemy."

A few days were spent thereafter in sight-seeing. The Commander-in-Chief who was directing Germany's great blow against England found time to visit the beaches of Dunkirk which had seen the last stand of the British Army, and then the train rolled on to Paris, where the royal suite was waiting – still at the Ritz.

Heyday of a Connoisseur

No one who was able to follow the somewhat intricate pattern of Reichsmarschall Goering's wanderings during the war has failed to be impressed with the amount of time which the Commander-in-Chief of the German Air Force was able to devote to visits to Paris. Between the fall of France and the end of 1943 he visited the French capital no fewer than twenty times. Each visit saw the special train rolling over French metals, its arrival dreaded by both German and French railway staffs, since it completely disorganized the time-table, and each visit saw it steaming back to Germany again much more heavily loaded than it had been on the outward run.

Reference has already been made more than once to the Marshal's passion – for it was nothing less – for the collection of art treasures. Soon after the achievement of power by the National Socialists in 1933 Hitler and Goering had conceived a plan whereby the latter was to form, by any means which suggested themselves to him, as magnificent a collection of art treasures as possible. These were to be his to enjoy during his lifetime, and on Goering's death were to pass to the German nation, when they would be housed in a magnificent museum whose site was frequently discussed but never definitely decided. At one moment it was suggested that Carinhall itself should house the collection. Already its ambitious founder saw his palace becoming a tourists' Mecca, and had made plans for the construction of a special railway-line from Berlin to the Schorfheide.

To assemble an art collection worthy of the German nation was, however, an expensive business, which could hardly be brought to a successful conclusion by even the most generous gifts of German industrialists alone. Moreover, Hitler himself had begun to collect *objets d'art*, and soon the competition between him and his "faithful Paladin" became so intense that an unwritten "findings keepings" agreement existed between the two men.

The fall of France, Belgium and Holland provided an ideal solution for Goering's difficulties. Here were art treasures of incomparable beauty and value, and thanks to the convenient arrangement by which the German occupation money stood at a 20 to 1 advantage *vis-à-vis* the currencies of the occupied countries, it was even possible to make a show of paying for whatever took one's fancy, and paying for it at very low rates.

Alfred Rosenberg, the "philosopher" of the National Socialist Party, had soon made the discovery that in wartime philosophy is at a discount. He had little to do and deeply resented his enforced idleness. Now a task was found for him. An organization styling itself the "*Einsatzstab Reichsleiter Rosenberg*" was established to collect, on Hitler's behalf, political material in the occupied countries for the furthering of the "struggle against Jewry and Freemasonry." In July 1940 the "Western Office" of this organization, which was already functioning in Poland, came into operation and Goering lost little time in extending its sphere of activity. On November 5, 1940, the Marshal issued an order in Paris formally authorizing the Rosenberg Organization to include in its duties the confiscation of "ownerless" Jewish art collections, and he contrived so to alter the terms of reference under which the organization worked that the collection of works of art became, in fact, its main business in life.

That other ardent collector, Adolf Hitler, promptly gave orders that the Rosenberg "Western Office", which technically came under his direct command, should forward all works of art confiscated under Goering's decree to Germany, where they were to be placed at the Führer's personal disposal. For the first time Goering set himself deliberately to stultify one of Hitler's orders.

Soon Goering and not Hitler became the dominating personality to whom the Rosenberg Organization was responsible. Rosenberg himself, although personally inclined to carry out Hitler's orders to the letter, was not politically strong enough to oppose the formidable Marshal. Moreover, Goering's command of the Luftwaffe enabled him to place at the disposal of the Rosenberg Organization transport and military personnel for escort duties which would not otherwise have been available to them, and to give military sanction to their looting. Although the art treasures collected by the Rosenberg Organization were in almost all cases confiscated, Goering himself, displaying not for the first time bourgeois scruples which consorted ill with other elements of his character, insisted that no sequestrated property should decorate the walls of Carinhall. He therefore appointed a French expert, M. Jacques Beltrand, to appraise any works of art which took his fancy in the Rosenberg collections. The objects chosen were then forwarded to Goering's headquarters in Berlin, but no money ever passed, although the bills based on M. Beltrand's valuation were sent to Carinhall, nor was any method of payment ever established.

Yet to exercise effective control of the Rosenberg Organization was not sufficient for so ardent a collector as Hermann Goering. He also employed his own agents and an extensive staff to deal with them. Headed by Doctor Erich Gritzbach, who

189

had so obligingly shared the royalties of his biography of Goering with Goering himself, the Marshal's personal staff undertook most of the business transactions involved in assembling his art collection. The financial side of these dealings was handled by the Ministerial Staff, headed by General Karl Bodenschatz, through whose hands passed such money as Goering was willing to pay for the objects which he acquired. Finally the Police Section, appointed by Himmler, whose duties lay as much in supervising the Marshal's movements as in protecting his person, accompanied him, twenty men strong, everywhere. They too made themselves useful in a variety of ways.

Every organization of the German State which might assist in ministering to Goering's passion was enlisted to help him. The *Devisenschutzkommando* (German Foreign Exchange Authority), which established itself in France, Holland and Belgium immediately after the occupation of those countries by the Germans, proved an invaluable ally. Whenever an official of this Authority discovered, in the vaults of a bank or elsewhere, an art collection which might be of interest to the Reichsmarschall, he lost no time in informing Goering's personal Staff of his find. The collection was then inspected, such articles as might interest the Marshal were removed from it and displayed with other loot upon the great man's next visit to the country concerned. In this manner no less than eighteen private collections were confiscated in France alone and at least two in Belgium.

Although Holland and Belgium produced many valuable treasures for the Marshal's pleasure, France was his happy hunting-ground. The Paris art market was by far the most active in Europe. With the fall of France, German buyers, their pockets bulging with invasion marks, descended like locusts upon the Paris art shows. Few French dealers could resist the temptation to fleece the ignorant Teuton, and that the ignorant Teutons, including Goering, for all his expert advisers, were sometimes thoroughly fleeced is a matter for no doubt whatever. Though Goering secured a certain amount of rubbish in France, he also obtained, at no personal cost, paintings, tapestries and statues, some of which have long been numbered among the glories of Western civilization. Although the bills for the objects confiscated by the Rosenberg Organization were never settled, a large amount of money did find its way from the Marshal into the pockets of the owners of treasures which he coveted. This money was drawn from the "Art Fund," controlled by General Bodenschatz but supervised by Goering's private secretary, Frau

Grundtmann-Kornatski, and after her death in 1942 by Fräulein Limberger, her successor. Of the sources from which money poured into the "Art Fund" only a few have been definitely established. In December 1940 the balance standing to the credit of this account was 3,000,000 marks, and it may be assumed that most of this money was provided from State funds.

Some of it, however, came from other sources. Generous Herr Reemtsma contributed no less than 500,000 marks in the course of 1943, Doctor Kurt Herrmann, a wealthy industrialist from Leipzig, paid 350,000 marks into the account in that year, and it became the custom for those competitors for Goering's favour who wished to give the Marshal a birthday present which he would really appreciate to pay into the "Art Fund" a sum of money sufficient to enable him to buy some treasure which he particularly desired to possess. Doctor Gritzbach was always ready to inform them of his master's needs.

The German currency laws which followed the Forces of Occupation throughout defeated Europe afforded for the Marshal many convenient loop-holes which enabled him to carry out deals quite impossible, even then, for anyone but himself to negotiate.

By January 1941 the Rosenberg Organization, working under the powers vested in it by Goering two months previously, had become an open scandal – a scandal which in the opinion of the military authorities was damaging to the good name of the German Army. In a secret memorandum addressed by the Military Commander in France to Berlin on January 29, the Army pointed out that the rights of the Reich as the Occupying Power were regulated by the Hague Convention on Continental Warfare, which Germany as well as France had ratified, and which therefore was binding upon both parties as Occupation Law. Article 46, paragraph 2, of this Convention prohibited in principle any seizure of private property except in so far as its confiscation was essential for the prosecution of war.

"Seizure of Jewish art property," the memorandum stated, "cannot be designated as confiscation of property essential for warfare, nor as a police measure in the interests of uniform economy in occupied territory. Therefore the German Reich, or Occupation Power, can neither – according to the Hague Convention – expropriate Jewish art property nor substitute itself in the place of the French State.

"The Military Commander within the limits of his Command has to act in accordance with the Führer's orders. But the

Führer's order is carried out in agreement with the order of the Reichsmarschall of November 5, 1940. The Military Administration is therefore exempt from any responsibility of contraventions of the Hague Convention concerning private property. . . . In order to express that the Military Commander in France is in no way responsible for the activity of the Rosenberg Organization, paragraph 6 of the Reichsmarschall's order should be amended as follows:

"(6) Further confiscation of Jewish art property will be affected in the manner heretofore adopted by the Einsatzstab Rosenberg under my [Goering's] direction."

The Reichsmarschall completely ignored this very proper protest. For him the Military Occupation Authorities were a convenient camouflage which he had no intention of abandoning. The Rosenberg Organization therefore continued its activities unchecked.

To give some indication of the extent to which Western Europe was stripped of her art treasures by the Marshal it is worth observing that, according to a list drawn up in October 1942, Goering had by then acquired for his own use in France, and France alone, 237 paintings, 15 stained-glass windows, 28 statues of various kinds, 51 pieces of furniture and 36 carpets and tapestries. The collection included 12 pictures by Boucher, whose delicate, rounded nudes appealed particularly to the Marshal's taste, 4 Cézannes, 13 Corots, 10 Dégas, 5 Van Goghs, 10 Renoirs, a Velasquez, a Reynolds, 3 Rubens and a very large collection of French and Flemish primitives. As an indication of the value set upon the pictures by Goering's "experts" it may be mentioned that the Reynolds "Portrait of a Lady" from the Rothschild Collection was officially valued at 12,000 francs. Van Gogh's celebrated self-portrait, in which the artist appears in a cap and turban smoking a pipe, at 500,000 francs and a Rembrandt at 150,000 francs.

These treasures – which by no means represent the whole of Goering's acquisitions in France alone – were for the most part chosen for his own collection. He was, however, shrewd enough not to reject the paintings of masters whose work had no appeal to him, or even those of painters who, in the Nazi terminology, were "degenerate." For although the paintings of, say, Bracque or Picasso might be condemned both by Goering's own taste and by the official taste of the Third Reich, there were still people in the world who admired them, and in that sense these works of art were, for Goering, as good as money. In the Occupied

Territories of Europe the acquisition of foreign exchange presented no difficulty to the Marshal. He could apply for and obtain as many French francs, Belgian francs or Dutch florins as he required for his transactions. But Swiss francs were in extremely short supply – so short that not even the Marshal of the German Reich could divert them from purposes essential for the prosecution of the war to purposes desirable for the building up of his own art collection. However, with a large number of good impressionist pictures in hand it was possible to approach Swiss dealers with good hope of obtaining from them the pictures which the Marshal required, and for which they would accept neither German marks nor any other currency of German-occupied Europe.

A single example, one of many such transactions, will suffice to illustrate all of them. In 1941 Goering gave twenty-five pictures by French impressionists – Corot, Daumier, Dégas, Van Gogh, Manet, Renoir, and Sisely – to a dealer in Lucerne. He received in exchange seven pictures, four of them by Lucas Cranach the Elder, one by Lucas Cranach the Younger and the two remainder German primitives. The total value of this collection was set at 169,000 Swiss francs. Goering's collection of "swaps" – to use the phraseology of stamp-collectors – consisted, at least as far as France was concerned, of rather less than 100 pictures, the artists ranging from Bracque and Modigliani to Chirico and Matisse. A good many of these useful canvases had been confiscated by the Rosenberg Organization from Jewish collections.

One other case deserves to be cited, if only because the letter which refers to it is one of the few actually signed by Goering which have been found in the complicated archives which deal with his art transactions. As a rule the Marshal preferred to keep himself strictly in the background, but on this occasion, perhaps because British property was involved, he emerged from his anonymity. The letter, dated from Rominten on November 21, 1940, is self-explanatory. It is addressed to Herr Fischböck, Germany's Industrial Representative in Holland, and runs as follows:

"DEAR PARTY MEMBER FISCHBOCK,

I am asking you a favour today which as Industrial Representative to Holland you will easily be able to grant me.

I have purchased from my Dutch art dealer 'D. A. Hoogendick & Co., Keisergracht 640,' some pictures, of which he owns a half-share, while the other half-share belongs to English art dealers – that is to say it is the property of enemy aliens. I have made the purchase by paying the Dutchman the price he asked – in other words I let him have his very considerable profit. Since, however, the other share in the pictures is the property of enemy aliens it must be paid into the account of a trustee appointed by yourself – or perhaps you yourself are the trustee. It is certainly my view that the profit of the English gentlemen should in no circumstances be included in my payment and that they should, at best, receive the value which the picture may have had for them when they bought it. In the case of some of the pictures the Dutchman told me quite plainly that he had calculated his own profit at 100 per cent. – in other words that the pictures had cost the Englishman only half what I paid for them and in some cases even less. Therefore a valuation should be made. Since I have already had the pictures removed to Berlin my expert, the German art dealer Hoefer, could be told to make the appraisal."

The letter goes on to list a Van Dyke portrait for which Goering would consider 10,000 florins a very fair half-share for the Englishmen, a Veronese for which the English owners, in his view, should receive no more than 5000 florins, and several less important canvases for which Goering quotes a very low price.

"I would be glad if you would tell me," the letter concludes, "how the share of the enemy alien owners is to be paid, so that the pictures may become my legal property. I suggest that the German expert – Mr. Hoefer – should make the appraisals in the manner in which I have suggested and submit them to you and then you can communicate to me where the payment must be made.
Thanking you in advance for an early reply,
With best regards and Heil Hitler!
(signed) GOERING."

No money was ever paid by Goering to the German custodian of enemy property in Holland.

In the spring of 1941 Goering paid another visit to France. As usual the Rosenberg Organization and his own agents displayed, in the Jeu de Paume, their choicest pictures, statues and tapestries for his inspection. But this time Goering was in Paris for work as well as for pleasure. The winter had not been a particularly happy one. The daylight bombing raids on London had proved more costly than the Luftwaffe could afford and had given place to the far less dramatic night bombing, which had equally failed to bring the English to their senses. At a meeting of Senior Air Force officers held at the headquarters of Air Fleet No. 3 in Paris, Goering girded bitterly at his officers for their failure to subdue Great Britain and told them also an interesting piece of news. The Führer, he said, intended to attack the Soviet Union, since if he did not do so the Soviet Union would, in the Führer's view, attack Germany. Goering added that he himself did not believe this – one of the few occasions on which he publicly admitted that his opinion and that of Hitler did not coincide – and gave his listeners to understand that the attack on Russia might be expected very shortly.

Senior officers of the Luftwaffe were in despair at the news. A party of engineers had recently been sent to Russia by Goering's closest friend, General Ernst Udet, now responsible for the entire supply and equipment of the Luftwaffe. The Russians, obligingly it must be admitted if, as Hitler thought, they intended to attack Germany, showed the German experts their aircraft factories and sent them back to Berlin, as they doubtless intended to do, in an extremely gloomy mood. The experts reported, for instance, that the output of the engine works at Kuybyshev alone was greater than the combined production of the six main factories which were producing aircraft engines in Germany. Milch, only too well aware of the difficulties which the Luftwaffe now increasingly faced in the West, begged Goering to represent to Hitler the folly of engaging a new enemy. "Now is the greatest moment of your life – your historic hour," Milch said. "You *must* prevent this war." As always Goering, a timid man of peace, agreed; but as always he feared to take any action himself, refused to approach Hitler in the matter, and ordered Milch on no account to do so himself. He declared, moreover, that if the engineers who had just returned from Russia gave the public any hint of what they had seen there, they would immediately find themselves in a concentration camp. As always Goering preferred not to face unpleasant facts.

Great Britain was unbeaten. Indeed she grew stronger every day, thanks to her own efforts and to the help so prodigally given by the United States. The German Embassy in Washington forwarded to Berlin alarming figures of American aircraft production, actual and potential; but these, like the news from Russia Goering preferred to disregard. "The Americans can make,

Fords and Chevrolets, I dare say," he said, "but they can't build aircraft!"

May brought with it a victory. For some time Goering had urged, with what force he had at his command, that the Luftwaffe should be allotted more than the single parachute division which at that time stood under his command. As usual he did not make his demand to Hitler with sufficient frequency or firmness and the Army got the men which he needed. Now his single parachute division was thrown into action in Crete under General Student. They succeeded in their undertaking. Crete was wrested from British hands, but of the Luftwaffe's single airborne division little more was heard for almost a year.

When on June 22, 1941, the German Army, much to the surprise of most of its members, was launched against the Soviet Union, Goering remained quietly at Carinhall. He did not approve of this new venture. The cheerful confidence which he had felt in the efficiency of his own Luftwaffe a year before had already begun to evaporate under the stubborn resistance of the British and the increasingly heavy blows which their bombers were beginning to strike at Germany itself. To add wantonly another enemy to the already sufficiently formidable hostility of the British Empire, to which might at any time be joined that of the United States, seemed to the Marshal folly. Now, therefore, he sulked in the Schorfheide as the German Army, having broken through the light Russian covering forces, began to meet serious resistance and found it unexpectedly tough. In Party circles it was expected that the war with the Soviet Union would last no more than six weeks. Goering did not believe this, but he seemed to have less and less say in things now. It was better to sit quietly at Carinhall, to travel peacefully to Rominten in June. When the great German attack on Moscow began in the autumn, Marshal Goering, Commander-in-Chief of the German Air Force, was shooting in East Prussia.

The Setting Star

REICHSMARSCHALL GOERING was not a superstitious man. Having forbidden the practice of astrology in the Reich since the early months of the war, Hitler himself continued to consult the stars, until at last his best-known adviser, an eminent Swiss astrologer, died in Buchenwald concentration camp for his temerity in predicting for Hitler and for his country a tragic outcome of the war. Many other leading members of the Party followed their Führer's example, but Goering, the materialist, scorned such attempts to peep into the future. Long after Germany's defeat it was reported that he did at one time employ a number of astrologers in the Air Ministry to cast the horoscopes of the Allied war leaders, but nowhere has it been possible to confirm this rumour.

November 1941 nevertheless brought two omens which even to a man robustly free of superstition might well have seemed sinister. Colonel-General Ernst Udet, Goering's old comrade-in-arms from the First World War, his best friend for the past twenty-five years, was now in despair. As *Generalluftzeugmeister* of the Luftwaffe it was Udet's responsibility to keep the Service supplied with all it might need for the successful prosecution of the war. When the enemy put into the air new and improved types of aircraft, so must Udet see to it that Germany herself had machines capable of meeting and defeating them. Radar, anti-aircraft guns, bombs, ammunition of all kinds – to supply these was also Udet's responsibility. More and more this genial, cheerful man perceived that without the full support of his best friend and Commander-in-Chief the ultimate defeat of the Luftwaffe was certain.

Even to an administrative genius the task which had been set to Ernst Udet might well have seemed impossible to fulfil. Udet was no administrative genius. A fighting officer of undoubted gallantry and patriotism and of more than ordinary ability, he was still, although no longer young, more at home in the cockpit of an aircraft than in the offices in which his days were now spent. Yet, served as he was by an enthusiastic staff, Udet might have mastered the difficulties which pressed in upon him had he received from Goering the support which he deserved. He did not receive it.

The fatal order of February 1940, by which Goering had suspended the development of new types of aircraft, lay heavy upon Udet now. He saw clearly enough that the happy carefree days when the Luftwaffe could count upon sweeping everything before it were over. The Battle of Britain had proved that, and worse might now follow:

"If we do not considerably enlarge the numbers of our fighter squadrons," he said in the summer of 1941, "and if we do not adopt a defensive attitude by 1942, the war is lost."

Goering, averse as ever from hearing bad news, living more and more in a rosy world of his own, a world into which the harsh realities of war were allowed to penetrate as little as possible, would not listen to such "defeatist" talk.

In the middle of November 1941 Udet travelled with a heavy heart to the special train "Asia," which at that moment lay on a siding near Rominten, Goering's hunting-lodge. The courtiers gathered about the Marshal noticed that the General seemed to have lost his usual cheerful manner. He was anxious and depressed, nor did his conversations with Goering during that visit do anything to remove his depression. General Udet returned to Berlin, and there, in his magnificent office in the Air Ministry, shot himself.

The German people learned of the death of one of their heroes from the newspapers, but of the true manner of his end they naturally learned nothing. An official communiqué to the Press announced, ironically enough, that General Udet had lost his life in an accident while he was testing a new type of aircraft and that the Führer had ordered a State funeral for him. Something had to be done to save face.

The funeral took place on November 21. In the great Hall of Honour of the Air Ministry in Berlin stood the coffin of the man who had been Goering's friend, covered with the German battle flag and surmounted by his steel-helmet and his sword. The leading fighter pilots of Germany, led by Colonel Galland, formed Udet's guard of honour, but here too one face was missing – that of General Mölders, Germany's Ace of Aces, recently appointed *"General der Jagdflieger,"* a new appointment which gave him supervisory powers over the whole Fighter Arm of the German Air Force. For Mölders too was dead – he had crashed in Germany as he flew back from the Crimea to Udet's burial.

Goering, standing behind a battery of microphones, delivered the funeral oration. He was visibly moved. He spoke of Udet as the founder of the Luftwaffe, his friend and adviser – an airman of genius. Even to himself he probably did not admit that the man who now lay in the coffin beside him had died because of that very friendship which the Marshal now celebrated. Prevented, as he saw it, from doing his duty in giving Germany the aircraft and equipment which her Air Force needed, hamstrung by Goering's refusal to face unpleasant facts and to take the action necessary to meet them, yet continually bullied to provide more and more aircraft by his Commander-in-Chief – when Goering could bring himself to think of such matters – Udet had preferred death to further friendship on such terms.

The funeral of Udet was followed by that of Mölders. As Goering stood by the open grave he turned to Colonel Galland and informed him then and there, before the earth had been shovelled over Mölders' coffin, that he was to be the dead man's successor.

In Germany rumours soon began to circulate. By those who were opposed to National Socialism, and in particular by many German Catholics, it was said that Mölders had been murdered by Goering's order on account of the Catholic faith which he had never ceased to affirm. Some months previously a letter written by the fighter ace to a priest, in which Mölders had deplored the lack of religion in the Luftwaffe, had been illegally printed and widely circulated in southern Germany. In fact, however, those who were close to Goering at this time seem to agree that the incident had very little effect upon the Marshal.

Soon it appeared that Galland, too, might be following in his predecessor's footsteps. His mother, a devout lady, had organized a petition against the closing of a Roman Catholic school in her neighbourhood, and one of Galland's interviews with Goering after his promotion was spent in explaining – as was in fact no more than the truth – that he himself did not share his mother's militant faith and had had no hand in promoting the petition.

Goering decided as usual that the best way of banishing unpleasant thoughts lay in travel, and on the day after Mölders funeral he set off to France to do his Christmas shopping, to inspect the latest pictures which had been collected for his approval, and incidentally to meet Marshal Pétain, the Head of the French "State."

This encounter, which was little more than a formality and which lasted only an hour, took place in the special train at Saint-Florentin, on the frontier between the Occupied and the Unoccupied zones of France. Thereafter Goering was free to spend a pleasant week in Paris – still at the Ritz, although a headquarters, which he never in fact used, had been found for the Marshal on the outskirts of the French capital. Until the Germans left France the château at Gros-Blois stood waiting for its master, its guard ready to turn out at any moment to welcome the Marshal. Now he preferred the Ritz.

The journey back to Berlin lay through Ghent, Antwerp,

Rotterdam and The Hague, and in each city Goering's expert produced treasures for his inspection and approval. That Christmas was a happy one at Carinhall.

January brought further travel. Already the Italians were proving more of a liability than an asset to their German allies. In Libya things were going none too well, and it fell therefore to Marshal Goering to journey to Rome; his purpose, to put fresh heart into the junior member of the Axis.

The days when Goering, a neophyte to the Fascist cause, had sat at the knee of Italy's successful Dictator, learning all he could and resolved one day to emulate the Master, were long past. Now the two men could scarcely abide the sight of one another. Although a genuine admiration for the Italian Dictator had always been one of the less comprehensible sides of Hitler's character, Goering no longer had any respect whatever for the Duce. Nevertheless, on this visit the German Marshal talked at length to Mussolini, and not unhopefully. Goering blamed all Germany's difficulties in Russia upon the cowardice and ineptitude of her Generals, but assured his host that the Soviet Union would certainly be defeated in 1942 and Great Britain by 1943. He succeeded in concealing his dislike of Mussolini and of the country which he ruled – those had been Hitler's orders. Things looked a little better in Libya as the days wore on, and on the whole the visit was a success.

In his diary, published posthumously, Count Ciano, who was Mussolini's son-in-law and Italy's Foreign Minister, gives a snapshot of Goering at this time:

"We had dinner at the Excelsior Hotel and during the dinner Goering talked of little else but the jewels he owned. In fact, he had some beautiful rings on his fingers. He explained that he bought them for a relatively small sum in Holland after all jewels were confiscated in Germany. I am told that he plays with his gems like a little boy with his marbles. During the trip he was nervous, so his A.D.C.s brought him a small vase filled with diamonds. He placed them on the table and counted them, lined them up, mixed them together, and became happy again. . . . To the station he wore a great sable coat, something between what chauffeurs wore in 1906 and what a high-grade prostitute wears to the Opera. If any of us tried a thing like that we should be stoned on the streets. He, on the contrary, is not only accepted in Germany but perhaps even loved for it. That is because he has a dash of humanity."

February, its peaceful routine broken only by a visit from Marshal Antonescu, the Dictator of Rumania, and by an extremely inauspicious call from Quisling, the Fascist traitor of Norway, who was shown out of the Marshal's study after a talk lasting only a few minutes, passed off peacefully enough at Carinhall. The month also gave Goering an opportunity of avenging himself upon at least one of the aristocratic Generals whose indecision and cowardice he lost no occasion to condemn. Sitting, on Hitler's orders, as President of the court martial, he tried General Count Sponeck on a charge of disobeying Hitler's orders by retreating on the Russian front and saw him sentenced to death, although the General spoke up bravely, asserting that he had done no wrong and would again act as he had acted in similar circumstances. The death sentence passed on von Sponeck was commuted to one of penal servitude for life, but the General was murdered in prison by the S.S. in 1944.

The deceitful British had fresh surprises in store for Marshal Goering that autumn, for now Nemesis was drawing very near and the harvest sown by inattention to duty, wishful thinking, and indolence must be reaped. The appearance of the "Mosquito" light bomber gave Goering a shock as severe as any which he had experienced during the war. This impudent little machine, built moreover of wood, a material which the Germans had long since rejected as unsuitable for the construction of modern aircraft, was able to fly over the Reich with impunity by daylight and to return home untouched, since no German fighter could overtake it.

"I'd have been glad," said Goering, referring bitterly to the Mosquito, "if somebody had bought *me* some wooden aircraft." Nobody bought him new aircraft, wooden or otherwise.

The German bombers were now proving as outdated as their fighters. Neither the Do 217 nor the Ju 88 could match the British "Beaufighter," whose depredations made night raids over Great Britain more and more costly. The morale of the Luftwaffe began to sink, and with it the morale of its Commander-in-Chief.

Still Goering refused to take part in technical discussions with his senior Air Officers, who, turning in disillusionment to Hitler, found in him a more ready listener. At last Goering's pasteboard façade, which for years had concealed from the Führer the true state of his Air Force, began to fall to pieces, and Hitler could see through the gaping rents in its fabric what lay behind that imposing sham.

Not even the memory of twenty years' association in a common struggle, not even Goering's still unshaken loyalty or the popularity with the German people which he retained, could save him now from Hitler's displeasure.

Spring and summer nevertheless went by pleasantly enough for the Marshal. A visit to Paris in March was followed by a more ambitious undertaking – at last, in July, the special train set off for Russia.

Kalinovka was, admittedly, some 500 miles behind the German front line, but here it had been decreed the special train should halt. In anticipation of the Marshal's visit, preparations had been made for his reception little less elaborate than those undertaken in Hitler's Field Headquarters near by. A special station had been erected for the Marshal's train, houses lighted and heated by a power station imported from Germany for the purpose had been built, and even a shooting-range stood ready for Goering's pleasure when the Marshal might display his skill with weapons of all kinds in safety. Goering spent two restful periods at Kalinovka during 1942.

In Germany, meanwhile, Goering's boast that the Reich was utterly inaccessible to enemy bombers had long since proved empty. The first heavy raids upon the ancient city of Cologne brought home to the people of the Rhineland the true meaning of air warfare. As far as they were concerned Goering's name was already "Meier," yet "Uncle Hermann's" popularity with the people who must now bear the brunt of his policy remained undiminished. Not that he visited them in their extremity. His summer was taken up with visits to Kalinovka, with the peaceful life of Carinhall, in arranging a magnificent funeral for his private secretary who had just died, in accepting from the Rumanians the Order of "Michael the Brave," a decoration which entitled its holder to wear a magnificent if bizarre uniform, and in telling those same Rumanians that Germany could spare them no aircraft. The summer of 1943 also brought unpleasant news.

In the months which had passed since the entry into the war of the Americans, those contemptible "builders of Fords and Chevrolets" of whom Goering had once spoken so lightly, it had become very evident to all who chose to see the truth, that the gloomiest forecasts of America's industrial potential and of her warlike might which had been made by Germany's experts had still not been gloomy enough. Yet Goering did not wish to see the truth.

In Africa General Rommel's offensive had been halted at the gates of Alexandria. Before him lay all the riches of Egypt, almost within his grasp yet denied to the Army of Germany and of her Italian satellite by a "red line" of defenders which every day grew less thin. In particular, the reports of large reinforcements of aircraft and aircrews flowing into Egyptian bases disturbed the heads of the Luftwaffe, and Galland, now a Major-General, himself went to Africa to investigate.

He returned disheartened, as Udet's engineers had returned from Russia a year before. In his brief-case he brought photographs of British airfields taken by German reconnaissance aircraft, from which Air Intelligence had deduced that, as against a force of at least 800 British aircraft of all types, the Luftwaffe in Africa could now oppose only 80 fighters. Goering once well enough versed himself in the interpretation of such air photographs as the primitive equipment of the First World War could provide, examined Galland's collection and promptly reached the decision which he wished to reach. At least 50 per cent. of the British aircraft shown in the photographs were, he declared, fakes – mere dummies of sacking and plywood good enough to deceive the idiots who were in charge of German Intelligence in Africa, but no match for the piercing eye of the Reichsmarschall. The Luftwaffe had no appeal from this decision, and later, when the battle of El Alamein had been lost, there could be no redress. Once again Goering had helped his British enemies to win a campaign.

From the end of 1942 Hitler's disillusionment with his "Paladin" grew slowly, but, under the pressure of events and of enemies at "Court," inevitably. Reinhardt Heydrich, Goering's most rancorous opponent, had been murdered in June by Czech patriots, yet the disappearance of that dangerous man brought the Marshal no relief. Martin Bormann, Chief of the Party Chancellery since the flight of Rudolf Hess to Scotland in 1941, was an enemy no less bitter than Heydrich and one far more closely in the Führer's confidence. As the Marshal's star sank, so Bormann, putting aside all pretence of friendship with Goering, sowed in Hitler's mind, on soil which Goering by his own actions had already tilled, the seeds of distrust which were to bear their harvest in due season.

The Furies crowded in upon Carinhall in 1943. January brought the first daylight raids on Germany by the United States Army Air Force, and proved even to an unwilling Goering the accuracy of Udet's prophecy made in 1941. Galland, now at the age of 30 chiefly responsible for Germany's fighter defences, told Hitler that so heavily armed were the American invaders that the Luftwaffe must put into the air at least three or four fighters in order to be sure of destroying each unescorted American bomber.

Alive to the situation at last, Goering cast his eyes round desperately for the fighters which did not exist, and even proposed that the Eastern front should be almost entirely stripped of fighter aircraft in order that the menace from the West might be more successfully encountered. He did not, however, dare to make this suggestion to Hitler. As usual he vented his fury upon his pilots. Such German fighters as were available were now equipped with extra petrol tanks, giving them an increased range of two hours' flying time. The tanks could be detached by the pilot in extremity, but Goering gave orders that this was never to be done except when the aircraft had actually been hit. Only after many pilots had been lost through obeying this order was it withdrawn.

In an address given to the Chiefs of the German Fighter Arm in the spring, Goering raved savagely against "the heroes of the Battle of Britain who lied for each other's Knight's Crosses," cursed them for poltroons and laid upon their shoulders the blame for all Germany's misfortunes in the air. Galland, himself decorated like most of the members of the Marshal's audience with the Knight's Cross, snatched the little piece of metal with its oak leaves and its swords from his neck and threw it on the table. His brother officers offered to follow his example, but Galland restrained them from making this gesture, although he himself did not wear the Cross again for a year thereafter.

In 1943 the birthday festivities which each January brought the Marshal a flood of gifts from his sycophants were, if possible, more gorgeous than ever, for this was Goering's fiftieth birthday. The story went round Berlin that presents whose value amounted to far more than 1,000,000 marks had been given to Goering on this occasion, including a Sèvres service of porcelain of 2400 pieces, in itself valued at 500,000 marks, a complete French hunting-lodge, dismantled and brought to Germany, where it was to be erected on one of Goering's estates, and hundreds of other gifts each one of which might have reasonably satisfied an ordinary man for many birthdays – not to mention Christmases.

Yet January 30, one of the great festivals of the National Socialist year, the anniversary of the Party's accession to power in 1933, brought fresh humiliation. In Russia the German armies, encircled at Stalingrad, were fighting desperately but without hope. As usual Goering had promised more than he could perform. He had assured Hitler that at all costs the beleaguered army should be supplied from the air, and that promise, inevitably, he failed to keep. While on January 30 Hitler, furious and mortified, sulked, a second-rate Achilles, in his headquarters, it fell to Goering to make the traditional speech at the gathering of "Old Fighters" of the Party. It was unfortunate for the founder of the German Air Force that an air-raid alert, coming in the middle of this oration, should have forced him to take refuge in the shelter.

The German army capitulated at Stalingrad and its Commander, Field-Marshal von Paulus, promoted to that rank by Hitler on the last day of January, had by early February begun to transfer his allegiance to his Russian conquerors. Now British bombs rained down on Berlin by night and American bombs on the industrial centres of Germany by day. Goering let the wave of disaster break over him at Carinhall, rousing himself occasionally to telephone to the Commanders of Berlin's anti-aircraft defences, to inquire about the night's bag of enemy bombers and to upbraid them if it did not seem to him sufficiently large. He informed the Luftwaffe that they had disgraced the good name of German arms, and that until they had retrieved their honour he would lay aside all his German decorations. The gesture infuriated the Luftwaffe, but the simple people of Germany were impressed.

Yet even now, as the real world began to crash about him, Goering continued to live for the most part in a world of his own. When the newly appointed German Minister to Stockholm, a diplomatic post in which Goering had always taken a particular interest, presented himself at Carinhall early in 1943, his host received him dressed in the bizarre uniform of the Master Hunter of the Reich, his enormous stomach encircled by a jewel-studded belt from which hung a dagger in a golden sheath. He changed his costume several times during the day of the Minister's visit, appearing at last for dinner in a violet kimono with fur-trimmed bedroom slippers.

April brought with it a visit to Rominten and an unhappy return to Berlin. While Goering had been enjoying the peace of East Prussia, daylight raids over Germany became more and more frequent. One day Goering decided that he himself would take a hand. As he sat in his command post in "Asia," which had brought him back from Rominten, the air-raid warning system reported a force of American bombers heading for Frankfurt.

At once, in every fighter station in Germany, the news that the Commander-in-Chief was taking over flashed by wireless and all available German fighters were directed to assemble over Frankfurt. They never found the enemy, who having dropped his bombs west of the Rhine had turned peacefully homewards to his English base. Now, however, the German fighters, picked up by radar, were themselves mistaken for the enemy and the Marshal ordered other fighters to intercept them. The German force, flying back to base, was astonished to find itself attacked not by Spitfires or Mustangs – which would in any case have been inconceivable – but by Messerschmitts. Meanwhile more and more German fighters were vectored by Goering's order upon his own aircraft. Many of them, hurtling to meet an imaginary enemy, ran out of fuel and were forced back. The German force lost several aircraft in one way or another and the news spread like wildfire throughout the Luftwaffe. The impression created by this, Goering's last attempt to command fighter operations in person, was not dispelled by the humorous telegram which he sent next day to the squadrons engaged.

Such thought as the Marshal still devoted to the affairs of the German Air Force was concentrated at this time largely upon the impudent, elusive Mosquito. As 1943 wore on the incursions of these aircraft over German territory became more and more intolerable, and Galland was ordered by Goering to raise a special fighter unit whose sole duty it would be to attack Mosquitoes engaged in photo-reconnaissance. Galland, realizing the impossibility of succeeding in such an undertaking with the obsolescent fighters at his disposal, refused to obey this order. Surprisingly Goering accepted this refusal but entrusted this task to others. The special squadron was formed, lost 100 aircraft in five months, and was then disbanded without having in any way seriously interfered with the operations of the British intruders.

Meanwhile Goering's star continued to sink. After the failure to supply the Stalingrad arm from the air, General Milch, now Udet's successor as *Reichsluftzeugmeister*, went to Hitler and urged that Goering should be removed from his appointment as Commander-in-Chief. He proposed, as Goering would never have done, that the Luftwaffe should be subordinated to the Army in the field for tactical purposes and put forward the suggestion, which Goering had considered but had never dared to mention to the Führer, that the Eastern front should be largely denuded of its fighter squadrons in order that Germany might be better defended in the West against the ever-increasing air power of the United States and Great Britain. Hitler listened to these proposals in silence, appeared to agree with them, but did nothing. Marshal Goering's star had not yet reached its nadir.

Between Milch and General Jeschonnek, the Chief of the Air Staff, relations were now very tense. The two men should have worked in the closest collaboration, yet now they had drifted far apart. Their Commander-in-Chief, whose duty it was to see that the relationship between the heads of his operational and supply branches was as harmonious as possible, had never interested himself sufficiently in their difficulties or sought to bridge the gulf which now lay between them. Yet both Generals faced the same basic problem. They were responsible to a thoroughly inefficient Commander-in-Chief.

Jeschonnek, incessantly berated as he was by Hitler as the failure of the Air Force became more and more apparent, was powerless, so rigid was the Party control over the Fighting Services, to take any effective action without Goering's support. He now learned the bitter lesson which poor Udet had learned only a few months before. The Marshal's support was never given and so Jeschonnek found the same way out of a life which had become intolerable to him as Udet had chosen. In August 1943 he too committed suicide, and this time Goering did not bother to return from Rominten for the funeral.

General Korten, the ninth officer to hold the post of Chief of the Air Staff in the twelve years of the Luftwaffe's existence, was appointed to fill the gap left by Jeschonnek's death. A few days later Goering took occasion to read Galland one of those insulting lectures to which that unhappy young officer had by now become accustomed.

Once more Galland had to stand, rigid, before his Commander-in-Chief while Goering laid the blame for all Germany's misfortunes upon the fighter pilots for whom he had failed to provide the machines which they needed. He harked back to the First World War, when, he told Galland, men had been real men and fighter pilots had not hesitated to intercept and engage the enemy wherever he was found. To him air warfare was still basically a matter of Fokkers and Sopwiths, a romantic affair unchanged in its essentials by the mastery which airmen had achieved over their element during the twenty-five years which had elapsed since Goering himself was a fighter pilot. Galland, a man of the new generation, listened grimly and made no reply.

The Western Allies landed in Sicily, and each day brought its fresh tale of reverses. Goering's reactions were characteristic. To use a phrase which was often on the lips of his Staff, he began to "think globally." A proposal that New York and the Panama Canal should be bombed by long-range flying-boats was accepted with alacrity by the Marshal. This was the kind of spectacular operation in which he delighted. It was agreed that while the actual damage inflicted on New York might be inconsiderable from the purely military point of view, the moral effects of such an attack could be far reaching. As for the Panama Canal, a few bombs well placed could, with any luck, force Allied shipping from American west-coast ports to take the long route round Cape Horn for some months while the damage was repaired.

For a few days Goering discussed this scheme with enthusiasm. The plan was not his, but he immediately took full credit for it. It was agreed that the flying-boats which were to carry out these raids should operate in close partnership with the Navy, whose submarines would enable them to refuel at sea when their missions had been completed. At last it seemed that Goering might be able to do something spectacular, but he had reckoned without the jealousies and antagonisms, by now irradicable, which Hitler's system of leadership had bred between the three German Services. Germany possessed no Joint Chiefs of Staff Committee which could make decisions upon matters in which one Service was required to co-operate with another. The Führer had deliberately denied to each Service all but the barest minimum of knowledge of the activities of its sisters. He alone was the connecting-link between the three. Nowhere, therefore, was there any real co-operation between the Navy and Air Force, except at the lowest level.

Admiral Doenitz declared that he had no submarines available for co-operation with the Luftwaffe in the raids which Goering proposed, and that in any case he regarded the whole scheme as wasteful and impracticable. By now the Marshal was in no position to insist that Hitler should bring his Admirals to heel. He had never, for that matter, insisted sufficiently about anything which concerned the welfare of his own Service. And so, reluctantly, he abandoned the plan to bring German bombs crashing upon Manhattan and instead turned his attention, with disastrous results, towards the secret weapons which might yet help to retrieve the failure of the Luftwaffe.

The experiments with long-range missiles which had been conducted from the island of Peenemünde, off Germany's Baltic coast, had not long been a secret to the Allies, for all the security precautions which surrounded them. In the summer of 1942 the place had been raided by the Royal Air Force and the establishment there put out of commission for five weeks. Now, in spite of periodical raids, the island was producing the "secret weapons" which might yet turn the war in Germany's favour. The development of the "V 1" was complete and that of the "V 2" almost so. Goering had ordained that by the end of the year the "V 1" must be thrown into the battle against Great Britain, but once again unexpectedly helpful to his enemies, he failed to see the potentialities of another weapon which had been developed in Peenemünde and whose efficiency had been proved.

This was the "F X" or "Guided Bomb," which, fired from an aircraft and steered towards its target by wireless control, was intended primarily to serve as a weapon against enemy warships. Unfortunately for the German Navy the design and production of this very efficient weapon was not their responsibility but that of the Luftwaffe, and Goering therefore had the final and still undisputed say in its future. He decided, without having seriously gone into the question or consulted the Naval experts, that the further production of the "F X" was, in the circumstances which now faced Germany, a waste of time. As in 1940, so now in 1943 he set his face against novelties, however useful to Germany's war effort, and ordered that the production of the "F X" should be stopped and the labour hitherto which had been assigned to it diverted to the production of still larger numbers of obsolescent fighters.

That Goering in making this decision did another great service to the Allies may be judged from the fact that, on August 14, 1943, German aircraft armed with virtually the only prototypes of this weapon which Germany possessed – had no difficulty in sinking, off Sardinia, the Italian battleship *Roma* as she sailed to join the victorious Allies. Admiral Doenitz, watching in the same month a demonstration of the weapon which would now be denied to his Navy, observed bitterly that he had not been able to see the Reichsmarschall for weeks and wondered where he was shooting at that moment. That "F X" was not used against the Allies as their forces approached the Normandy beachheads a year later may be ascribed to the mercy of Providence and to the Marshal's lack of foresight.

The Ruhr and the Rhineland, in which most of Germany's war-industry was centred, were now scorched day and night by

Allied bombers. Not only were the factories upon which the Luftwaffe relied for its bombs and guns, its ammunition, and its aircraft crippled by the bombs from which Goering had proved powerless to protect them, but manpower was also running short. Milch, responsible as he was for the whole equipment of the Air Force, knew that it was useless to apply to the Commander-in-Chief for any priority in manpower. Never in all his years of association with Goering since the foundation of the Luftwaffe in 1934 had the Commander-in-Chief been willing to lay such requests before Hitler. How could he now, deprived as he was of the Führer's confidence, succeed in what he had previously not even been prepared to attempt?

And so Milch turned to the concentration camps, from which Himmler was willing to provide on a strictly economic basis supplies of low-grade slave labour which might somehow suffice to keep the wheels of the German aircraft industry turning. Milch made no mention of this arrangement to his Commander-in-Chief. The whole subject of concentration camps was extremely distasteful to the Reichsmarschall, nor would Milch's chance of succeeding in his approach to Himmler be improved if Goering took a hand in it. The slaves of the Gestapo were therefore herded into Germany's aircraft factories, there to work long hours, their pay credited to the Gestapo and fed on concentration-camp rations, until they died or, proving themselves physically unfit for further work, became by Himmler's standards ripe for extermination. Goering, in Carinhall, cared for none of these things.

By December 1943 a large number of launching sites, built chiefly with requisitioned French labour, stood ranged along the Channel coast ready to hurl the flying bombs, upon which so many of Goering's hopes were set, against London. It might be possible, it seemed, to obey to the letter the Marshal's order that the attack on the British capital was to begin by the end of the year. Yet in December the Royal Air Force struck, and by the end of that month 57 per cent. of the launching-sites had been successfully attacked, despite the ingenious camouflage with which the Germans had sought to protect them. Once again Goering's plans had miscarried.

On the last day of November, the anniversary of the Munich *Putsch*, Goering spoke over the wireless network to the German people – for the last time had he but known it. He took as his theme the holding by the last gallant 300 defenders of Sparta of the Pass of Thermopylae against the might of Persia, and urged his listeners to defend Germany no less stoutly against the ring of foes which now threatened her existence. Speaking of the effects of the Allied air raids, of which during a brief visit to the Rhineland and the Ruhr he had just seen something with his own eyes, Goering did not attempt, as other Nazi orators had done, to belittle them.

"Even if every city in Germany is razed to the ground," Goering said, "the German people would still survive. It would be hard, of course, but the German people existed before there were any cities at all, and we may even have to live in holes in the ground. But the end of everything would come if the Bolsheviks poured in. If Berlin vanished from the face of the earth it would be dreadful but not fatal. The German people had existed in the past without Berlin. But if the Russians reached Berlin the German people would have ceased to exist."

Nemesis

As the year 1944 opened, the threat of invasion hung heavy over the Reich, and now not from the East only, where the German armies tried vainly to stem the Russian tide, still relatively far distant from the frontiers of their country. The threat also came from the West.

Intelligence reports showed that the attack on the Continent which the British and American leaders had long promised would certainly take place before the year was out, and Hitler made no secret of his fears. He rounded savagely upon Goering, who had failed him, and Goering, flinching beneath the Führer's reproaches, delivered in a voice so loud that it penetrated the thick doors of his study and was audible to those waiting in the ante-room outside, humbly admitted his miscalculation. The Americans, he confessed, had more than justified themselves as builders of aircraft and as airmen. He had underestimated them. Yet he still assured the Führer all would soon be well, since the Transatlantic enemy had now overreached himself. His reserves of men were almost exhausted, and of what use were many aircraft if the men to fly them were lacking?

Hitler, unimpressed by these arguments, sought by any means to fill the gaping voids in the German air defences which Goering's optimism and carelessness had created. At Berchtesgaden the whole question was discussed. From having always favoured the production of bombers rather than fighters, both Hitler and Goering were now brought to the realization that fighters they must have. A production rate of 5000 fighters a month was hopefully suggested by them as a target still within the range of the German aircraft industry, and was rejected out of hand by experts with a truer knowledge of that industry's present capacity than had the Führer and the Commander-in-Chief of his Air Force.

Nevertheless Hitler was still obsessed with bombers – his whole character, and for that matter Goering's, inclined him to give blows rather than to parry them. In spite of the fact that development of new aircraft had been at a virtual standstill for four years, one splendid machine, first designed in 1938, was ready to go into production – the Me 262 jet-fighter. There, had Hitler only seen it, lay a real chance of striking a blow at the Western Allies when they invaded France. The Royal Air Force, thanks to the genius of Sir Frank Whittle, was as far advanced in the design of jet aircraft as were the Germans, yet had the Me 262 been produced in really large numbers as a fighter, the Allied landing in Normandy would have proved an even more painful and difficult enterprise for the invaders than it in fact was. But Hitler, his obsession with bombers still unexorcised, directed that the Me 262 should be produced not as a fighter but as a fighter-bomber. Formal orders were given by the Führer himself that this aircraft was never to be referred to save as a "Jabo" (*Jagdbomber*), and Professor Willi Messerschmitt went dismally back to his drawing-board to incorporate into the design of the fighter the modifications which would be necessary before it could be employed for bombing and which would hold up its production. For this salvation the Allies may thank in some degree the Mosquito fighter-bomber.

Goering's failure was now completely manifest and the prestige of his Air Force almost at its lowest ebb. The master of Carinhall sat brooding in his palace, taking himself once or twice a week to Berlin for *Lagebesprechungen* in Hitler's Chancellery which for him, and for the officers who accompanied him, were torture. At these meetings, attended by the leaders of the three Services, Hitler never missed an opportunity of venting his spleen upon the man who had once been his favourite. The Marshal's A.D.C.s, sitting outside the conference room, heard the Führer's voice raised in passionate anger against their Chief and sometimes, greatly daring, took it upon themselves to close the steel doors of the chamber, the ordinary wooden doors not being sufficient to exclude the sounds of Goering's humiliation from the world outside. As the Marshal's Staff sat waiting for the ordeal to end, officers of the other Services passing through the ante-room would ask them how many German aircraft the Luftwaffe had shot down in the past twenty-four hours, and pass sneering on their way. The degradation was almost too bitter to be borne, and Goering, when he returned to Carinhall after one of these meetings with Hitler, used to shut himself away for three or four hours during which he sat alone, his huge form slumped in a chair, apparently incapable of speech, or movement. Yet now there was no redemption, and Goering in his heart knew it.

As the first British and American liberators set foot upon the soil of France, Goering was at Veldenstein. Taking his cue from the Führer, and taking it willingly since it coincided with his own hopes, he professed to welcome the invasion since the German High Command now knew where to strike their counter-blow. As Chairman of the Ministerial Council for the Defence of the Reich (for Goering had been deprived of none of his offices by Hitler, however deeply he might have fallen out of favour), he spent the days which followed the first Normandy landings in desultory conversation with this and that industrialist, conversations which led nowhere. At no time did he even consider a visit to the Western front, and indeed had he made such a suggestion to the Führer it would almost certainly have been vetoed. For by this time Hitler knew too much about Goering's "trips of inspection," which he dismissed as laughable.

And so, while the Western Allies hammered across Normandy and the Russians drove towards Poland, the Marshal sat in impotent idleness.

The morning of July 20 broke calm and sunny. At last Goering was going to visit the "front" – that is to say he was going to make a short excursion from Rominten, where he was now staying, north-eastwards towards the Lithuanian frontier, for now the front had come very close to East Prussia and the Russians were threatening Kovno. For two hours the file of cars – the A.D.C.s, drivers and escort – awaited the Marshal's pleasure, until the news of the event which had just taken place caused all plans for the journey to be cancelled. A bomb had exploded in Hitler's conference room during a meeting between the Führer and his Staff. Although Hitler himself had escaped death, some of his officers had not been so fortunate. Goering at once drove to the "Wolf's Lair."

At long last the "opposition" had taken action, and action in which Goering was not formally involved. The conspirators in the "20th of July Plot" included General Beck, who as long ago as 1938 had endeavoured to enlist Goering's support against Hitler at the time of Munich and had himself resigned his appointment as Chief of the General Staff in protest against Hitler's policy. They included Count Helldorf, apart from Goering himself the last survivor from among the Reichstag plotters and a man who had no better reason to trust the Marshal than had General Beck. They included Field-Marshal von Witzleben, another officer who had once toyed with the idea that Goering might throw in his lot with the opposition and had then dismissed it on the grounds that the Marshal's character was too unreliable, his reputation for loyalty to his friends and associates too doubtful.

It is not probable, therefore, that Goering was in any sense formally implicated in the plot of July 20, yet those who were on duty that day at Rominten, and through whose hands passed all teleprinter messages and telephone calls for the Field-Marshal, cannot resist the belief that their master had, in fact, some foreknowledge of the plot. Had the plan of the conspirators succeeded, had Hitler lost his life and the assassins been able to set up the Military Government in Germany for which they had made the most detailed plans, it is not unlikely that the Marshal would have hastened to make common cause with them. The strange delay in the departure of the Commander-in-Chief on his visit to the front, a departure which was due to take place at 10 a.m. and which was finally cancelled more than two hours later, seems to lend some colour to this supposition. According to some of those who were at Rominten on that day and who are still able to tell the tale, Goering, having got wind of what was afoot, was unable to resist the temptation to wait, close to the spot where the murder was to take place, in order that he might lose no time in learning its result. With this end he postponed a trip which, had it started on time, would have seen him innocently bowling along an East Prussian highroad at the time when the bomb exploded in the "Wolf's Lair," but would equally have seen him out of touch for a few hours with the course of events.

The plot had not succeeded. Hitler still lived, and Goering, hastening to his Headquarters to congratulate, ordered the Luftwaffe, in terms very similar to those which he had issued during the purge of 1934, to wipe out any officers, soldiers or civilians of whatever rank who might take up cudgels in defence of those who had sought to kill the Führer.

Four days after the attempt a curious incident took place which well illustrates the abasement into which Goering had now fallen. On July 24 an Order signed by him was published throughout the Fighting Forces, of which he was still, in rank, the senior officer:

"The Reichsmarschall of the Great-German Reich, as Senior Officer of the Fighting Services, in his own name and in that of General-Field-Marshal Keitel and of Gross-Admiral Doenitz, has reported to the Führer that all the branches of the Services have requested, on the occasion of the Führer's preservation from death, that the "German Greeting" (Nazi Party Salute) should be introduced throughout the Services as a symbol of loyalty to the Führer and of the closest co-operation between the Fighting Services and the Party. The Führer has now given his approval of this proposal. Salutes will therefore henceforward be rendered, with immediate effect upon the appearance of this Order, by giving the "German Greeting" instead of bringing the right hand up to the head-dress as heretofore."

This Order was laid before Goering for his signature although he had never been consulted about it, and it came to him as a complete surprise. Indeed he, who had always taken pride in being a soldier rather than a mere Nazi, did not agree with the terms of the Order, which emanated from Hitler himself. Yet he had no choice but to sign it and to allow it to be issued in his name. To those closest about him he complained bitterly that Hitler was treating him now as no more than his office boy, but once again there was no protest. To have protested would in the circumstances have been unwise.

Although the tide of war lapped each day closer to Carinhall the last agonizing struggle for Germany's existence which had now begun seemed to have scarcely any connection with the Marshal's life. By October Himmler's ascendancy over Hitler, even in matters directly connected with the Air Force, seemed complete. He, and not the Führer, conveyed to the Commander-in-Chief of the Luftwaffe the order that the Me 262 was now to be sent into action as a fighter. He, and not Goering, appointed a certain General Kammler as the Führer's personal representative on the War Production Board for all matters concerned with jet aircraft. Goering's feeble riposte in appointing General

Kammhuber as his own representative in opposition to Kammler merely served to increase the confusion which already surrounded the Me 262 to such a degree that few aircraft of this type took the air as fighters until April 1945, when their intervention could not possibly influence the course of the war in Germany's favour.

Yet still Goering cast around for some miracle which might retrieve his fallen fortunes and prestige. He did not scorn to blame Udet for the Luftwaffe's decline, and early in November 1944 he gave vent to his wounded feelings in a furious harangue, which lasted three and a half hours. Again the Marshal repeated the accusations of cowardice, slackness and treachery which he had so often hurled at the senior officers of the Fighter Arm. But now he addressed himself not to the senior officers only but to the men whom they commanded. His speech was recorded in part, and on his order circulated down to squadrons in the field. It had an appalling effect on morale.

Still searching for whatever might conceivably retrieve his own position and that of his Service, the Marshal, as Commander-in-Chief still exercising authority, though now without prestige, summoned the leading officers of the Air Force to the "Parliament," held at Gatow airfield near Berlin, today a station of the Royal Air Force and the British civil airport in the German capital. After telling the assembled officers that they were free to make any criticisms and suggestions which might occur to them, short of attacks upon his own person, the Marshal left the gathering, and returning to Carinhall awaited a report on the deliberations. This was presently brought to him by Galland, and its terms included, as an essential preliminary to any real reform in the Luftwaffe, the request that the leading members of the Commander-in-Chief's personal staff should be replaced by other officers who enjoyed to a greater degree the confidence of the Service. Goering, who had admittedly never shown much faith in "parliamentary" methods, reacted to this request by awarding on the same day the "Golden Pilot's Badge with Diamonds" to Colonel von Brauchitsch, his principal A.D.C., and thereby annihilated what little prestige he still enjoyed with his own Service.

Yet it might even now be possible to perform a miracle, and Goering at Galland's suggestion selected the day-bombers of the United States Air Force, whose raids upon Germany became ever heavier and more painful, as the victims whose destruction should restore his standing with the Führer and with the Service which he still commanded. *Der Grosse Schlag* – "The Great Blow" – was planned for November 12. Two preliminary conditions were essential for the success of the operation – a very large sortie of American bombers over Germany (which Goering, from bitter experience, had every reason to believe would be provided) and clear weather. Given those conditions, 11 *Gefechtsverbände* (fighter formations) would take off to intercept the intruders – the largest fighter force that Germany could muster. Goering believed – and found some senior officers to share his confidence – that with a possible loss of 200 fighters and 150 pilots "the Great Blow" would destroy between 400 and 500 American bombers, and cause such destruction of morale and material in the "Yankee" Air Force that the German aircraft industry might for a time be spared from their crippling blows. Then – and this was the hope which Goering, as usual more realistic than Hitler and the fanatics who surrounded him, admitted privately to some of his senior officers – it might be possible to hold off the Russians in the East until the Allies had entered Germany and could, with what remained of the German Forces, deny the Reich to the Muscovite invader.

Needless to say this aspiration, confided in the strictest secrecy to a few trusted subordinates, was not communicated to General Eisenhower's headquarters.

But "the Great Blow" was never struck, for the weather remained dull and cloudy and the German fighters' hopes of successfully intercepting a large force of American bombers in such a way as to destroy it were brought to nothing. The Fortresses, droning high above the clouds, flew in as usual over the Reich, dropped their bombs and returned to their bases with no more than normal loss.

General Galland, as was now customary, bore the brunt of the Marshal's disappointment. At Christmas he was received by the Commander-in-Chief, assured of Goering's personal liking for himself, and abruptly sent on leave. The weather remained bad. American bombers continued to prowl almost unmolested by day and British bombers to prowl by night. Civilians in their shelters, when they heard German fighters take the air, used to say, half in earnest, that the alert must now be over; and the men of the German fighter squadrons, grounded and impotent, lost heart and openly cursed their Commander-in-Chief. However, von Rundstedt's offensive in the Ardennes, which had now opened and seemed to be going well, offered some hope, and

217

Goering hung the Knight's Cross of the Iron Cross about his neck again.

No longer was Carinhall a safe retreat, the inviolable fortress of the second man in the German Reich. The guard company, 120 strong, still kept watch and ward around the great house, but the avengers were very close now. On Christmas Eve von Rundstedt recognized that his effort in the Ardennes had been in vain and sought to break off contact with the enemy. Only Hitler's orders that the offensive was to continue at all costs restrained him. Russian tanks had reached East Prussia and the way to the heart of Germany seemed to be open to them. At last the thing which Goering had dreaded since 1938 was indeed upon him. He had done nothing to prevent war; war had come and now was lost, and with it was lost everything that Goering had snatched for himself in twenty-two years of political piracy. His eyes turned towards the West. There might still be some hope of compromise.

There had been a time, after all, when he had had English friends, and he believed that he still enjoyed some popularity, if not in Great Britain, so sorely tried by his bombers, then at least in the United States, which thank goodness had never felt the weight of the Luftwaffe in its days of greatness. The Marshal believed that if only he could make contact with the West he, and only he, of all the leading men in Germany, might reach an agreement which would save Germany from the Russian invasion now threatening her. That belief, that hope, obsessed his mind, but he dared take no positive steps to put it to the test. Did not his reputation with the Führer stand low enough already?

And so a miserable Christmas, in which the hand of dissolution seemed already to have touched everything in Carinhall, a Christmas at which the presents were fewer and less valuable than in former years and the fun, what there was of it, very false, led into a sombre new year. Once more Goering summoned his senior officers to Berlin, once more he accused them of cowardice and lack of resolution. He found them in an ugly mood, particularly Galland and his brother officers of the Fighter Arm. They complained bitterly that the long-awaited Me 262 had not been delivered, and Goering, helpfully, threatened to have them all arrested and shot if they continued to voice these complaints.

In a fit of impotent rage Goering did have Galland arrested and then ordered his release. He sought a scapegoat now for the failure of his fighters, and that scapegoat should, if it could be managed, be Galland himself. Upon his release the young General, informed of what was afoot, knowing that three members of the Air Force Judge-Advocate-General's Branch had been ordered to present a convincing case against him for dereliction of duty, planned like other distinguished officers of the Luftwaffe before him to commit suicide. He told his close friends, members of his former Staff, that he felt that his conviction had already taken place in advance. He would not desert to the West. Instead he would shoot himself.

That night Albert Speer, Reich Minister of Armaments and War Production, an able clear-sighted man, distinguished moreover for the moral courage which Goering had always lacked, heard of Galland's decision and reported it immediately to Hitler, who ordered all proceedings impending against the General to be cancelled forthwith. He had known nothing of them until Speer had brought him the news.

Now Galland must face another interview with the master of Carinhall. Knowing the facts as he did, he was not impressed by Goering's claim himself to have quashed the proceedings against him, but he jumped at the offer of a unit of Me 262's which he might himself lead into battle. That, after the enervating atmosphere of the Luftwaffe Staff and of the court which surrounded his Commander-in-Chief, would be to see life once more.

Meanwhile the lorries had begun to roll away from Carinhall. A great part of the Marshal's art collection had left the mansion for the Kurfürst deep shelter near Potsdam, where its treasures would be safe from Allied bombs. The Carinhall shelter itself had received much of the hoard and some articles of secondary value had been stored elsewhere – in the manor-house at Ringenwalde, fifteen miles from Carinhall, where Frau Goering's brother, Dr. Sonnemann, lived with a number of his sister's friends who like himself had been bombed out of their homes in Berlin, in the little farm at Gollin, on the Carinhall estate, and at Mauterndorf.

Now with the Soviet armies so close to the capital everything must be carried to safety in the south. The collection, which in 1939 had numbered some 200 objects, now contained over 2000 works of art, including 1375 paintings, 250 sculptures, 108 tapestries, 200 pieces of period furniture, 60 Persian and French carpets, 75 stained-glass windows and 175 *objets d'art* of various kinds.

During the first week of February 1945 the special train rolled out of Forst Zinna station, bound for Neuhaus in Franconia. In his extremity Goering had turned again towards his boyhood home, for Neuhaus station served the Castle of Veldenstein, and it was here that the Marshal proposed to conceal a great part of his hoard.

Goering had acquired the Castle of Veldenstein some time before, and it was now being rebuilt like all his other houses to suit the taste of its owner. The castle, standing perched on an eminence at whose foot clustered the brick houses of the little town of Neuhaus, its white tower a local landmark looking out over the wild pine-forests of the Franconian mountains, was almost a replica of the toy castle which had been such a feature of the model railway at Carinhall. A company of pioneers, seconded to the Marshal from more urgent duties even in this desperate hour of Germany's military fortunes, was at work on the task of reconstruction as the special train drew in to Neuhaus.

This first consignment contained only the smaller and more portable objects contained in his collection, since the rooms at Veldenstein were small, judged by the Marshal's usual standards of accommodation, and the corridors narrow.

On March 13 a second shipment left Berlin for Veldenstein, and the third and last consignment, containing everything left in the Carinhall and Potsdam shelters, was made ready for despatch at the beginning of April. The fate of this argosy will be told later.

Goering could do nothing now but await the inevitable end. The miserable "Führer briefings" were still held in the Chancellery, and Goering still attended them, driving from Carinhall through the reek and rubble of Berlin, past haggard gangs of civilians erecting flimsy defences against the Russian armour, past tattered, slouching, untrained units of the *Volkssturm*, the German "Home Guard," whose formation had been ordered by Hitler in the previous October.

Then, after the usual horrible meeting with a Führer whose insanity was now apparent to all who saw him, back through the dark littered streets to Carinhall. Sometimes an air-raid alert – they seemed nowadays to follow one another with hardly a break – drove Goering into a Berlin shelter, and there he was still greeted with affection by the people whom he had helped to ruin. On these occasions he tried to speak words of encouragement, to hold out some hope of victory in this last hour, and his hearers responded eagerly even now.

Sometimes, too, when he saw a dark figure signalling **from**

the roadside, Goering ordered the car to stop and took aboard the wanderer, marooned by the breakdown of Berlin's Transport Services. Then the hitch-hiker, perched in the back of the car beside Captain Klaas, most junior of Goering's A.D.C.s who always accompanied him on these expeditions, would perceive on the shoulders of the bulky figure who sat beside the chauffeur the flash of gold and would ask in a whisper who the officer in front might be. When he learned the identity of his host the passenger sometimes tried to jump out of the Mercedes, feeling that it was not well for a simple man to become entangled, however fleetingly, with such a mighty person as Reichsmarschall Goering. For to the German people, stunned and staring defeat in the face, Goering was still a great man. The effects of twelve years' propaganda are not easily effaced.

On January 12, 1945, Goering's fifty-second birthday, the armies of the Soviet Union rolled forward again in Poland and East Prussia. In less than a week they had broken through 250 miles of the German front. By the end of the month Gleiwitz and Katowice had fallen and the Head of the German Four Year Plan, the President of the Reich Defence Council, saw the coal, steel and oil of Upper Silesia snatched from him. In that month more than 200,000 Germans were killed and 75,000 taken prisoner on the Eastern front alone. The Luftwaffe as an airborne force had virtually ceased to exist, and the flower of its young men now fought grimly as ground troops, though no longer under Goering's Command. He had no Command worth mentioning any more.

Once again Goering wondered whether he might not attempt Hitler's overthrow, and for a time his mind went back to an old alliance. With Himmler he had once brought about the destruction of Röhm. Since then not only had the two men ceased to be allies – they had become bitter enemies. But now Himmler too was in partial disgrace, his credit with Hitler reduced by the man whom Goering also counted as his most bitter foe – Martin Bormann. Perhaps it might be possible to do something with Himmler . . . perhaps. Goering pondered in the empty vastness of Carinhall, while the hammers of the packers thudded in the picture gallery and their steps sounded clear and hollow on floors which had once been carpeted. He pondered, and again he reached no decision.

Emmy Goering had passed her nights lately in the deep shelter at Carinhall and her days in giving what help she could to friends bombed out from Berlin, to anybody who seemed to need her

assistance. She had for some time past made a habit of collecting from her friends the addresses of poor families, preferably with many children, to whom she sent food and clothing – the clothing largely drawn from the stocks of a Luftwaffe which had in effect ceased to exist. Now, on January 30, it was all over. The Eastern front had broken, and it seemed broken finally. The Russian offensive was not to be halted by such desperate, improvised measures as the Germans were now forced to devise. One hundred and fifty German Divisions had been shattered by Marshals Koniev, Zhukov and Rokossovsky, and the road to Carinhall lay open to the invader.

Quickly Frau Goering packed a few clothes and personal belongings, including some of her jewellery. Then accompanied by her best friend, Frau Bouhler, she drove from Carinhall for the last time in a special train which waited to carry her to Berchtesgaden. Hitler himself had ordered all women and children to leave the mansion.

As the train pulled out in the twilight of a winter day the Marshal stood waving to his wife and little daughter. He had promised them that if all seemed irretrievably lost he would die in action, and he wept as the red tail-light of the last coach vanished into the gloom. Carinhall, when he returned to it, was even lonelier than had been the flat in Badenschestrasse after Carin's death.

Between the beginning of February and the early days of March the Germans lost on the Western front 100,000 men. By March 7 the Americans had occupied Cologne, by March 23 the Second British Army under General Dempsey and the Ninth U.S. Army under General Simpson had crossed the Rhine in force. By March 25 the west bank of the Rhine was entirely cleared of its German defenders. East Prussia was lost to the Soviet Army; now the Russians had crossed the Polish frontier into Silesia, were driving through Czechoslovakia towards Saxony and striking down from the Baltic towards Berlin. The morale of the Army had collapsed. Field-Marshal Keitel had found it necessary to issue an order decreeing that any officer who helped a subordinate to leave the battle area by issuing him with a false pass or other papers would be treated as a saboteur and sentenced to death. The war was almost over.

Yet Hitler now pinned his faith on saboteurs. Trusting to the German love of all that is weird and sinister – that same twist in the national character which had produced the *Fehmgerichte* – he ordered Himmler to organize the "Werewolves." Recruited at

first from the ranks of the "Hitler Youth." the Werewolves soon enlisted members of the regular fighting services and began their operations in Upper Silesia, behind the Russian lines. By the end of March they were ready to go into action in the West, ordered by their lunatic leader to use any means, no matter how shameful, to destroy the enemy. Goering, the realist, had no hand in this enterprise, believing rightly that the Werewolves had no hope whatever of success. In fact, sugar was occasionally put into Allied petrol tanks, a few nails strewn across country roads and one or two German "collaborators" murdered in true *Fehmgericht* style. That was the limit of the Werewolves' contribution to Germany's defence.

Meanwhile, as Emmy Goering and her friends sat filled with anxiety in the peace of Berchtesgaden, the quiet villages about them, nestling among the Bavarian Alps, became filled with fevered, hopeless activity. To them came now the principal members of the Berlin Ministries, bringing with them lorry-loads of files and archives. Here, in the mountains which he had loved, the Führer had decided National Socialism's last stand should be made. This was "National Redoubt," against which, from east and west, Russian and American columns were moving. It seemed that the family of the Reichsmarschall might still find themselves living in a battlefield.

Every evening the Marshal rang up from Carinhall inquiring after the health of Emmy and the child, declaring that he was desperately lonely, reaffirming his determination to die with his face to the enemy rather than surrender. Yet was he not still the second man of the Reich? Might he not even now accomplish something which it was not in the power of the Führer or of anyone else to achieve? Goering had always believed that he could handle foreigners. Could he not handle General Eisenhower?

In the meanwhile Carinhall must on no account fall into the hands of the Russians, who were now all too close to the house. On Goering's orders heavy bombs were laid in the cellar and in all parts of the building where an explosion might be most effective. The officer commanding the guard company was ordered to detonate them as soon as Russian troops reached the park which lay about the palace. Only in Carin's tomb was no bomb laid. Although he might now never join her in the great pewter coffin in which she lay, Goering decided that her rest should not be disturbed by him. The coffin remained in the brick vault.

On April 20 another of the dreaded "Führer briefings" took place. The spearheads of a Russian army had been reported at Lübben, only sixty miles south of Berlin; if any Nazi leader wished to leave the lost capital by road he must now seize his last chance. Hitler abandoned the whole idea of defending the Bavarian Redoubt. He would remain in the capital to await whatever might befall. This decision, announced by the Führer himself over what remained of the German wireless network in what was to be his last Birthday Speech to the German people, in no way accorded with Goering's plans. Now, having spent several weary hours in the group about Hitler, his presence there no more than a matter of routine, the Marshal plucked up courage and asked the Führer whether he too should stay in Berlin, or whether he might not leave for Bavaria, since he felt that he could make himself more useful on the Southern front which was without any national leader of importance.

Hitler's reply to this suggestion gave a measure of the disgrace into which his "faithful Paladin" had fallen. The Führer, far from making the scene which Goering had feared, agreed to the suggestion in a completely off-hand manner.

"Yes, of course, that's quite understood, my dear Goering," said the Führer, and with that phrase ended the tragic association which in twenty-three years had brought both men to heights of power which have been rarely equalled in history; and to ruin the like of which history has yet to see repeated.

Hardly saying good-bye to his companions in the command post, Goering went out into the night and returned, for the last time, to Carinhall. All preparations for departure had already been made. The Marshal's lorries were loaded, his personal car and the cars of his Staff were ready. Again the pestilential enemy aircraft whose successes had destroyed his reputation interrupted the last preparations. Till 1.20 a.m. on April 21 an air-raid alert kept them in the shelters, and only at 3 a.m. did Goering himself leave his palace for ever.

Save for a few servants and guards, the house which Goering had left was now empty. Almost all the beautiful things which it had contained, of which, however they may have been acquired, the Marshal was sincerely proud, had been carried away. A few pictures too large and cumbersome for quick and easy removal remained on the walls, a Greek Venus, legitimately his, since it had been a present from Marshal Balbo, still stood in the picture gallery, and a few pieces of delicate French furniture in the music room and the main hall. Otherwise all had been removed, and

the Kurfürst shelter too was empty, save for a few tapestries.

On April 12 the last shipment of art treasures had left Berlin in the special train; at Reichenhall it joined another train, loaded with much of the loot which had originally been taken to Veldenstein and had now, on Goering's orders, been repacked. Both trains reached Berchtesgaden on April 16.

The Marshal's escape-route, lying between the armies of his advancing enemies, ran south-westwards to Brandenburg and Belzig and thence south-eastwards to Dresden. In the early morning Goering reached Teplitz in what had once been the Sudetenland area of Czechoslovakia. Here a halt was made for breakfast, and Goering for the first time in many years sat down humbly with his Staff in a common restaurant and accepted whatever might happen to be on the menu. The news of his presence flashed round the little town, and in a few minutes the square outside the hotel in which the Marshal sat was black with people. They cheered and shouted, and when at last Goering came out of the restaurant crowded round him, slapping him on the back, wishing him well. It was, as Goering afterwards said, using a phrase of which he was very fond, "one of the most beautiful moments of my life."

The Marshal reached Berchtesgaden in the afternoon and was rejoiced to see his wife and daughter both well and Emmy striving to be cheerful. In the meanwhile, up in Berlin, Hitler, screaming with rage, had demanded that the whole High Command of the Luftwaffe should be hanged immediately, had withdrawn from Carinhall Goering's guard battalion, and was very evidently sinking into the last stages of paranoiac insanity.

Down in the south Goering wrestled, as he had sometimes wrestled before, trying to determine where his duty and his self-interest now lay. In his Birthday Speech Hitler had promised his people "a glorious German victory," and it might be that even now the Führer was right. If he were proved right, and if in the meanwhile Goering had obeyed his instinct and approached the Western Allies without Hitler's authorization, even such reputation as he still retained with the Führer would be lost. On the other hand, how could the Führer be right? What possibility was there of anything but defeat, and was it not both sensible and prudent that the second man in Germany – not, like the Führer hemmed in Berlin but free within limits to move about – should attempt to save what he might from the wreckage? For twenty-four hours Goering turned the matter over and came to no decision.

On the evening of April 22 General Koller, who had succeeded Korten, at one remove, as head of the German Air Staff, received in his headquarters at Berlin a verbal report on Hitler's condition. The Führer, he was told by General Christian, had had a breakdown and believed that it was useless to continue the war. He himself refused to leave Berlin, and although his courtiers had spared no effort to turn him from this decision, he persisted in it, and had been joined in the Chancellery shelter by Dr. Goebbels, his wife and children. Other members of the Staff had been told by Hitler that they might leave the Bunker when they chose and go where they pleased.

Koller, a well-trained staff-officer, immediately decided to report this conversation to his Commander-in-Chief. He accordingly telephoned to the Marshal's Staff at Berchtesgaden and was told that Goering wished him to fly southwards immediately. Before leaving, however, he visited his opposite number in the Army, Field-Marshal Jodl, at his headquarters near Krampnitz. According to Jodl, Hitler had said that he himself could no longer continue to direct the defence of the Reich and that what remained to be done must be done by Goering. To this Jodl had objected that the troops would not fight for the Reichsmarschall:

"Fight?" Hitler asked. "What do you mean, fight? There's not much more fighting to be done. When it comes to negotiating, Goering can do it better than I can."

Primed with this news, Koller took off from Berlin at 3.30 a.m. and arrived at Berchtesgaden at noon on April 23.

The newcomer was immediately called in to a conference at which Goering, his Chief A.D.C., Colonel von Brauchitsch, and Philip Bouhler were present. No sooner had he heard the news which Koller brought than Goering sent for Dr. Lammers, the head of the Chancellery, and asked him to bring with him the Law of June 29, 1941, in which Hitler had formally appointed his successor. Lammers brought the document in a tin box and they all studied it together. Its terms were unequivocal:

"Should illness or any other cause prevent me even temporarily from carrying out my duties and should I be unable to give personal instructions concerning the execution of my functions during the period of my indisposition I designate as my successor in all my capacities the Marshal of the Great-German Reich, Hermann Goering."

An Appendix to this document signed by Hitler at the same time, ran as follows:

"In view of the Law of December 13, 1934, on the successor of the Führer and Vice-Chancellor, I hereby abrogate all former dispositions and designate as my successor the Marshal of the Great-German Reich, Hermann Goering. Immediately after my death members of the Government of the Reich, Governors of the Reich, the Army, the Civil Service Officials of the National Socialist German Workers Party, the formations of the S.A., the S.S., the National Socialist Motor Corps and the National Socialist Flying Corps will swear an oath of allegiance to his person."

These documents seemed to put the position quite unequivocally, and Dr. Lammers, who had himself countersigned both of them when they were drawn up, confirmed that in the event of Hitler's death they conferred full powers upon Goering. Anxiously Goering mentioned rumours which he had heard that Bormann planned to murder him and himself to assume power on Hitler's death, but Lammers assured the Marshal that no such intention existed, since if it had he would have known it.

Was Hitler still alive, Goering inquired? Koller said that he had been alive when he himself had left Berlin, but might for all he knew now be dead. Would it therefore not be well to make a signal by wireless in order to clarify the position? Everyone present at the little conference agreed to this plan, and Goering dictated the signal at such length that Koller was obliged to warn him that with wireless communications in their present state it had no likelihood of reaching its destination in that form. At last Goering and his Chief of Staff drafted a signal together and Goering dictated the final version. It ran as follows:

"H.Q. 23–4–45. My Führer. Do you agree that in consequence of your decision to remain at your post of battle in the fortress of Berlin and in conformity with your decree of 29–6–41 I should immediately assume as your successor the whole Government of the Reich with full liberty of action in internal and external affairs?

Failing a reply by 2200 hours I shall presume that you have lost your liberty of action.

I shall then consider the preliminary conditions specified in your decree to have been fulfilled and I shall act for the good of the People and the Fatherland. Cannot express in words what I feel for you in these the darkest hours of my life. You know it. May God protect you and bring you here as soon as possible in spite of everything.

Your faithful HERMANN GOERING."

Goering followed this telegram with one to Hitler's A.D.C., Colonel von Below, informing him of the action that he had taken and ordering the Colonel to hand Goering's telegram to the Führer in person. He further warned both Ribbentrop, his inveterate enemy, and Jodl of the steps he had taken, and suggested that if no reply were received from Hitler within the time limit which he had suggested they should join him at Berchtesgaden for a conference.

When these signals had been despatched Goering sat down with his friends and planned the future. Assuming, as one was almost entitled to assume, that no reply were received from Hitler by 10 p.m., Goering's first step would be to issue an appeal to the Armed Forces and the Nation. All Ministers of the existing Government were to be replaced, and Ribbentrop especially should be got out of the way as soon as possible. Count Folke Bernadotte, head of the Swedish Red Cross, should be invited to visit the Marshal immediately in order that he might advise on the best manner of approaching General Eisenhower. Goering asserted his willingness to fly personally to the Allied Commander-in-Chief. In the meanwhile he demanded that the forces guarding Berchtesgaden be reinforced, and was offered 100 anti-aircraft guns by the local Commander.

At long last it seemed, tragic though the circumstances were, Goering had achieved his ultimate ambition. He was Führer of the German Reich, no longer the second man in Germany but its Leader. The evening dragged slowly by while the Marshal awaited word from Berlin which he hoped would never come. It did come. Hitler was still very much alive. The signal which Goering read, while his hand shook, was written in his crispest style:

"The decree of 29-6-41 does not come into force without my special authority. There is no reason to suppose that I am not a free agent. I consequently forbid any action being taken in the sense indicated by you.

ADOLF HITLER."

But if Hitler was a free agent when he sent this telegram the man who received it was not. Punctually at 10 p.m., the hour at which Goering had announced that the time limit which he had given for a reply from Hitler would expire, a party of S.S.

entered the house. Its commander, Obersturmbannführer Frank, came straight to the point. The Marshal of the Great-German Reich was under arrest!

For a few moments Goering could not believe his ears. Then he realized that Bormann had won a round. It must be on his orders that he was now a prisoner, and certainly the telegram which arrived soon after announcing that Goering and his family had been condemned to death and signed "Führer" could not come from anyone but Bormann. On the other hand the signal forbidding Goering to assume the powers for which he had asked could have come from no one but Hitler himself. Clearly then, Hitler lived; but equally clearly Bormann, seizing his opportunity, was taking advantage of the man's demented condition to avenge himself upon his old enemy.

Goering dictated and sent, with permission of his captors, signals to Ribbentrop, Himmler and Jodl, informing them that Hitler lived and cancelling the conference to which, in the signal sent that morning, he had summoned them. These radiograms were duly received.

Bormann had done his work well. As the Marshal, denied even the society of his wife by the S.S., sat miserably in the little house at Berchtesgaden, Eigruber, the local Gauleiter (Party Governor), ordered out the Home Guard on grounds that the security of his *Gau* was threatened and announced that all who opposed Adolf Hitler in his area, including Goering were to be shot. A few hours later the plans of this overzealous official were cancelled, but just before midnight on April 24, Kaltenbrunner, Heydrich's successor and a man scarcely less sinister than Heydrich himself, paid a short visit to Berchtesgaden and left again quickly without speaking a word to the prisoners, who included besides the Marshal himself all Goering's A.D.C.s

Next day the "Brains Trust" arrived in a despondent mood. General Loerzer and "Pilli" Koerner peeped timidly into the house in which Goering was confined, spoke to the S.S. guards, found that they would not be allowed to communicate with their friend, and while offering to visit him daily, if he required their services, departed with seventy-eight crates of assorted property and were never seen again by Goering until the war was ended.

In the meanwhile the Luftwaffe, such as it was, was under a new Commander-in-Chief. General Ritter von Greim, Air Officer Commanding-in-Chief, Air Fleet 6, with headquarters at Munich, was ordered to fly immediately to Berlin, and before leaving he spoke to Koller.

The Chief of Staff had a very fair idea of the purpose which lay behind the summons to von Greim, but when that officer attacked Goering as a traitor, Koller leapt to his defence.

"I can quite understand why he didn't stay in the Bunker." Koller said, "because he hadn't a single friend there. He had only enemies about him, men who instead of helping him have fought him and the Luftwaffe in the most malevolent and insidious way for months – one might say for the past two years. What would happen to us if all those responsible for the conduct of the war were locked up in a Bunker? It is not for me to defend the Reichsmarschall. He had too many faults for that, and Heaven knows he had made life difficult for me and treated me badly enough. He threatened me with a court-martial and death for no reason, threatened to shoot German Staff Officers in front of the assembled General Staff, but in spite of all that I can't change or falsify the facts of what occurred on April 22 and 23. The Reichsmarschall has done nothing which can be thought treasonable."

The monotony of captivity was unpleasantly broken on April 25. Suddenly the prisoners were hustled without ceremony into the deep air-raid shelter which lay behind Goering's house, and there they all sat, captives and captors, while American aircraft, flying low and unopposed, rained bombs upon the Führer's little village. Within half an hour Goering's house had vanished. Hitler's house was half-destroyed and that of Martin Bormann completely wrecked – which may have given the Marshal some consolation. There was nothing for it but to continue living in the shelter.

Koller flew back to General Headquarters at Fuerstenberg near Berlin on April 26, found that nobody there was very interested in anything that might have happened to Goering. Marshal Keitel refused to discuss the matter with him at all. Himmler, with his habitual caution, declared that "The Reichsmarschall affair is unfortunate business," but would say no more. Admiral Doenitz, after expressing his conviction that Goering had meant well, did not commit himself further and broke off the conversation to go to lunch. Loyally Koller did what he could for his old Chief, but nobody listened to him. Goering was not even a pasteboard Marshal now.

On the evening of April 26 General von Greim reached the Chancellery in Berlin after an adventurous flight from Munich, during which he had been twice forced down by Russian fighters and had been wounded in the leg.

As he lay in the sick bay of the Bunker, Hitler came to his bedside and declared that, as Koller had already suspected, he had summoned von Greim in order that he might appoint him Commander-in-Chief of the Luftwaffe in Goering's place. Goering, the Führer said, had betrayed and deserted both him and Germany. He had negotiated with the enemy behind Hitler's back. He had taken refuge in Berchtesgaden against Hitler's orders and had then had the impudence to send the Führer a telegram asking to be named as his successor. Consequently, Hitler went on, he had ordered Goering's arrest, had deprived him of all his titles and offices, and now appealed to von Greim to make what he could of the shambles in which his predecessor had left the Luftwaffe.

If Hitler's animosity against Goering was due to Bormann's machinations, then Bormann had done his work well. As Hitler was speaking to his successor in Berlin a telegram reached the prisoner at Berchtesgaden, and this time also the Führer's distinctive style was sufficient guarantee of its origin:

"Your actions are punishable by death. Because of your valuable services of the past I shall refrain from instituting proceedings if you will voluntarily relinquish all offices and titles, otherwise other steps will have to be taken."

As he sat in the stuffy atmosphere of the Bunker, the stench of ordure in his nostrils – for no proper sanitary arrangements for so large a party had been made – his wife and child, his A.D.C.s and servants gathered pell-mell about him, Goering's feelings on reading this telegram were bitter indeed. April 29 brought some relief, although it brought also further separation from his wife. Putting forth all his powers of persuasion, Goering persuaded Frank that he would be no less securely guarded in his own castle of Mauterndorf than in the filthy conditions which now prevailed in the Berchtesgaden shelter. Accordingly, while his wife and child remained for the present in Berchtesgaden, the Marshal – if he may still be so described – was taken under heavy guard over the few miles which separated the Berghof from Mauterndorf.

Poor, loyal Koller was in the meanwhile having the worst of both worlds. He had written a scrupulously accurate report of the Marshal's activities at Berchtesgaden on April 22 and 23 only to find that no one would read it. Goering, out of touch with his former Chief of Staff, persisted in believing that he had never delivered this report to the Führer as he had promised to do, and that he had not even tried to deliver it. Koller, too, it seemed, had abandoned him, and he spoke of him as a "rotter without a spark of decency." Yet Koller still did what he could to help his fallen master.

On May 1 the Guard Commander at Mauterndorf received a telegram from Berlin, signed this time not by Hitler but by Bormann. It seemed to set a seal on Goering's death sentence.

"The situation in Berlin is deteriorating. If we should fail you will be responsible with your honour, your lives and the lives of your families that the traitors of April 23 do not escape."

Standartenführer Brause, who was now responsible for Goering's custody, did not at all relish the tone of this signal and contrived to apprise Koller, who visited him that day, of his doubts. "Does the Luftwaffe mean to rescue Goering by force?" Brause asked, half hopefully. "If so, of course the S.S. would be hopelessly outnumbered." Koller, to test the temper of the S.S. man, replied bluntly that he had no intention of attempting a rescue since, in view of Brause's orders, he would only be rescuing a corpse. Thereupon Brause undertook to protect Goering's life against his own men if a determined attempt to release the Field-Marshal were made by the Luftwaffe, and Holler asked Field-Marshal Kesselring, who was now Commander-in-Chief of all forces in the West, to provide troops for the rescue. Kesselring agreed to this suggestion, but with a caution which was habitual in him insisted that Doenitz, who had that day been officially appointed as Hitler's successor, should first be consulted.

In the meanwhile the prisoner's loneliness was somewhat relieved by the arrival of his A.D.C.s, Colonel von Brauchitsch, Major Mühr and Captain Klaas, who had been allowed to leave Berchtesgaden and join him. Two days passed without word from Kesselring. The conditions of Goering's confinement were now considerably relaxed, and he was able to walk with his A.D.C.s in the grounds of the castle. By May 4 Reichenhall, north of Berchtesgaden and therefore even farther north of Mauterndorf, was in American hands, and Berchtesgaden itself was reported to be surrendering. At 5.30 p.m. on that day General Pickard of the Luftwaffe, reconnoitring the castle at Mauterndorf, was astonished to see Goering leaning over a fence which bordered the roadway. The Marshal lost no time in giving the General a verbal message which he was to bring to Koller.

In the first place the message said Goering's person was to be protected and Luftwaffe troops sent for this purpose. Koller should then send an officer to Eisenhower suggesting that Goering should come to meet him, bringing with him Field-Marshal Kesselring, and that they should have a "man to man" talk which would not be binding on either side. Goering went on to explain to the fascinated Pickard that he believed his name had "a good ring" abroad and that something might still be achieved by negotiation with the West. The signals ordering his arrest, he added, had been sent by Bormann when Hitler was already dead – a statement which in the light of subsequent knowledge he found to be false – and he insisted upon the fact that he was the Führer's legal successor. He was the most popular of all leading Germans, he said, in the eyes of the outer world and especially in the United States.

Pickard went away and Goering returned to the castle. Another day dragged by and on May 6 the Armistice was signed. By this time Goering was a free man. A few Air Force troops had at last arrived at Mauterndorf and the S.S., thoroughly demoralized, had been only too glad to hand over their inconvenient prisoner and themselves to withdraw as far into the background as possible. Recounting the incident afterwards to American interrogators, Goering allowed his imagination to run away with him as he had so often done in the past with more disastrous consequences, and depicted that last scene as a heroic deed of derring-do in which he had played the principal role.

According to his version of the rescue, a detachment of the Luftwaffe, marching along the road which skirts the park at Mauterndorf, had been horrified to see their Commander-in-Chief surrounded by S.S. In an instant Goering perceived that his own troops outnumbered the guards. He lost no time in taking command: "I am commanding this detachment," he roared. "Attack the S.S.! Forward! Left right, left right! Hurrah!" The S.S., dismayed by these tactics, took flight. Goering had regained liberty for himself by his own powers of command.

The facts are less dramatic. Luftwaffe troops had been asked by Kesselring to take over, and the S.S. were only too willing that they should do so.

Without a second's delay Goering, after his liberation, set the keys of the wireless transmitter tapping as they sent a long signal to Hitler's successor, Admiral Doenitz. The radiogram, dated May 6, merits quotation, since nothing could better reveal Goering's state of mind at this critical time:

"Radiogram to ADMIRAL DOENITZ:

Are you, Admiral, familiar with the intrigue, dangerous to the security of the State, which Reichsleiter Bormann has carried on to eliminate me? All steps taken against me arose out of the request, sent by me in all loyalty, to the Führer, asking whether he wished that his order concerning his successor should come into force. . . . The steps taken against me were carried out on the authority of a radiogram signed Bormann. I have not been interrogated by anybody in spite of my requests and no attempt of mine to justify my position has been accepted. Reichsführer S.S. Himmler can confirm the immense extent of these intrigues. I have just learned that you intend to send Jodl to Eisenhower with a view to negotiating. I think it important in the interests of our people that, besides the official negotiations of Jodl, I should officially approach Eisenhower, as one Marshal to another. My success in all the important negotiations abroad with which the Führer always entrusted me before the war is sufficient guarantee that I can hope to create the personal atmosphere appropriate for Jodl's negotiations. Moreover both Great Britain and America have proved through their Press and their wireless, and in the declarations of their statesmen during the last few years, that their attitude towards me is more favourable than towards other political leaders in Germany. I think, that at this most difficult hour all should collaborate and that nothing should be neglected which might assure as far as possible the future of Germany.

GOERING, Marshal of the Reich."

When this telegram reached his headquarters, Admiral Doenitz glanced at it and filed it without bothering to dictate a reply.

Still Goering did not lose hope that he might be allowed to play a leading role in the situation, which, tragic as it was for Germany, yet seemed to him wonderfully dramatic. On May 7 he despatched his chief A.D.C., von Brauchitsch, to the nearest American headquarters, bearing letters to General Eisenhower, in which he requested an interview with the Allied Commander-in-Chief. After encountering considerable difficulties, since all roads were choked with traffic of one sort or another, von Brauchitsch delivered his letters at the headquarters of a Texan division and was ordered to return to his master with instructions that he should proceed to Fischhorn Castle, where he

234

would be placed under American protection. When on May 8 General Stack reached Fischhorn with thirty men to take charge of the distinguished prisoner, he was annoyed to find that Goering had not arrived. He could still not make up his mind, but this time the Americans made it up for him. A sharp order from General Stack brought him hurrying from Mauterndorf, and after a long and tiresome delay in a traffic block, from which he had to be extricated by American troops, Goering stood at last face to face with an enemy General.

Goering exuded friendliness at this meeting. Every ounce of "soldierly presence" that he could muster was thrown into the scales, and General Stack, although scarcely as effusive in his prisoner's view as he might have been, behaved politely enough. More painful was the interview with a score of American journalists, male and female, which followed. This was very different from the occasional meetings with the Foreign Press which the Marshal had been accustomed to arrange from time to time during his days of power. Now he was in no position to patronize the journalists or to instruct them in what they should write. He found the whole thing very humiliating; only when the flag of Texas, emblem of the Division to which he had surrendered, was produced and the Marshal was invited to place himself before it for purposes of photography did his spirits revive. He drew himself up proudly before the Lone Star and almost preened himself as the shutters clicked. Then he returned to dinner with General Stack while his A.D.C.s were accommodated in an Officers' Mess.

The dinner had disastrous consequences. *Stars and Stripes*, the United States Army newspaper, reported indignantly next day that the notorious Goering had been dined and wined royally by an American General and that his A.D.C.s had been allowed to eat chicken. At once a strict regime was introduced. Goering and his three A.D.Cs. were lodged in two communicating rooms. Their food was supplied from field-kitchens and Goering was constantly interviewed, not by interrogating officers only, but by journalists of all kinds and sometimes by people who, drawn by mere curiosity, were nevertheless allowed to see the captured Marshal.

Still no word came from Eisenhower, and the possibility that Goering might even now be allowed to play some decisive role in determining Germany's destiny became more and more remote. Since, by some oversight, the prisoners had not yet been deprived of their arms, Goering and Brauchitsch withdrew to the smaller of their two rooms which had been given to Goering for his personal use and discussed whether they should not commit suicide there and then. From the treatment they were receiving, from Eisenhower's silence, and from such news as reached them from the outside world, it was clear that Germany's future would be decided by the victors, and by the victors alone. For some hours the whole topic of suicide was discussed, and then came news which drove it from Goering's mind.

There would, it seemed, be a trial of some kind at which the leaders of National Socialist Germany who had fallen into Allied hands would be arraigned on charges as yet unspecified. Here was an opportunity to shine! Although Admiral Doenitz had for a few days assumed the nominal government of Germany in the Führer's name, Goering was unquestionably now by far the most eminent survivor of the Nazi hierarchy. On him more than upon any former colleagues who might be charged with him would fall the duty of giving to the German people and to the world the last defence of National Socialism. It was very evident that the attention of all civilized humanity would be directed towards the dramatic trial which was to take place and therefore, in the first instance, towards Hermann Goering. Even now he could be the Führer of what remained of National Socialism, and the chance was too good to miss. All thoughts of suicide were abandoned and Goering submitted with surprisingly good grace to his imprisonment.

Judgment Day

WHILE American troops were removing from the Berchtesgaden shelters the cream of Goering's art collection, finding to their dismay that some of it, notably furniture, books and documents, had been looted from three coaches of the special train which had been provisionally hidden in the tunnel at Berchtesgaden station. Goering flew off to "Ashcan," a camp at Mondorf in Luxembourg designed as a sort of purgatory in which eminent prisoners might await trial. He found the inmates sharply divided between the supporters of Admiral Doenitz and his own adherents, and he immediately resumed leadership of his own group. There were some painful meetings in "Ashcan." The

Marshal's own brother, wretched, in plain clothes, was brought in one day and bitterly attacked by the Marshal for cowardice and disloyalty. Bruno Loerzer also found his way to "Ashcan," and this too was an unpleasant meeting.

Imprisonment brought with it other privations. Since his second cure at the Långbro Asylum Goering had not reverted to that addiction to morphine which had once threatened his sanity. Neither at the time of his final arrest nor in the days of his greatness could he be described as a morphine addict. It had been his habit to take paracodeine, a very mild morphine derivative, and this was now gradually denied to him by the authorities. He looked and felt all the better for the change. Now he could no longer shake a few little tablets into his hand whenever he chose and swallow them – the tablets, made to his special order, were so small that 100 of them, which Goering was quite apt to swallow during a normal day, amounted to a dose of not more than four grains of morphine. Paracodeine had become a habit with him, just as cigarettes are with many people a habit, and it affected him little more than cigarettes might affect a heavy smoker.

At the time of his capture Goering weighed 20 stone, and now, under the careful treatment of American doctors – treatment to which he submitted with good grace – he lost weight rapidly. By the time he reached the prison in Nuremberg he tipped the scales at only 15 stone.

At Mondorf, as later in Nuremberg prison, Goering impressed his American captors and interrogators by his shrewdness, the excellence of his brain and the admirable grape-vine system by which he contrived to learn a great deal more than he should have learned about all that went on around him. At Mondorf, where the conditions of his imprisonment were far less severe than they later became after his move to Nuremberg, the fallen Marshal had contrived to discover by tea-time each afternoon the gist of all that had passed at the policy meeting which the American officers of the camp attended each morning.

Goering answered most of the questions with which he was plied openly and frankly. One one occasion at Mondorf he was invited to explain why Hitler had chosen to declare war on the United States.

"I suppose," Goering answered, "that the Führer declared war on America because he believed that Roosevelt would declare war on Germany if he didn't, and Hitler wanted to get his blow in first."

The American who sat opposite the Marshal as he pronounced this opinion suggested that if, instead of challenging the United States, Hitler had publicly expressed, before the Reichstag, the German Government's regret at the Japanese bombing of Pearl Harbour, Roosevelt would have found it very difficult to carry his country with him into a war against Germany, so strongly did Isolationist sentiment still persist in many parts of the United States.

"If I believed that," Goering declared, "I'd go straight upstairs and take my own life!"

"That might be a little difficult," the American said. "Precautions against that sort of thing are pretty strict here."

The Marshal smiled, strangely.

"A man can take his own life at any time he pleases," he said.

Of all the many topics which were discussed at that time between Goering and his captors the topic of Hermann Goering was the most popular with the prisoner. He had taken with him into captivity a large assortment of photographs, some of them of his wife and child, but the majority of himself. These he loved to autograph and present to any American officer who was willing to accept them. He was, as he took every opportunity of explaining to anyone who would listen, *"ein Renaissancemensch"* – a man of the Renaissance, and he cited his passion for jewels – especially emeralds – and for fine clothing in proof of this assertion. It was equally characteristic that the two circumstances of his detention which he most resented were the facts that he had been deprived of his medals and decorations and that he was obliged to eat all his food with a spoon, since knife and fork were forbidden to him. "It simply isn't civilized to eat like this," he would protest at every meal, but the prison rules remained unchanged.

One of the unexpected pleasures of captivity was, for Goering, the opportunity which presented itself from time to time of making life unhappy for his despised enemy Joachim von Ribbentrop. On one occasion in Mondorf Ribbentrop had lied, stupidly and obstinately, during his interrogation until the very considerable patience of the American who was expected to swallow these falsehoods came to an end and he permitted himself the luxury of telling the former Foreign Minister exactly what he thought of him.

Ribbentrop had no other recourse in his abasement but to take to his bed, which he did, and there Goering paid him a visit of condolence. During one whole hour, which must have been a very amusing one for the Marshal, Goering played upon the cowardice of his enemy, describing to him in graphic detail the exact appearance which execution by hanging gives to the face of the victim and speculating at length just how Ribbentrop's face would appear when the hangmen had had their way with him. Goering left the man's room with the comfortable feeling that the slights and contempt with which Ribbentrop had assailed him for years were now receiving their just reward.

Goering was delivered to Nuremberg Gaol in September 1945. The cell in which he spent the last year of his life has been described often enough. It was 9 feet wide and 13 feet long, approached by a thick wooden door which faced a barred window set high in the opposite wall. The furniture was simple. A steel bed, and opposite it a water closet and washbowl with running water. A straight wooden chair and a table completed the furnishings. A panel in the door, provided with a trap opening inwards which could be lowered at will from the outside, enabled meals to be passed in to the prisoner, and gave the guards a view of him at all times. Only when he was actually seated on the lavatory was the inmate of the cell invisible to watchful eyes from the corridor, and even then his legs and feet could be seen.

The rules of Nuremberg Gaol were strict. At no time, even during the cold winter nights, might Goering lie in bed unless his head and both his hands were outside the bedclothes. If he cuddled down snugly into the blankets he would be awakened and forced to place his hands outside them. Cell searches took place at least once a week, and sometimes much more frequently, while the prisoner stood naked in a corner of his hutch. One shower-bath was allowed each week and prisoners might keep one set of their own clothing and several changes of linen and underwear in the cell. The guards, under the orders of Colonel B. C. Andrus, whom Goering cordially hated and nicknamed "The Fire-Brigade Colonel," had the strictest orders never to communicate with the prisoners except in matters of duty. The mighty were indeed fallen.

Goering's chief preoccupation during the first days of his imprisonment at Nuremberg was with his family, from whom he had not heard directly since his capture. Frau Goering had in the meanwhile been arrested and was now herself in a German prison. Only when he was able to receive letters from her and to write to her did Goering's mind appear to be comparatively at ease. Thereafter he submitted with surprising cheerfulness to the rigours of prison discipline, and managed to strike up comparatively friendly relations even with his guards, to whom he sometimes spoke of America, a country which he had never visited but which interested him, of their families and of the happiness which awaited them at home.

The Marshal's defence had been entrusted to Dr. Otto Stahmer of Kiel, and Dr. Walter Siemers, briefed to defend Admiral Raeder, also played a large part in preparing Goering's answer to the charges brought against him. Both these lawyers and their assistants worked under great difficulties, for it was almost impossible to induce the accused man to take seriously the accusations which he would have to face. Goering, quite certain that his conviction was a foregone conclusion, could see no purpose in bothering his head with an elaborate defence to the indictment. His counsel visited him regularly and came away deeply depressed after each interview since as conscientious lawyers they were anxious to present their client's case in the best possible light, and in this they had no co-operation from the client himself.

During these visits the talk would turn on every conceivable topic save that of the impending trial, nor was Goering's attitude, even when legal matters were discussed, a very helpful one. He gave full play to a sardonic sense of humour. Once, after Dr. Siemers had patiently tried to explain to the Marshal a point in the indictment, Goering observed reflectively: "You know, Siemers, we made a great mistake with people like you. We ought to have wiped out all you intellectuals who were never good National Socialists. Well – some day we shall wipe them out, but when that day comes you apply to me and I'll see that you're all right."

Goering was convinced that such defence as he needed could well be supplied from his capacious and extremely accurate memory. From his point of view the trial had only one purpose – that he might appear in Court as the Führer, the last great representative of National Socialism, and there expound his creed, so that his words might go down in German history and the Nazi legend might live. As he said to one of his counsel: "Ten years hence, you know, there'll be a statue to me in most German houses. A very small statue, I dare say, but it will be there!"

Finally, after weeks of persuasion, the prisoner was induced to take a serious interest in his case, and then the energy with which he set to work astonished the lawyers, although it would not have astonished anyone who had worked closely with him in his days of greatness. In a few hours he rushed through the indictment, answering it crisply point by point, and thereupon dismissed his lawyers with the air of a man who had at last performed a tedious job which he had been putting off for weeks and of which he was glad to be relieved. Henceforward he could sit back and enjoy life – for in a sense he was enjoying life. There was no doubt that the whole world was looking, fascinated, at the drama of Nuremberg, in which he was playing the leading role. Goering, the actor, was well content that it should be so.

On March 8, 1946, the witnesses called by the defence on behalf of the former Reichsmarschall Goering began to take the stand. There they all were – the old friends. Bodenschatz, once of the Richthofen Squadron and later head of his military household; Erhardt Milch, whom he had once invited to commit suicide back in 1937; Berndt von Brauchitsch, his Chief A.D.C.; "Pilli" Koerner, who had always been close to his side in bad times as in good; Field-Marshal Kesselring, Birger Dahlerus. One after the other they filed into the witness-box and gave their evidence.

Goering, separated only by Hess from his enemy Ribbentrop, sat in the dock, earphones adjusted, dark glasses over his eyes, as these spectres from the past went through the motions of giving evidence in his defence. It was evident that the defence would begin on a note which was, for Goering, extremely painful. On the night of March 24–25, 1944, seventy-six officers of the Royal Air Force escaped from Stalag-Luft III, at Sagan in Silesia. Only three of them made good their escape, eight were detained by the Gestapo on recapture, fifteen were returned to camp after they had been caught and fifty were shot by the Gestapo. How far had Goering any personal responsibility for this great crime? How far, moreover, did he acquiesce in Hitler's order that captured Allied airmen, who had supposedly attacked German civilians, were to be treated as outlaws.

On March 4, 1946, Colonel Smirnov of the Russian Panel of Prosecutors had read the official British Report on the Sagan murders, and it was now for Goering to prove that he had had no hand in a crime which was, in fact, inconsistent with his character. Perhaps, as he heard the Russian advocate read the deadly account of the massacre, he may have thought for a moment of Captain Beaumont to whom, long ago, in a war which for all its beastliness and squalor had been, at least as far as he was concerned, a comparatively chivalrous affair, he had

241

brought cigarettes, chocolate and comforts in a German prison camp. Now he was charged, in effect, with the murder of fifty British officers in this second war in which he was now the leading German protagonist.

Goering's exact part in the Sagan murders, or in the lynching of enemy airmen forced down in Germany, can never now be known, but in the light of what is now known of his character it is not unreasonable to suppose that the evidence given on the subject by Colonel von Brauchitsch is in substance accurate. Once again, it seems, moral cowardice made Goering become an accessory to a crime of which he did not at heart approve. In his evidence before the Tribunal, von Brauchitsch said this:

"In the spring of 1944 the number of civilian air-raid casualties by machine-gunning increased suddenly. These ·attacks were directed against civilians working in the fields, against secondary railways and stations of no military importance, against pedestrians and cyclists, all within the homeland. This must have been the reason for Hitler giving not only defence orders but also ordering measures against the flyers themselves. As far as I know, Hitler favoured drastic measures. Lynching was to be countenanced. . . . The Commander-in-Chief (Goering) and the Chief of the General Staff expressed their opinion that a most serious view must be taken of these attacks directed solely against civilians. Nevertheless, no special measures should be taken against these flyers – a suggestion of lynching and of not affording protection to those who baled out could not be agreed to. In view of Hitler's instructions, however, the Luftwaffe was forced to deal with these questions. They tried to prevent these ideas of Hitler's, of which they disapproved, from being put into practice. A way had to be found and the solution was to pretend that measures would be taken which were not actually carried out."

"In your opinion, therefore," Dr. Stahmer asked the witness, "could we say that the measures directed by Hitler were not carried out by the Air Force?"

"Yes," the witness replied. "It can be said that the measures directed by Hitler were not carried out. As confirmed by the Commanders of the Air Fleets, airmen did not receive any orders to shoot enemy flyers or to turn them over to the S.D. (Security Police)."

Once again, it seemed, Goering, not daring resolutely to oppose the orders of his Führer, had hoped by evading them to modify their worst effects and thus to salve his own conscience.

So it had been with Emmy's Jewish friends soon after their marriage, so it had always been. To oppose Hitler openly, to risk the consequences of that opposition would have been too much. Yet conscience did nag and could to some extent be stilled by half-measures. As usual, half-measures had led the Marshal to disaster.

On March 15 Goering gave his own account of the affair, and in the light of present knowledge of the relationship between the two men in 1944 the explanation does not seem unreasonable. At the time of the shooting at Sagan, Goering, as was not unusual, had been on leave. On his return to duty he had been told of the shooting and had immediately spoken to Himmler, who had assured Goering that orders for the massacre had been given personally by Hitler in spite of his own opposition to them. Notwithstanding the disfavour in which he stood, Goering had approached the Führer and had pointed out that the wholesale murder of British prisoners of war might well lead to reprisals against captured German airmen, and that the whole incident had lowered the morale of his own Service. Hitler had answered angrily that since German pilots shot down over the Eastern front were in any case liable to be lynched, he did not see why their counterparts on the Western front should necessarily be spared from the same fate. Goering told him that the two fronts "really had no connection with each other." Protesting again, in June 1944, against the encouragement given by the Party to civilians to lynch enemy airmen who had been shot down, Goering was met by Hitler's furious retort: "I know perfectly well that both Air Forces have come to a mutual agreement of cowardice."

"We have not come to an agreement of cowardice," Goering replied, "but somehow we fliers have always remained comrades, no matter how much we fight each other."

To Hitler, the undistinguished private of the First World War, such high-flown phrases meant little, but undoubtedly they meant much to the former Commander of the Richthofen Squadron – indeed some of his past actions had proved that. Yet they did not mean enough to nerve the Marshal to resolute action against manifest evil.

On March 18 Mr Justice Jackson, the Chief American Prosecutor, began the cross-examination of the prisoner. He proved no match for Goering. Inadequately briefed, without a sufficiently accurate knowledge of the facts on which his case was based, Jackson gave Goering the precise opportunity which he sought. Although he relied in cross-examination almost entirely upon his own memory, Goering was able to give his opponent as good as he got, and to use the witness-box as a platform from which to address the German people and the world. He did not seek to deny most of the accusations, often diffuse and sometimes even trivial, which the American Prosecutor directed against him. Often by tripping Mr. Justice Jackson on a matter of detail he was able to score heavily against the prosecution, and whenever he did so the smile which lit up his face showed that he fully appreciated what he had done. He subjected Mr. Justice Jackson to the treatment which he had once meted out to his schoolmasters. Not content with answering questions, he persisted in giving long explanations admirably calculated to put his case in the best light before his own countrymen, if not before the Tribunal.

At last the American Prosecutor was driven to violent protest:

"I respectfully submit to this Tribunal that this witness is not being responsive, and has not been in his exmination, and that it is perfectly futile to spend our time if we cannot have responsive answers to our questions. . . . This witness, it seems to me, is adopting and has adopted in this box and in the dock an arrogant and contemptuous attitude towards the Tribunal which is giving him the trial which he never gave a living soul, or dead ones either."

That evening Goering left the dock well pleased. He had caused his adversary to lose his temper and the congratulations of his fellow prisoners were very welcome. Doenitz had long since renounced any claim to be the Leader of the Party in the dock. Goering held that position and now, he felt, he had proved his claim to it.

When Sir David Maxwell-Fyfe, K.C., Deputy Chief Prosecutor of the British Panel, rose on March 20, the eighty-sixth day of the trial, to continue the cross-examination, the atmosphere of the Tribunal changed. The British Prosecutor knew his brief thoroughly, whereas Goering had not even bothered himself with a brief. Now Sir David concentrated on the weakest points in the prisoner's armour, and it was soon clear that his shots were telling. Slowly, meticulously, the British Prosecutor took the prisoner through the whole affair of the Sagan murders. He extracted from him an admission that they had been known not only to the Gestapo and the ordinary police but also to the Luftwaffe Director of Operations and to Field-Marshal Milch. Was it conceivable that it should also be unknown to the Commander-in-Chief? The witness attempted to evade the question and was sharply called to order by Lord Justice Lawrence, the President of the Tribunal. Goering did not, he protested, wish to shift the responsibility on to the shoulders of his subordinates, but he was not present at the time when the order to shoot the escaped officers had been given by the Führer. Was it true, Sir David finally asked, that the news of the escape from Sagan had been passed not only to the High Command, the Director of Operations Air Ministry and Inspector General of Prisoners of War, but also to Goering's own A.D.C. That was, Goering admitted at last, true. He had denied it on the previous day.

Sir David passed on to the negotiations with Dahlerus which had preceded the outbreak of the war and from that to the question of concentration camps. Goering was being driven back to his last defences, yet the opportunity of glorifying National Socialism, of defending the dead Führer, must not be lost.

"I think you told the Tribunal," said Sir David, "that right up to the end your loyalty to the Führer was unshaken. Is that right?"

"That is correct," Goering answered.

"Do you still," Sir David insisted, "seek to justify and glorify Hitler after he had ordered the murder of these fifty young flying officers in Stalag-Luft III."

"I am here," Goering answered, "neither to justify the Führer, Adolf Hitler, nor to glorify him. I am here only to emphasize that I remained faithful to him, for I believe in keeping one's oath not in good times only but also in bad times, when it is much more difficult."

During his re-examination of his client, Goering's own counsel, Dr. Stahmer, gave his client an opportunity of summing up his attitude in a manner highly satisfactory to himself:

"As to responsibility," Goering said, "one must differentiate between formal and actual responsibility. Formally I bear responsibility for all departments and offices which were under my command. Although I could not possibly have seen or known beforehand everything that was issued or discussed by them, I must nevertheless assume formal responsibility, particularly where we are concerned with the carrying out of general directions given by me. Actual responsibility I see in those cases in which I personally issued orders or directives, including, in particular, all acts and facts which I signed personally or issued authentically, but I mean these facts only and not so much

245

general words and statements which were made during those twenty-five years here and there in small circles. In particular I want to say the following, very carefully, about responsibility: The Führer, Adolf Hitler, is dead. I was regarded as his successor in leading the German Reich. Consequently . . . I acknowledge my responsibility for having done everything to carry out the preparations for the seizure of power and to make that power firm in order to make Germany free and great. I did everything to avoid this war, but after it had started my duty was to do everything to win it."

With that Goering left the witness-box. The sins of twenty-five years had been brought home to him. Better able than most of his colleagues in the dock to distinguish between good and evil, he had chosen to sin against the light and had not protested against the misdeeds of others. At least now, born actor that he was, he did not, as he sat in the dock at Nuremberg, seek to evade the responsibility.

When at last, on October 1, 1946, Goering sat convicted and waiting for sentence, he still contrived to draw for a moment the limelight to himself, and away from Lord Justice Lawrence who rose to condemn him to death. As the President spoke the first words of the sentence Goering pointed energetically to the earphones on which the German translation of the English Judge's words was borne to him and indicated that he could not hear. The President interrupted his reading of the sentence while guards fiddled with the connections of the earphones. Then, since all seemed to be in order the reading began again and was again interrupted by Goering as before. Only after repairs had been made a second time was the President able to read the sentence of the Tribunal through to the end. When he had heard it Goering took off the earphones, rose, and left the dock. As he passed out he said to the American guard on the doorway: "Well, I got the top sentence anyhow!"

Escape

THE day after sentence had been passed, Goering, through his lawyers, petitioned the Allied Council in Berlin "that he might be spared the ignominy of hanging and be allowed to die as a

246

soldier before a firing squad."

He had no real expectations that this request would be granted, nor was it granted. Thereafter he determined to find his own way out.

He was encouraged in this determination by the suicide at Nuremberg of Robert Ley, leader of the Nazi "Labour Front," who succeeded in strangling himself with a towel while seated on the lavatory in the only corner in the cell in which every part of his body was not visible to the guards. Three days before he was destined to lead the sorry file of condemned men to the gallows, which were being set up in the gymnasium of the prison, Goering had a last interview with his wife. Emmy, brave in her best hat, saw, through the grille which stood between her and her husband in their last moments together, the prisoner advance impetuously towards her, dragging behind him two American soldiers to whom he was handcuffed. He smiled cheerfully: "You see, Emmy," he cried, "I'm still leading!" (*Ich führe immer noch*).

It has been suggested that the capsule of poison which enabled Goering to take his own life was passed from the lips of his wife to his own during their last kiss or that she contrived to smuggle it to him in some other manner. The official theory, advanced by the Commission of Inquiry which sat after Goering's suicide, suggested that the poison had been hidden in an incision in the body or sewn into the navel. In later years more than one German has come forward with the claim to be the man who supplied the poison to the Marshal.

It will probably never be known for certain just how Goering contrived to receive the poison, but the theory which has the support of his defence counsel, and in particular of Dr. Siemers, who spoke to him just before he committed suicide, seems at least as plausible as any other yet advanced, and perhaps on the whole more probable. Among the comforts which Goering was allowed to receive in prison was a ration of cigars – twenty-five of them each week from his own stock. It is not possible for even the keenest guard effectively to search a cigar for a concealed object without destroying the cigar itself. At most, a fine needle might be inserted, and even then not too thoroughly. There is some reason to believe that the tiny ampoule was hidden in a cigar, perhaps one of a consignment sent for by Goering just before his execution was to take place.

In the prison gymnasium the principal executioner, Staff-Sergeant Woods, and his assistants worked throughout October 15 in preparing the two gallows of which Goering was to be the first victim. For him, with his 15 stone, only a short drop would be needed. The prisoner spent his last day in writing, and in those hours his thoughts went to his family and to the German people. He wrote to his wife and to his stepson, Thomas von Kantzow, in Sweden; but first he wrote his Testament to the German people, and the contents of this document, which was impounded by the American authorities, have never been divulged. The Testament, it may be presumed, sought to justify the actions of Adolf Hitler and his Government to those whom they had brought to ruin. It is also reasonable to suppose that it may have contained advice similar to that which Goering gave to his A.D.C.s when, at Fischhorn, he had at last abandoned all hope of himself taking any hand in the regeneration of Germany:

"It is all over. Germany as we have known it is finished, and it would be folly for you to cherish any illusions that she will be allowed to set herself upon her feet again. Yet you must seek to help your country, and that you can do by helping those Foreign Powers which seem to have Germany's interests most truly at heart. But they must be the Western Powers. Never, in any circumstances, must you help Russia, which seeks the utter destruction of Germany!"

On the evening of his last day on earth Goering ate his supper and spoke for a while to the Rev. Henry F. Gerecke, the Protestant Chaplain of the prison. Then he laid himself down on the bed, his hands outside the coverings as prison regulations required, and seemed to the guards as they peered in occasionally to be dozing. Suddenly, at about 10.45 p.m., the prisoner's body was seen to jerk in violent convulsions. A doctor and the chaplain were immediately summoned, but it was too late. At 10 minutes to 11 Goering died in the clergyman's arms.

Since the poison which he had taken required, for its rapid effect, to be dissolved in acid, and since an ampoule containing a lethal solution would have been too large for easy concealment, Goering had taken the crystals and had allowed his own stomach acids to work on them very slowly. He had lain quietly until, the poison having entered his system and a stomach-pump being useless, he could no longer repress the agonizing contraction which had convulsed his whole body. At least he had died by his own choice and not by that of his enemies, and he had avoided the noose.

In Stockholm, two women, whose affection for their brother-in-law had never wavered, knelt that evening, praying for his soul while candles burned on an improvised altar before them. Carin's sisters – Fanny, Countess von Wilamowitz-Moellendorf, and Countess Mary von Rosen – had not forgotten the man who had given happiness to a beloved sister. Suddenly Countess von Wilamowitz-Moellendorf stood up and blew out the candles. "It is all over," she said. "He is dead. I know it." The time was 11 p.m.

Epilogue

CARINHALL is a pile of rubble. The heavy charges of explosive which had been laid beneath the great house upon the orders of its master were fired as the Russian Army approached the Schorfheide, leaving no more than a smoking ruin to greet the victors. Today the entrance to the palace alone remains to remind the passer-by of vanished glories. It is flanked by two columns bearing the Goering coat-of-arms and surmounted by marble lions.

A hundred yards away to the northward stand the ruins of little Edda's fairy-tale palace, a replica in miniature of Frederick the Great's pleasure house, Sans Souci, near Potsdam. Nothing is left of its tiny grocer's shop, its miniature theatre, the salons and bedrooms, all of a size suitable for a very small person. The fountain in the formal garden which fronted this wonderful toy is dry and broken.

Russian bullets brought down the elks and bison, the roedeer and stags of which the Master Hunter of the Reich had been so proud, and Russian cooking-pots received their carcases. Today wild-boar and rabbits range the game preserve unchecked. They have become so numerous that they now constitute a pest, yet the gamekeepers, deprived of rifles and shotguns by their Russian rulers, can do nothing to check them.

The tomb of Carin, in which her husband had hoped to join her, is desolate. In 1945 ghouls broke into the vault, hoping to light upon jewels or other valuables, but finding nothing, departed, leaving its occupant undisturbed. The place has a sinister reputation in the surrounding countryside, and no peasant will now willingly go near it.

The Marshal's private bathing-beach on the Grosse Döllinsee is, however, much favoured by local anglers.

The Reichsjägerhof at Rominten is not even in Germany any more, since what was once East Prussia is now, for the most part, a province of Poland. It too is destroyed, and its site no more than a place of memories for the few Germans who have not yet been deported from the neighbourhood.

Of all the properties which once acknowledged the Marshal as their owner, only one still retains a connection with his family. Mauterndorf came to him not by sequestration or bought with funds dubiously amassed but through the normal process of inheritance. Today Frau Goering claims it as her own, although her claim has been contested by the Austrian Republic and by the brothers and nieces of Frau von Eppenstein, by whose will the Marshal inherited the estate.

For some time after the war Frau Goering lived very quietly in Franconia with her daughter and the faithful Cilly, once Carin's maid-of-all-work, who had stood by the family in good times as in bad. Frau Emmy's loyalty to her husband is quite unshaken, as is that of his daughter. At the school which Edda attended the child had at first to contend with the gibes of her schoolmates. She never flinched from them nor denied her father's goodness to her.

"If you'd known him," she used to retort, "you'd never call him a criminal!"

Soon Edda came to be accepted, not as the daughter of the Reichsmarschall, the little girl whose childhood was a fairy-tale in itself, but as a pleasant, well-mannered child, reserved and shy in her manner, intelligent and good looking.

Goering has no resting-place. His body was burned, with those of his companions who died on the scaffold, and his ashes scattered. It is not for him to claim the Divine mercy which Montluc invokes in his *Siege of Sienna*:

"Those are the laws of warfare; very often one must be cruel in order to defeat the enemy. God must be very pitiful towards us, who do such great evil!"

Hermann Goering's sin of commission, and even more of omission, were black indeed. The ruins of Warsaw, Rotterdam, London, Berlin and of scores of towns and cities up and down Russia and Western Europe still mutely reproach his memory. The dead of those cities and of the concentration camps will bear witness against him before a more august Tribunal than that which he has already faced.

Yet, strangely, at that supreme Judgment, Goering will not lack at least two advocates. Two voices which will beyond doubt speak in his defence will be those of the women whom he loved and married, who knew him best, and knowing him loved him still.